EGAN'S RATS

EGAN'S RATS

THE UNTOLD STORY OF THE PROHIBITION-ERA GANG THAT RULED ST. LOUIS

DANIEL WAUGH

CUMBERLAND HOUSE
NASHVILLE, TENNESSEE

EGAN'S RATS
PUBLISHED BY CUMBERLAND HOUSE PUBLISHING, INC.
431 Harding Industrial Drive
Nashville, TN 37211-3160

Cover design: Gore Studio, Inc.
Text design: John Mitchell

Library of Congress Cataloging-in-Publication Data

Waugh, Daniel, 1977-
 Egan's Rats : the untold story of the prohibition-era gang that ruled St. Louis / Daniel Waugh.
 p. cm.
 Includes bibliographical references and index.
 ISBN-13: 978-1-58182-575-6 (hardcover : alk. paper)
 ISBN-10: 1-58182-575-7 (hardcover : alk. paper)
 1. Crime—Missouri—Saint Louis—History. 2. Prohibition—Missouri—Saint Louis—History.
I. Title.

 HV6795.S2W38 2007
 364.1'0660977866—dc22

                                                              2006039557

Printed in the United States of America

1 2 3 4 5 6 7—13 12 11 10 09 08 07

To my son, David,
for being the best thing in my life.
This book is for you, kiddo!

CONTENTS

PREFACE

I think it all started with me back in 1987, when my mother and I saw the movie The Untouchables on the big screen at Chicago's Biograph Theatre (the same movie house that John Dillinger was killed coming out of). At the tender age of ten, I was fascinated by what unfolded on the screen before me—Kevin Costner, Sean Connery, Andy Garcia, Robert DeNiro, and a whole ton of Tommygun, Prohibition-era violence. I was dazzled. At the time, I had only the vaguest idea who Al Capone was, thanks largely to Geraldo Rivera's ridiculous attempt to cut into his old vaults. But after seeing this movie, I wanted to know more. Within a week, on late night TV, I had seen a rerun of 1973's Dillinger, featuring Warren Oates as the outlaw and an ultra-violent, exaggerated version of his exploits. I was hooked. Like young Todd Bowden in Stephen King's story "Apt Pupil," I had found my GREAT INTEREST.

Twenty years ago, the Internet was a military novelty that hadn't yet seen the light of day, so I went down to the library and checked out a large, blood-red copy of *Bloodletters and Badmen* and read of the exploits of Capone, Dillinger, "Baby Face" Nelson, and "Bugsy" Siegel. These were guys who were tough, who lived by their own rules, who took absolutely no crap from anyone. Most importantly, these were guys who were the exact opposite of who I was at that time. No matter what I put up with at school, at night I could live vicariously through their stories, even though they'd been dead for decades, and everything would be all right. Then something occurred to me.

9

All the gangsters I read about were largely from either New York or Chicago. Luciano, Capone, Lansky, Accardo, the masterminds of Murder Inc.

Didn't my hometown of St. Louis have any gangsters in the old days? I asked myself. All I found in most books was a cryptic entry about the Egan's Rats, the same three tired paragraphs about how the gang, led by "Jelly Roll" Egan, dominated the city during Prohibition, and how Fred "Killer" Burke was suspected of pulling Chicago's St. Valentine's Day Massacre. I decided to do my own research and found that the Egan gang was much more complex than most people knew. "Jelly Roll" wasn't the nickname of Tom Egan but of a later rival of the gang, and the Egan's Rats only ran St. Louis during four years of Prohibition. I also discovered stories that were previously unknown, buried deep in obscure microfilm copies of ancient St. Louis newspapers.

This book is my attempt to illuminate the untold story of the Egan's Rats. I would like to make clear that I am not trying to glorify the men or their crimes, some of which were extremely vicious. Although nearly a century has passed, some scars may not have healed. If anyone who reads this book is hurt or offended in any way, I offer my sincerest apologies.

Most of the material contained herein is based directly on St. Louis newspaper accounts. In particular, the latter chapters of the book draw heavily from Egan gangster Ray Renard's confession to the *St. Louis Star* in February and March 1925. Before Joe Valachi, before Henry Hill and Sammy the Bull, there was Ray Renard, and his testimony provides a fascinating glimpse into the everyday workings of the Egan's Rats. Most events and conversations are taken directly from his statements. Any factual mistakes in this book are mine alone.

This book is my best attempt to tell their story, and I hope that you, the reader, will enjoy what I've written, for that would make everything worthwhile.

Daniel E. Waugh
St. Louis, Missouri

ACKNOWLEDGMENTS

First and foremost, I would like to offer thanks to God, for without Him, this book would not exist. Thanks also to my parents, grandparents, brothers, and sister Michelle for your love and guidance over the years, for teaching this kid right from wrong, and for putting up with me when I got difficult. Much love to my wife, Renee, and the rest of the Cobb family.

Thanks to the staffs of the microfilm departments at the Detroit Public Library, Toledo Public Library, University of Michigan Undergraduate Library, and especially the St. Louis Public Library. Special thanks to Chris Geels for offering knowledge and advice to me in the salad days, and to historian Walter Fontaine, who was kind enough to share with me his considerable knowledge of St. Louis's underworld in a series of e-mails. Special thanks also to Ann Tinsley, who graciously spoke of her ancestor Thomas Camp (aka Fred Burke).

Additionally, I want to thank Mario Gomes and Taylor Pensoneau for boosting my confidence when it was low, and give a big shout out to Rick Mattix and Bill Helmer, who know more about Prohibition-era crime than perhaps anyone else in the country. Their support and suggestions were invaluable to me; I couldn't have done this without them. I'd like to thank as well all my friends at Laclede Street for providing moral and alcoholic support over the years.

All photos are from the author's collection unless otherwise noted.

PROLOGUE

Dint Goes Across the River

WEDNESDAY, FEBRUARY 17, 1943, was a typical winter day in St. Louis, Missouri. The city's residents went about their business under a gray, forbidding sky as the temperature pushed steadily into the forties. For most folks, the main thing on their minds was the war. The Big One. It had been more than a year since the bombing of Pearl Harbor, and St. Louis, like the rest of the country, had converted most of its industry to support the burgeoning war effort, and many of the area's males were either overseas or on their way.

There had been good news from the front. Two weeks earlier, the last of the German 6th Army, freezing and starving, had surrendered at the Russian city of Stalingrad. Just a week earlier, American troops in the Pacific had finally secured the island of Guadalcanal. But today, on the seventeenth, there were setbacks. Rommel's panzer divisions continued to push deeper into Tunisia, capturing three American airfields and setting the stage for what would be a showdown at the Kasserine Pass a few days later.

Today also was the day New York Yankee star outfielder Joe DiMaggio was sworn into the Army, proudly declaring, "They can put me where they think I'll do the most good. I haven't asked for anything special." Joltin' Joe would spend most of the war touring with a baseball team.

By 5 p.m., the leaden skies were deepening over the town, and by 6:30 it was completely dark. Families throughout the area settled into their evening routines, many crowding around their radios for entertainment.

At the edge of the northeastern tip of the city lies the hilly, tree-lined suburb of Riverview Gardens. In a simple yet elegant bungalow at 10036 Shelton Drive, a stocky, middle-aged man is having dinner with his wife in the kitchen. The man is glancing through a newspaper as he eats, catching up on the day's events. There was a time when the man himself was frequently in the papers, often on the front page. His name still occasionally made it into print today, but he didn't get as much of a kick out of it now as he had when he was younger.

After supper, the man puts on his overcoat and hat and bids his wife farewell, telling her he is "going across the river." As he strides toward his Ford sedan, dressed in off-the-rack outerwear, the man looks like an average hard-working man, which in fact he is—a master plumber with offices in the city at 1436 Franklin Avenue. But just one look at his pasty face and hard brown eyes would tell you that he is something else, as well.

William Patrick Colbeck, "Dint" to his close friends, is the former leader of the once-fearsome Egan's Rats gang. He had taken over the leadership reins from Willie Egan himself after the latter was gunned down on Franklin Avenue. Twenty years ago, he'd had the entire city under his thumb and was rolling in dough. Dint had made a lot of friends in those days—and a lot of enemies.

On his command million-dollar heists had been carried out and rival gangsters shot to pieces. Dint had rubbed elbows with all of the city's elite, the mayor, the chief of police. He was a Midwestern version of the Pied Piper. He had what everyone wanted: bootleg whiskey.

One thing Dint Colbeck and his friends hated was a snitch. Keeping your mouth shut had been ingrained in all of them since they were kids, running around with the rest of the Egan's Rats. A snitch was the worst thing in the world to be. And yet it was a snitch that had done in Chippy, Steve, Ol, Red, and the rest, a man they'd all known and trusted. And then, in the blink of an eye, it was all over.

Sixteen years in federal prison had mellowed Dint Colbeck, but it would be extremely foolish for anyone to underestimate him. Others had made that mistake in the past and paid for it in blood. Upon his release in November 1940, Dint had paid a visit to police headquarters and declared that he was "going straight." And since then, it appeared that he had kept that promise. But the rumors swirled.

Was Dint Colbeck *really* going straight? Police began hearing whispers that Dint was trying to get back into the action—muscling in on the East Side gambling clubs, participating in election fraud, depending on his reputation to instill fear. His old comrades-in-arms from the Rats were out of prison, but they weren't necessarily in his corner. Dint and the whole bunch had been questioned about the murder of a racetrack tout in June 1941.

But despite the rumors, Colbeck is traveling alone on this February night. He has no gun on his person, and the trunk of his Ford contains no pistols or sawed-off shotguns, just a set of plumber's tools. Just as he told his wife, Dint is heading across the river to the East Side.

Where Colbeck went once he crossed into Illinois is unknown. He may have gone to the Hyde Park Club in Venice, a popular joint that Dint was rumored to "have a piece of," or possibly another destination in Venice, East St. Louis, or Madison.

It seems certain that at some point during his trip, Colbeck had contact with Monroe "Blackie" Armes, an ex-bootlegger and hit man who formerly had worked for the Shelton mob, which had dominated criminal activity in southern Illinois for years. Why Dint would meet the dangerous Armes without a gun is a mystery. For their part, the three Shelton brothers—Carl, Earl, and Bernie—had largely switched their activities to Peoria recently, but they were still rumored to have some interests on the East Side. Interests that would be compromised if Dint Colbeck were indeed trying to muscle in on the action.

Perhaps Dint met up with his old friends David "Chippy" Robinson or Steve Ryan. He would have been relaxed around them and not felt the need of a firearm.

Wherever Dint Colbeck went that night, it was a relatively short trip. He had left his wife in Riverview Gardens at 8:30 p.m. and by 10:35 was driving onto the McKinley Bridge, heading back into St. Louis. Dint switched on the Ford's radio and perhaps spun the dial between the various stations offering news or entertainment, such as Fred Waring's *Pleasure Time* show on KSD, Gene Krupa on KXOK, Blue Barron's orchestra on KMOX, Les Brown on KWK, and *Night Patrol* on WIL.

Dint's Ford was back in St. Louis shortly after 10:40. Back on the North Side, where he was born and raised, Dint felt more relaxed. There were virtually no lights because of the wartime blackout, and when he turned south onto Ninth Street, it was pitch black. Why he decided to head south, instead of north toward Riverview Gardens, is not known. Perhaps he'd noticed a persistent set of headlights in his rearview mirror as he came across the bridge.

As he cruised along at a sedate pace, Dint saw a dark sedan pull alongside and then suddenly cut him off at the corner of Destrehan, crowding his car to the right. Colbeck jammed on the brakes and yanked the emergency brake.

Before he could react, a Thompson submachine gun opened up with an ear-splitting chatter, belching orange flame. Pain erupted behind Dint's left ear, and he sprawled sideways as the world went topsy-turvy and started to turn dark. And then there was nothing at all.

The murder of William "Dint" Colbeck was a top media item in St. Louis for the next few days, competing for space with the various military actions of the day. It was a violent echo from the past, a past in which bootleggers had ruled the day and graphic accounts of gang warfare screamed from the pages of the city's newspapers. Police suspected Colbeck may have been killed for attempting to "muscle in" on East Side gambling enterprises. Or perhaps he was slain by someone from the old days who still harbored a grudge, maybe from the Egan-Hogan gang war of 1921–23. A score of Dint's comrades were questioned, but as had happened so many times before with gang murders, the hit on Dint Colbeck would never be solved.

And so it was that, once again, the name Egan's Rats had grabbed the public's attention. Few St. Louisans today are aware of the Rats, but at one time they were some of the most fearsome men in the city. Dint's murder in February 1943 was perhaps the last major footnote in their story, but the history of the Egan's Rats spans more than half a century, beginning around 1890, the same year that Dint Colbeck was born.

SNEAK THIEVES

THEY CAME OUT of the slums east and north of downtown St. Louis, sandwiched between the burgeoning skyscrapers and the muddy Mississippi River. Living in rickety tenements and tarpaper shacks, many of the inhabitants were Irish immigrants, having fled to America in the mid-nineteenth century to escape the great potato famine. Soon, however, the area was populated by Germans, Bulgarians, Dutch, Jews, and blacks. Almost any and all, it would seem, were crammed into the district.

Looking around the neighborhood, one wouldn't think any of the city's prosperity had touched it. Those who worked made barely enough to get by, and those who didn't usually spent their time trying to steal from those who did. Burglaries, robberies, and rapes were all too common. Most dwellings didn't have such "luxuries" as electricity or indoor plumbing. The streets were paved with uneven cobblestones, and some of the lesser-traveled thoroughfares were dirt. Garbage piled up on the avenues, and the stench of waste, both animal and human, was always in the air. Diseases were rampant and took their toll on the residents, especially young children.

It was in this tough neighborhood that Martin Egan lived with his family. Their flat at 1011 Collins Street was in the heart of what was then called the "Kerry Patch," so named because of the large number of Irish immigrants who lived there. Egan was a rough-and-tumble man who kept a saloon at Second and Carr streets. He scraped together enough money to support a wife, Annie, and a burgeoning family. Their first child, Martin Jr., was born about 1870. A daughter, Catherine, followed on November 27, 1872, and another son, Thomas, arrived on November 1, 1874. Then came James, Nellie, Mamie, and finally William, who was born on June 7, 1884. The family regularly attended mass at St. Patrick's Catholic Church at Sixth and Biddle streets, and the children would soon be attending parochial school.

Annie Egan had just given birth to a fourth girl, Katie, when disaster struck in late November 1886. The entire Egan household was stricken with a serious disease which would take the lives of both Annie and teenaged Martin Jr.. James Egan never totally recovered and developed chronic lung problems which would send him to an early grave. Infant Katie did not survive for long, dying on September 20, 1887, possibly from diphtheria.

Having lost his wife and two children, Martin Egan threw himself into his saloon business. Fifteen-year-old Catherine immediately became the woman of the house, with the two younger girls, Nellie and Mamie, helping. Three-year-old William was probably too young to remember his mother and siblings, but Thomas, at an impressionable twelve years of age, probably felt the losses more than anyone else. Now, deprived of his mother and older brother, and with his father increasingly absent, the boy took to the streets, looking for male companionship and ways to get money. Money that couldn't be had in a classroom overseen by nuns.

Tom Egan's best friend was a skinny, loquacious kid from across the street. This boy, six years older than Egan, had a charming manner and a shrewd mind, but his affable exterior concealed a hair-trigger temper and tremendous strength. With the death of Martin Jr., the boy became the closest thing Tom had to a big brother.

Born on March 3, 1868, Thomas Elwood Kinney lived with his family at 1012 Collins. Tom, accompanied by his younger brothers Mike and Willie, briefly attended school but was soon hawking newspapers on street corners in the Fourth Ward. It was during this juvenile stab at employment that many believe Kinney earned the colorful nickname that would follow him for much of his life.

The newspaper-selling business was a brutal one in the late-nineteenth century. Boys regularly engaged in vicious fights over bundles of newspapers, corners to sell them on, and the proceeds of their work. Newspaper bundles were left at certain corners early each morning for the newsboys. Tom Kinney, eager and enterprising, was always the first one there and grabbed the largest bundle, whether it was intended for him or not. He always made a point at the end of the day to square accounts with his victim.

One morning, a kid who wasn't familiar with this complained to a neighborhood beat cop, who explained, "That little Kinney sneaked the papers!" The policeman, a burly Irishman named Grady, spoke with a heavy brogue, so "sneaked" came out sounding like "snaked." Thereafter Tom was known as "Snake" Kinney. Others, however, sneered at the story and declared that Kinney got his moniker by being shifty and devious.

By 1886, Kinney was working in a local pool hall. He was very proficient with a cue and made lots of money by beating well-heeled opponents. Noted as the neighborhood pool shark, Snake's reputation began to grow. He and Tom Egan would share a lifelong love of the game of billiards.

Soon both of Kinney's parents were dead, and he took to more serious employment. Snake measured lard for a while and caught on as a hardware salesman for Sligo Steel. Eventually, however, his employment was terminated after he got drunk one night and crashed the company's horse-drawn wagon.

Kinney soon found his true calling in local politics. The Fourth and Fifth Wards were solidly Democratic, and he was elected to the Democratic City Committee in 1890 at the age of twenty-two. Snake loved working for the poor and downtrodden, putting his natural sense of honor and fair play to work for the masses. His friendly, outgoing manner opened many doors, and he was soon well known in the city's political circles. The Fourth Ward became the city's Democratic stronghold because of Kinney's amazing ability to get out the vote. The first time Snake was elected to the House of Delegates, he beat his Republican rival by tallying an astounding 4,000 votes while his opponent claimed less than 100.

While his erstwhile buddy Snake Kinney was establishing himself as a ward politician, Tom Egan was carving a much tougher reputation on the streets of the "Bloody Third District," as it was called by the St. Louis police. Egan hung around with other kids from the neighborhood, notably Harry Horrocks, William "Skippy" Rohan, Dave Hickey, Willie Gagel, John "Guinea Mack" McAuliffe, William "Red" Houlihan, Thomas Lamb, Michael "Mickey Mack" McNamara, Eddie and Tim Kelleher, and the Caples twins, Jerry and Will.

Known as the Ashley Street Gang, these young men constituted the original nucleus of what would one day become the Egan's Rats.

Most of the Ashley Streeters had childhoods identical to that of Tom Egan. Surrounded by crushing poverty, boredom, and a bad neighborhood, these boys, with devil-may-care mischievousness, schooled themselves well in the arts of purse snatching, pickpocketing, burglary, drunk rolling, and armed robbery. They terrorized virtually all businesses as well as other gangs in the area. These gang wars bore little resemblance to those of today. Instead of nine-millimeter handguns and TEC-9 machine pistols, the Ashley Streeters brawled with their fists, brass knuckles, lead pipes, bricks, knives, and the occasional revolver. They were known for their brutality and fearlessness, and word of the gang's bad pedigree spread quickly.

While the criminals of the future learned their trade in the early 1890s, the last of the American West was being tamed. Desperados like Sam Bass, Billy the Kid, and Missouri's own Jesse James were long dead. In October 1892, while Tom Egan and his pals were rampaging in St. Louis, the Dalton Gang was shot to pieces while trying to simultaneously rob two banks in Coffeyville, Kansas. The Doolin Gang was being run down in the Indian Territory, soon to be known as Oklahoma. With the exception of a few robberies by Butch Cassidy and the Wild Bunch, the days of the horseback bandits were fading away. A new form of criminal was emerging in America's cities: the gangster.

The Ashley Street Gang victimized shops and homes in the neighborhood, as well as those in the neighboring Fifth Ward. They roamed the busy downtown streets, among the booming build of the early 1890s, always ready to snatch an unsuspecting lady's handbag as she emerged from a department store or remove a wealthy-looking gent's pocketbook on a crowded streetcar. The crew also swiped anything and everything that wasn't bolted down—booze, tobacco products, jewelry, chickens and geese, as well as the occasional horse-drawn carriage (a prelude to modern-day car theft). There wasn't a crime the Ashley Street boys wouldn't commit.

Unlike the modern image of the immaculately dressed gangster, the Ashley Street thugs looked like bums: rough shirts and patched pants, well-worn leather shoes, fingerless gloves, topped off by knit caps or slouch hats. During the winter they wore woolen overcoats and waist-length jackets with the collars turned up. Perhaps they sported a fancy derby stolen from someplace. If one of them changed his underwear twice a week, he was considered to have excellent hygiene. Their diet was poor (vitamins hadn't been discovered yet), and their faces and bodies displayed the effects of inadequate nutrition. Rarely, if ever, did they see a dentist, and various tooth ailments probably kept the boys in constant pain.

For entertainment, they would take in a vaudeville show at one of the many theaters of the area, particularly those in the entertainment district around Broadway and Carr. One of these joints, the Standard Theater, was a special hangout for the city's gangs. The Standard boasted as a doorman a fifty-something gent with a tall frame, hook nose, ice-cold eyes, and a six-shooter under his arm. This man was none other than legendary former bank robber Frank James.

Tom Egan grew into a man of medium height, with a muscular build, dark hair, and cold blue eyes that peered out at the world in a penetrating stare. He had small, delicate hands, which was surprising because he was known as a fearsome fist fighter, often beating taller, stronger opponents. A large scar ran lengthwise across his forehead, due to a violent blade fight at some point during his youth. Egan was renowned for his calm in a crisis and did not know fear.

This from-life sketch of Tom Egan, namesake of the Egan's Rats, shows a face that, as one journalist noted, "is somewhat weather-beaten, like a sailor's."

Years later, a journalist would provide this view of Tom Egan:

"His face is weather-beaten, somewhat like a sailor's, with the scar of a bullet wound on one cheek. The touch of his hand is soft, even dissolving to the grasp. But beneath his urbanity, his relish of a good story, his ready smile, lurks the quiet presence of danger. His coal-like eyes seem to smolder, 'needing' in Carlyle's vivid phrase, 'only to be blown.'"

His close friend was John McAuliffe, a handsome youth who was known as the fashion plate of the bunch, going out of his way to swipe fancy clothes, hats, and coats. Known as "Guinea Mack," he also was greatly feared in the neighborhood. Another pal was Harry Horrocks, a black-haired youth whose undersized build concealed a vicious nature. Egan and Horrocks were often rousted by the police in each other's company in the early 1890s. Most of the other boys had their inevitable run-ins with the law as well. Especially Dave Hickey, who had the disturbing habit of going free while his accomplices got sent to the city workhouse. This would eventually erode his standing in the gang and lead to a violent confrontation with Tom Egan himself.

By far the boldest of them all was William "Skippy" Rohan. Like Egan and Horrocks, he stood only about five and a half feet tall but was as tough as nails. He was handsome (except for several scars and a prominent chipped tooth,) with chestnut hair, gray eyes, a thin mustache, and droopy eyelids that gave him a perpetual sleepy expression. While most of the boys on rare occasions would exercise at least *some* caution, Rohan did not. Skippy would rob anyone, anytime, and damn the consequences. On one occasion, in 1892, when two detectives tried to arrest him, Skippy got to his gun, shot one of them and pistol-whipped the other in a fierce struggle.

His good looks and daring ways made him popular with the ladies, and it wouldn't be long before Skippy Rohan was known as the most notorious criminal in the city. Rohan's bad reputation and crimes would land him in jail more often than not in Chicago as well as St. Louis.

During these early days of criminality, Tom Egan received his first major jail sentence. A series of indictments racked up through the winter and spring of 1893 had caught up with him. On June 3, the eighteen-year-old Egan was sent off to serve a year in the city workhouse at 4200 South Broadway, breaking rocks, washing sheets, building tables, and doing other menial tasks. But the city of St. Louis had not heard the last of Tom Egan. Indeed, he was just getting started.

While Egan was completing his postgraduate criminal study at the St. Louis City Workhouse, Snake Kinney was throwing himself and the rest of the gang into the Democratic political scene. Since the separation of the city and county in 1876, St. Louis held

Harry Horrocks, left, and Dave Hickey were childhood pals of Tom Egan and original members of the Ashley Street Gang.

elections every two years. Each election day Snake and his thugs would man the polls in the Fourth Ward, stuffing ballot boxes, voting as many times as they could for the Democratic candidate of their choice, and intimidating or beating anyone who tried to vote differently.

In fact, most street gangs across the city in the 1890s had political interests as well as criminal. Local ward politicians, both Republican and Democratic, used vicious thugs to enforce their will and ensure the desired election results. In this case, the Ashley Street Gang was no different than the dozens of others that terrorized St. Louis neighborhoods.

On February 14, 1894, Snake Kinney went into the saloon business, opening in Martin Egan's old saloon at the southwestern corner of Second and Carr, right around the block from his home. The elder Egan and several others lived in the rooms upstairs. One of the Ashley Street boys, James "Jimmy the Rat" Collins, was the bartender. On that Valentine's Day, the future Egan's Rats had their first notable headquarters.

In those days, and today to some extent, saloons dotted neighborhoods across St. Louis, serving as a home away from home for the denizens of the ward. The saloon served as both a social and a political gathering place. The saloonkeeper often threw a lot of weight behind whatever political party he so desired. This resulted in a lot of individual fiefdoms set up across the town.

Snake Kinney's saloon was a microcosm of other Fourth Ward saloons. The small, virtually airless building was an important place for the local factory workers, dock wallopers, and other working men who would come into the place to ease the strain of their day with a few drinks. Music was provided by a fiddler and/or piano player. Free lunch was offered to the patrons, usually consisting of a table holding various types of lunchmeats, bread, and cheeses. Between the smells of the "free lunch" sitting out in the open, spilled beer and whiskey, tobacco smoke, sawdust, and the odor of the customers (in the 1890s, most people didn't know how to *spell* deodorant, let alone use it,) the stench of the saloon could be quite rank to the untrained nose.

Most of Kinney's clientele came from criminals, especially his buddies in the Ashley Street Gang. Fights broke out almost hourly in the joint, and mild-mannered neighborhood residents soon learned to give the place a wide berth. Unsuspecting well-dressed patrons who happened to wander into the place would often have something slipped in their beer, usually chloral hydrate, and while they were unconscious the boys would rifle their pockets for valuables. The victims would awaken on the sidewalk or in a back alley a while later, scratching their heads and wondering where the hell they were.

The police immediately began a campaign of harassment against Kinney in order to get his liquor license revoked. Local beat cops dubbed his place "The Robbers Roost."

Thomas "Snake" Kinney, best friend of Tom Egan and a future Missouri state senator, was the first street and political boss of what would become the Egan's Rats.

At 1:30 on the morning of October 17, 1894, the streets of North St. Louis were virtually deserted. Except for an occasional nocturnal pedestrian or a carriage quietly clip-clopping along the cobblestones, there was no action. A perfect night for a burglary.

Thomas Egan and an unknown companion stood at the front door of William Mordieck's saloon at 1026 Cass Avenue. Egan was quickly chiseling away at the lock while his buddy's eyes scanned the darkened streets for passersby. They intended to enter the saloon and steal whatever cash or valuables they could find.

Ever since his release from the workhouse four months earlier, Tom Egan had resumed his place in the Ashley Street hierarchy, robbing and assaulting with utter abandon. Tonight, however, was destined to be different.

The saloon had a private watchman, Edward Funck, who saw the two youths trying to jimmy the door. Startled by the interruption, Egan yanked a revolver from his pocket and opened fire. Patrolman Patrick Walsh, attracted by the shouts and shots, rushed up the street with his gun drawn. He opened fire on the two burglars. The nameless one escaped but Tom Egan was not as lucky. A bullet struck him on the right side of his neck, passed upwards through the jaw, and exited through his left cheek. Egan collapsed in a heap and was taken to the City Hospital via the dispensary.

Despite being shot clean through the head, Tom Egan would survive and escape being charged, thanks to Snake Kinney's influence. He would, however, be left with an ugly scar on his left cheek, just above the corner of his mouth.

Egan's fleet-footed partner was never identified but was rumored to be Dave Hickey. Indeed, there was tension between them when they were both shipped back to the workhouse for

Michael "Mickey Mack" McNamara, a daring and violent member of the Ashley Street Gang, gained notoriety after escaping from the Four Courts in September 1894.

yet another caper the following spring. Many other members of the Ashley Street Gang were there as well, including Eddie Kelleher, who had effected a daring escape from the Four Courts building the previous September, along with fellow Ashley Streeter Mickey Mack McNamara and five others.

The morning of June 3, 1895, began like any other for the inmates of the workhouse. Prisoners arrived at their workstations after breakfast. By 7:30, Tom Egan, Dave Hickey, Eddie Kelleher, Guinea Mack McAuliffe, and Pat Kennedy were in the quarry breaking rocks with large macadam hammers. The men used empty blasting-powder kegs to sit on while performing their backbreaking work. According to Egan, someone swiped Hickey's keg and he demanded Egan's. The latter brought his macadam hammer up and crushed the bigger boy's skull with a fierce blow. Hickey fell without making a sound, blood coming out of his ears.

Despite the fractured skull and the fact that prison and media officials thought he would die, Dave Hickey survived. Amazingly, he continued to run with the Ashley Street Gang and never ran out his friends again.

With one swing in the rock yard of the workhouse, Tom Egan had firmly cemented himself as the leader of the Ashley Streeters. His swift and brutal solution to the Dave Hickey problem sent a powerful message to anyone who thought to cross him.

The night before Thanksgiving, November 27, 1895, several of the Ashley Street Gang gathered in the back room of Snake Kinney's saloon to indulge in some holiday cheer. Present were Tom Egan and his father, Martin, John McHale, Richard Walsh, Willie Gagel (who had just been released from the penitentiary after serving a three-year stretch for burglary), and the Caples twins, Will and Jerry. Even Dave Hickey, completely recovered from his fractured skull, had joined his buddies for a "growler" of beer. The boys settled in, boiled a couple of chickens on the stove, and drank freely throughout the night. Soon Tom Egan bid his crew farewell and left, while his father went upstairs to bed.

The party continued into the early hours of Thanksgiving morning, and soon the men were all extremely drunk. At 4:30, an argument ensued between nineteen-year-old Jerry Caples and Willie Gagel, perhaps, as the papers said, over who had bought the most drinks, or maybe it was one of the many other things men find offensive in the myopic state of drunkenness. The squabble grew in ferocity until the two men bolted from their seats.

Caples intended to settle matters with his fists. Gagel, however, whipped out a pistol and aimed it at his adversary. The gun misfired twice, whereupon Caples rushed Gagel, but the former was so intoxicated that he was easily overpowered by the muscular ex-convict. With the others yelling at him to stop, Gagel pinned Caples's face to the dingy table with one hand, and with the other placed his revolver against the back of the kid's head and fired a bullet into it.

Gagel swayed drunkenly for a moment, just before he was shoved out the back door and told to get lost. He made his way down Carr Street toward the river, eventually hopping a Chicago-bound freight train.

The Ashley Streeters were enraged over the murder of young Jerry Caples. Especially Tom Egan, who made it known that he would kill Willie Gagel at the first opportunity. Indeed, when he was apprehended almost a year later in Chicago, Gagel eagerly pleaded guilty and went to prison for a ten-year term, figuring the state pen at Jefferson City would be a safe refuge from the wrath of Egan.

The slaying of Jerry Caples marked the first time a prominent member of the Egan's Rats (although still technically the Ashley Street Gang) had been murdered. It would be far from the last.

By 1896 it was obvious that St. Louis was a city on the rise. Its population had passed the half-million mark, and prosperity was evident throughout the business section. New skyscrapers were being erected with stunning regularity, radically altering the city's skyline in a short time. Electric trolleys now crisscrossed the city, and telephone usage was slowly climbing.

The one black mark of the year against the city occurred on May 27. That day, in the midst of severe spring thunderstorms, a huge tornado (Category 5 on the modern-day Fujita scale) ripped through the South Side on a northeasterly course and across the river into East St. Louis, killing and injuring hundreds while causing millions of dollars worth of damage.

Not everyone who passed through St. Louis was impressed with its modern amenities. While visiting from New York, muckraker Lincoln Steffens turned his nose up, writing:

> Go to St. Louis and you will find the habit of civic pride in them; they still boast. The visitor is told of the wealth of the residents, of the financial strength of the banks, and of the growing importance of the industries, yet he sees poorly

paved, refuse-burdened streets, and dusty or mud-covered alleys; he passes a ramshackle fire-trap crowded with the sick, and learns that it is the City Hospital; he enters the "Four Courts," and his nostrils are greeted by the odor of formaldehyde used as a disinfectant, and insect powder spread to destroy vermin; he calls at the new City Hall, and finds half the entrance boarded with pine planks to cover up the unfinished interior. Finally, he turns a tap in the hotel, to see liquid mud flow into wash-basin or bath-tub.

Snake Kinney and his thugs increasingly found themselves in conflict with the rival gangs of the surrounding neighborhoods. Men like John J. Ryan and John McGillicuddy, known as "Cuddy Mack," ran crews of hoodlums who were indistinguishable from the Ashley Streeters, and they even worked for the Democratic Party on Election Day. These were all desperate men engaged in desperate enterprises, and the jealousies and resentments that arose between them, often fueled by alcohol, led to several violent incidents between the gangs.

By far Kinney's greatest rival in the mid-1890s was twenty-eight-year-old George Higgins. Known as "Baldy" for his perpetually shaved head, Higgins was a large man who often acted the part of a bully. Frequently drunk, he would fight at the slightest provocation, often using a gun or knife to make his point. While working the polls on Election Day in November 1894, Baldy Higgins engaged a man named Thomas Stapleton in a drunken shootout, endangering the lives of countless bystanders. Both men emptied their pistols, but only Higgins scored a hit, on Stapleton's leg, which would lead to the latter's death by blood poisoning a month later.

Acquitted on the grounds of self-defense, Higgins became bolder and even more belligerent, taking great pains to antagonize Snake Kinney and the Ashley Streeters. Observers on both sides agreed it was only a matter of time before one of the men killed the other.

A small group of reporters from the paper visited Snake Kinney's saloon, and their experiences were recounted in an illustrated article in the September 6, 1896, edition of the *St. Louis Post-Dispatch* that paints a vivid picture of Kinney's place and other rough joints in the Third District:

In less than a minute a policeman appeared at the front door and peeped in. He glided up the sidewalk to the rear entrance, and a moment later a mysterious Woman in Red slipped through the door and beckoned to Kinney. They held a whispered conversation, and in less than another minute every habitué of the place knew the character of the strange visitors and their mission.

Doubtless this all came about through the hypnotic influence of Mr. Kinney's beer.

Among the crowd present was one powerful fellow who claimed to be an ex-policeman. He pretended to be hopelessly drunk, but when drinks were ordered he sprang from the floor where he had fallen and "lined up" at the bar with the others with remarkable agility.

He then resumed the part he had been instructed to act and sat down at a table, apparently falling asleep, but none of the visitors sat down to talk, as he had expected and hoped, so that he could report to Kinney, and he never failed to hear the clarion voice that ordered the drinks.

That is one of the iron-clad rules of the house. When drinks are ordered everybody is expected to drink, whether he is invited or not, and to fail to "line up" would be to lay one's self liable to expulsion from "Snake" Kinney's charmed circle.

The bartender is a villainous looking youth (Jimmy "The Rat" Collins), and the gang by which he is surrounded daily and nightly is surpassingly tough. Nearly every member of it has "done time" in the penal institution of which Gov. Stone is president, and all they know is to drink beer and advance the interests of "Snake" Kinney.

But the public must not judge Mr. Kinney too harshly. Some of these men can vote, and those who can't vote legally can stuff ballot boxes as well as anyone else, and these are matters which must be attended to.

Being a gentleman and a man of influence, it devolves

upon Mr. Kinney to attend to these little details of an election, if the country is to be wrenched from the gaping jaws of damnation, and consequently he must keep the voters and the 'pushers' in line, especially as the polling place is right across the street from his emporium.

If these gentlemen become engaged in a controversy in the course of their patriotic struggle, and cut and shoot and kill each other, and thereby lessen the voting population, that is a misfortune which it is beyond the power of Mr. Kinney to avert.

Patriotism, like politics, makes strange bedfellows.

One of the chief attractions of Mr. Kinney's place is the spacious 'can yard' in the rear, where the ladies and gentlemen of the neighborhood congregate to partake of the succulent "growler" and shoot folly as it flies, or each other, if occasion demands.

The mysterious Woman in Red appears to be the queen of this bohemian realm and the confidante of the proprietor.

In this Bower of Love nightly revels are held, and a man was stabbed to death there last Christmas Eve, but the policeman on the beat, being under the hypnotic influence of the beer, takes no notice of these nocturnal orgies, because it is Mr. Kinney's "vish."

The statesman-proprietor became very uneasy at the protracted stay of his visitors, and finally called one of them aside to plead for leniency in view of an anticipated write-up in the paper.

"You fellows ought to be easy with me," said Kinney. "I don't run no tough place down here, as you can see. I'm an honest man—just as honest as you are—and anybody will tell you so. Just ask any of my friends. They will tell you that 'Snake' Kinney is all right.'"

At the end of their visit, the reporters noted the entire neighborhood had been alerted to their presence and ogled their departure. Furthermore, they later wrote, "The mysterious Woman in Red followed at a safe distance, accompanied by another damsel in flowing robes, and they did not turn back until the party had proceeded eight blocks. ... Mr. Kinney's system is admirable."

The remarkable article provides a glimpse into the working relationship between Kinney and the local police. Indeed, the sarcasm of the author is evident.

The mysterious "Woman in Red" was, in all probability, Catherine Egan, sister of Tom. Kinney had been courting her for quite some time, and they would soon marry, making the Kinneys and Egans family as well as best friends.

Just two weeks after the article went to print, Snake Kinney's feud with Baldy Higgins finally came to a head. At 6 a.m. on September 20, 1896, Kinney, his brother Mike, Tom Egan, and several associates were drinking in Frank Moore's saloon, near the intersection of Sixth and Morgan streets. The men had attended a wedding the previous afternoon and had been celebrating nonstop since then. A beer joint owned by Louis Cella was a few doors down at the corner, and one of Kinney's group staggered into the latter bar, promptly running into Baldy Higgins and his gang. Kinney's associate was badly beaten in the melee and he made his way back to Moore's to tell them what happened.

Snake led his boys out into the street, the men pulling knives, blackjacks, and brass knuckles as they prepared for an epic street brawl. Baldy and his crew spilled into the intersection, ready for action. The two chiefs instantly went for each other, landing haymaker blows and grappling as they rolled around on the horse dropping-strewn pavement.

The respective groups watched their leaders wrestle in the street. The powerful Higgins pinned Kinney to the ground, drew a large knife, and tried to plunge it into his chest. Snake managed to get his revolver out, shoving it against Baldy's left armpit and pulling the trigger. Shot through the lungs, Higgins rolled off Kinney, who jumped up, panting and adrenaline-crazed, and pointed his smoking pistol at Baldy's gang. "Now, if any of you want to take up the fight, come on!" The boys backed off while Kinney and his party repaired to a saloon at Seventh and Franklin for more drinks, where the police found them a short time later.

George "Baldy" Higgins lingered in the hospital until the morning of September 22. Snake Kinney was held immediately after the shooting but was released on a $500 bond provided by

Jim Cronin, saloonkeeper and prominent Democratic politician. Kinney's men had visited Higgins's attending doctor and "persuaded" him to write a note to the judge saying how Baldy was recovering. When Higgins died, Kinney was re-arrested, although the gang boss ultimately was acquitted on the grounds of self-defense. The poor doctor was left to explain why he had signed the note proclaiming his patient's good health just a few hours before Higgins died.

The strings Snake Kinney was able to pull in escaping murder charges were an indication of how far he had come. The man who signed his bond, James Cronin, was one of the best-known political figures in the city. Although only in his early thirties, Cronin looked about twenty years older, with his sizable paunch, handlebar mustache, and cranky demeanor. He represented the First Ward in the House of Delegates, as well as operating his saloon. Cronin was a blacksmith by trade, having worked as a kid in the shop of Ed Butler, who, in 1896, exerted more control over St. Louis than did the mayor or the ward aldermen.

THE BUTLER
MACHINE

BORN IN IRELAND in 1838, Ed Butler ran away from home at the age of twelve and landed in New York. By the end of the Civil War he had moved to St. Louis, where he eventually opened a blacksmithing shop at Tenth and Walnut. Here he employed many stray young toughs from the streets, boys who would grow into men that would do his bidding.

Acquiring great wealth through shrewd business practices (including gaining the horseshoeing contract for all mule- and horse-drawn street railways), Butler soon entered city politics, anointed himself with the title of "Colonel," and before long soon held sway over the House of Delegates. Like any good political machine, the Butler combine dispensed and received favors as needed, from city, state, and even federal officials. Many fat envelopes were passed back and forth to ensure bill passage, candidate support, civic projects, no-bid construction contracts, and countless other things. The Colonel kept himself insulated by using middlemen, or "boodlers," to carry messages and/or bribes, but his real strength lay in the gangs of thugs who enforced his will at the polls.

The Butler political machine had a hand in every law passed in St. Louis in the 1880s and '90s. While the machine itself was referred to as the "Combination" or the "Push," the goons who worked the polls were called "Indians," presumably because they were on the warpath every Election Day.

Despite the fact that he was a Democrat, Colonel Butler was truly bipartisan in spirit, backing whichever candidate served his best interests. When some of his home-party enemies elected E. H. Noonan mayor in 1889, Butler responded by backing the Republican city collector, Henry Ziegenhein, who won the next election handily. Butler's brash and often brutal tactics won city elections for Republicans in 1893, 1895, and 1897. In the midst of this intra-party squabbling, however, lay the seeds of Colonel Ed Butler's eventual demise.

In a sense, Snake Kinney and his band of thugs were a single cog in the Butler machine, the most powerful political force in the state of Missouri. Most of the heady stuff, however, was lost on the low-level hoods who, except on Election Day, were garden-variety criminals rather than political agents. Emboldened after the killing of Baldy Higgins, the Ashley Street boys went on an extended crime spree.

The weekend of November 7-8, 1896, saw the boys especially out of control. Wanted for numerous armed robberies, Mickey Mack McNamara and Dan O'Leary engaged two detectives in a spirited gun battle at the corner of Ninth and Franklin streets on Saturday night. The latter was seriously wounded in the gunplay. In the dead of Monday morning, with the whole precinct looking for the gang, both Tom Egan and Thomas Lamb were arrested in a house on North Broadway.

Most of the "top-liners," as the boys called newspaper head-lines, were dominated by William "Skippy" Rohan, whose ultra-violent criminal career reached a pinnacle in the summer of 1897. On the night of June 16, Skippy and three others capped a week-long robbery spree by holding up the bar of Caspar Beim-fohr. Things went south and the German saloonkeeper ended up getting shot. The four men fled, and Rohan at first took refuge in The Rookery at Fifteenth and O'Fallon streets.

The Butler Machine

The Rookery was a large, three-story building with narrow, dark corridors and steep stairs, and filled with garbage, criminals, lunatics, and drug addicts of the worst order. Police never entered the structure except in sizable force. The Rookery had a lot in common with the more famous bastion of lawlessness, the Old Brewery, in the Five Points district of New York.

Most smart criminals had the sense not to stay in The Rookery any longer than they had to, and one night was more than enough for Skippy Rohan. The next day he relocated to the home of Alice Parsons, a black woman with whom he was romantically involved. She lived at the rear of 1218 Fifteenth Street, and it was in the alley behind her place that Skippy would be cornered by four police officers who somehow had learned of his location.

Rohan fought like a bear, swinging and gouging with utter abandon after failing to get to his revolver in time. Parsons herself joined in the melee, jumping on an officer's back and smacking away until she was thrown off. Rohan eventually was subdued by a full nelson and vicious revolver "taps" to his skull.

Caspar Beimfohr's son identified the locked-up desperado as one of the robbers that had shot his father, and Skippy Rohan was bound over for trial. The gangster knew that only one man had known his whereabouts, twenty-year-old Carl Lohrman, his brother-in-law and protégé, who had been with Rohan during the ill-fated holdup. Regardless of whether his youthful understudy was actually responsible, Rohan thought he was, and that alone was enough to seal his death warrant.

And so it was that Carl Lohrman was lured by Tom Egan and

William "Skippy" Rohan was the most notorious member of the fledgling Egan's Rats, known throughout St. Louis as an incorrigible menace.

Guinea Mack McAuliffe to a meeting at Snake Kinney's saloon on the night of August 9, 1897. What was discussed no one knows, but after leaving the joint, Lohrman walked four blocks west to the intersection of Sixth and Carr, where his archrival Mike Bresnehan was waiting for him. Before the former could utter a greeting, the latter plunged a knife into Lohrman's stomach and ripped upward, leaving him writhing in agony on the sidewalk. Lohrman died the next day, and Bresnehan was arrested and sent away for a short stretch in prison after feeding the police a prearranged story about killing his enemy in self-defense.

It is unknown whether Skippy Rohan's sister ever learned that her husband may have been killed on her brother's orders.

Despite the revenge that had been extracted, there was still an unimpeachable witness against Rohan in the form of Caspar Beimfohr's son, giving the locked-up thief serious misgivings. Later, Skippy said he had bribed the jailer to let him out of his cell. However it went down, Skippy Rohan and two accomplices, Buck O'Malley and Sport Heffernan, escaped from the city workhouse on August 30, 1897. After robbing a saloon for funds a few days later, Rohan and his pals fled to Chicago. While escapes were not altogether uncommon at the workhouse (Harry Horrocks had pulled off a similar stunt a year earlier), the ease with which Skippy bolted led to disciplinary action against several turnkeys and a complete revamping of security.

As for St. Louis's most notorious crook, he and his two partners were recaptured in December. When Rohan finally went to trial in May 1898, he was acquitted. While heading to prison on a separate burglary charge, he declared that he had found the Lord and promised to reform. Unfortunately, this would prove to be a hollow promise.

Skippy Rohan's crimes notwithstanding, Snake Kinney and the Ashley Streeters kept a low profile through the late 1890s. The men who would soon become the Egan's Rats were not even regarded as the toughest gang in the city. At the moment, that unsavory distinction belonged to the Walnut Street Gang, which operated on its namesake between Sixth and Twelfth streets. They were led by Edward Dwyer.

A barrel-chested man of medium height, with a pasty face, beady eyes, and a body mapped with more than two dozen bullet and knife scars, Dwyer was notorious throughout St. Louis. Known as "Bullet" because of his frequent involvement in gunplay, he was a mean, sadistic drunk, and was never without a revolver or large knife on his person. Dwyer thought less about killing a man than he did about blowing his nose. As a boy, he had worked in Colonel Ed Butler's blacksmith shop, and he always turned out at the polls to help his benefactor.

Bullet Dwyer's right-hand man shared his taste for alcohol and violence. Born in New York City in 1876, brought to St. Louis as a boy, William Condon was soon hanging around Butler's blacksmith shop and learning the horseshoeing trade. Following the older Dwyer's lead, William soon fell into a life of crime. Standing five feet eight and weighing 193 pounds, the stout gangster was known as "Tough Bill" because of his penchant for fisticuffs. Condon had been shot and stabbed so many times his torso seemed to be a relief map from hell. When drunk, even his closest friends became nervous. The only person who wasn't afraid of Tough Bill Condon, it seemed, was his pal Bullet Dwyer.

The Walnut Street Gang was noted as having the ear of Colonel Butler himself, due to the fact that its two leaders had worked in his shop as boys. So, too, did Jack Williams, a former police officer who served as Colonel Butler's liaison to the city's underworld.

The *Post-Dispatch* described Jack Williams as "... a handsome fellow, with a frank, open countenance, and a magnificent physique. He is as bold as a lion and is liked by everybody connected to the Police Department." Born in 1873, Williams joined the ranks of Butler minions after a long apprenticeship in the blacksmith shop. What set Williams apart from the rest was his good attitude and amiable demeanor, and like Skippy Rohan, he was known as a ladies man.

Jack joined the police force in March 1896, and in less than a year he was promoted to detective. Williams notched a good arrest record and showed no qualms about wading into a violent crowd, swinging his fists and nightstick, until he captured his

Edward "Bullet" Dwyer, above, and William "Tough Bill" Condon were leaders of the Walnut Street Gang, considered to be the main rivals of the Kinney Gang by the turn of the twentieth century.

man. However, Williams was often disciplined for spending his duty hours in saloons drinking with old pals. One reprimand too many got Williams bounced off the job in May 1898.

Williams soon opened a saloon at Nineteenth and Chestnut streets, which served as a hangout for the Walnut Street boys and any other Butler men who happened to wander into the area. The neighborhood surrounding Williams's saloon was known as Chestnut Valley but more often was called the "Bad Lands" by locals, due to its high crime rate and large number of saloons, brothels, and rickety tenements.

Jack Williams was lauded by his friends and hated by his enemies, who dubbed him, "Bad" Jack. But Williams found his true calling as a saloonkeeper and top Butler henchman, and he first came to the media's attention on the afternoon of March 16, 1899. On this gray, chilly day, the Republican primary was being held in the city. Bad Jack Williams, accompanied by Bullet Dwyer, Harry Horrocks, Coxey Holden, Tim Kelleher, and a couple of others, invaded the Nineteenth Ward, intending to wreak havoc at the polls located at North Grand Avenue and Natural Bridge Road.

The Butler men headed directly for the saloon of Republican State Senator Tom Martin, located at that intersection. A large mob of men milled around the corner, and there was much arguing and commotion. Election Days were seldom peaceful in St. Louis. The men stomped into the place intending to vote but were ejected by a large horde of Republican suitors.

Outside the saloon the turmoil grew. Harry Horrocks responded to the threat by socking one of the offenders in the face with a pair of brass knuckles. Upon seeing this, a congressional committeeman, Edward Damman, whipped out a revolver and a fired a shot that ripped through the top of Bullet Dwyer's bowler. Jack Williams drew his own gun and fired blindly into the crowd killing two men, Edward Kassenbaum and Bud Pierce. Williams and his men fled the angry mob in the confusion. Bad Jack Williams surrendered soon after but was acquitted on a plea of self-defense.

Despite all the Election Day incidents in the past, the shootings of March 16 seemed to call the citizens of St. Louis to action. Colonel Ed Butler had had his run of the city for more than a decade, and it seemed he would stop at nothing to achieve his ends. But public sentiment began to turn against the Butler machine.

By the end of the 1890s, Snake Kinney could sense change in the political winds, as well. By now, he was also a father, with Catherine having given birth to a daughter named Florence. Having reached his early thirties, Kinney was no longer satisfied with being a dutiful understudy of the aging Butler. He had come quite a long way, financially and politically. Tom Egan and the boys reflected that success. They no longer dressed like lowly street urchins but in the finest suits and hats, and tooled around in expensive coaches. No more "ankle express" for the Ashley Street crew. Although, by this time, they were usually referred to as the Kinney gang. The coming year was an election year, and with the dawn of the new century, Thomas "Snake" Kinney, Tom Egan, and their gang would make their power play in St. Louis politics.

The twentieth century dawned ice-cold in St. Louis, the temperature hovering in the teens. On New Year's Night, 1900, Snake Kinney went out carousing with Tom Egan, Harry Horrocks, Sam Young, and a few others. They busted up Mike Fleming's saloon at Twenty-third and Cass, stealing nearly $500. New century or no, for the moment it seemed that things hadn't changed a bit.

A few days later, the Democratic City Committee was reorganized by Harry B. Hawes, head of the police board of commissioners. Those in the minority, including Snake Kinney, Cuddy Mack, John Ryan, and "Kid" Sheridan, quickly looked to regroup their losses. Kinney, seeing the disarray that the city's Democratic leadership was in, decided to run for the House of Delegates the following April.

At the time no one seemed to notice Kinney's decision, nor pay attention to his ambition. The city had more important things to worry about, such as the recording of the new census and the budding war in China, soon to be known as the Boxer Rebellion. The Butlers then lost one of their "best" men.

A feud had been brimming within the ranks of the Walnut Street Gang for some time. Even the best of friends, Bullet Dwyer and Tough Bill Condon, were in conflict. On the evening of May 3, 1900, the two met in Condon's saloon at Tenth and Walnut and began fighting. After bystanders patched them up, they sat down and continued drinking all through the rest of the night.

The sun was rising as the two inebriated thugs carefully made their way two blocks west to Jim Cronin's saloon. At 7:30, the two began squabbling again. Condon clawed out a .32-caliber revolver and shot Dwyer twice through the chest, the close-range blasts setting his clothes on fire. Dwyer staggered into the front doorway and fell dead, while the extremely intoxicated Condon unsuccessfully snapped his gun a third time over the body. Not surprisingly, the authorities dismissed this an act of crooks killing other crooks and Tough Bill Condon went free.

Whatever was left of the Walnut Street Gang gravitated to Bad Jack Williams's saloon, where Bill Condon established himself as Jack's second-in-command. Williams and his men would find themselves aligned against Snake Kinney in the months leading up to the St. Louis municipal election.

Kinney, in the meantime, had broken ranks and struck an alliance with police board chairman Harry Hawes, who would use Kinney's gang as his personal army in the coming months. Other Democratic gangsters like John J. Ryan and Cuddy Mack were left out in the cold, fueling their resentment toward the

Fourth Ward boss. In saloons and political clubs across the city, supporters of each camp frequently squared off against one another.

Trouble initially reared its head on October 1, 1900, when saloonkeeper Oliver "Curley" Keyes, rumored to be friendly with Snake Kinney, forcibly ejected a bunch of Butler goons from his place at Twenty-second and Chestnut. Tough Bill Condon happened upon the squabbling men and ended the debate by shooting Keyes dead.

Retaliation of sorts came in the early morning hours of November 6, 1900, when members of the Kinney gang invaded the Bad Lands, spoiling for a fight. At 3 o'clock, in the street in front of Mike Churchill's saloon at Twenty-third and Chestnut, a gun battle erupted between the opposing sides. Frank Hussey was seriously wounded in the stomach. The injured man was transported to City Hospital by none other than original Ashley Streeter Mickey Mack McNamara, who now worked as a cabman and just happened to be on the scene when Hussey was shot by his old pals. Frank's brother Dan and half-brother Lawler Daly removed him from the hospital at gunpoint, saying that he could recover just fine at home, which he did.

The Kinneys struck again in late January 1901, when Guinea Mack McAuliffe shot and killed a Butler "Indian" named Foxy Regan in a dive bar at Third and Biddle streets. Tom Egan was arrested as a witness but didn't say a word while McAuliffe beat the rap.

In the spring of 1901, just before the election, Kinney tried to bag two of his rivals in one fell swoop. William "Red" Houlihan, who had just got out of jail after trying to kill a cop in the alley in back of the Standard Theater, was designated by Snake to assassinate both Ryan and Cuddy Mack.

Sometime after midnight on March 15, 1901, Red Houlihan infiltrated Ryan and Cuddy Mack's saloon at the northwest corner of Sixth and Franklin. Upstairs, in the bar area, were Cuddy and John "Skinny" Golden. Houlihan instead went into the basement to get John Ryan. In an impressive display of hand-to-hand combat Ryan overpowered Red and shot him in the back as he tried to escape. Ryan faced no charges for killing Houlihan but Snake Kinney never forgot, especially after he was overwhelmingly elected to the House of Delegates a few weeks later. He then closed his saloon at Second and Carr and devoted himself full-time to politics. His brother Mike was elected constable of Justice Halloran's court, with Guinea Mack McAuliffe as his deputy. The constable positions under various city judges were highly prized by the town's gangsters, as constables were permitted to carry firearms and even make arrests if necessary.

Upon his swearing in, Snake Kinney pledged an oath that typified the graft and corruption in St. Louis city politics. A pledge worthy of the Mafia itself:

> I do swear before Almighty God that ... I will vote and act with the Combination ... that I will not at any place or any time reveal the fact that there is a Combination ... that I will not communicate ... anything that may take place at any meeting. ...
>
> And I do solemnly agree that, in case I should reveal the fact that any person in this Combination has received money, I hereby permit and authorize other members of the Combination to take the forfeit of my life ... and that my throat may be cut, my tongue torn out, and my body thrown into the Mississippi River.

Two weeks after the try on Ryan's life, the Butler hoodlums committed a prank that would shock much of the city.

The Williams Gang's territory bordered the city's Chinese neighborhood, which was derisively referred to by white St. Louisans as "Hop Alley." Toward the end of March, one of the most important leaders in the Asian community, Gam Lee, passed away, and his constituents planned to give him a grand funeral. His body was laid out on the night of March 28, 1901, in a house at the rear of 712 Market Street, encircled by candles and burning incense.

That same night, at Bad Jack Williams's place at Nineteenth and Chestnut, the top Butler gangsters were drinking heavily and making snide remarks about the passing of the Chinese leader. In the course of their conversations, the boys concocted a scheme to steal Gam Lee's body, walk him into Williams's saloon *Weekend at Bernie's*-style, prop him up at the bar, and "serve" him drinks by pouring whiskey and beer down his throat.

A wagon sped toward "Hop Alley," driven by John J. Ryan, Tough Bill Condon, and a large, smirking goon known as "Dutch Louie" Fingerlin. At 9:30 p.m. the three men forced their way into the house past several guards who were apparently under the influence of opium. The three picked up the coffin, gingerly stepped out to their wagon, and took off. An alarm was sounded by a black man who was on the premises, Speedy Miller, and soon a large number of Chinese flooded the streets, crying that Gam Lee's body had been stolen.

Detective-turned-gangster "Bad Jack" Williams was Colonel Ed Butler's personal liaison to the St. Louis underworld.

Miller chased after the men on foot and kept them in sight until they got to Ninth and Walnut. He queried passersby about the speeding wagon. The three body snatchers, despite their drunkenness, soon realized the folly of their ways. One of them, probably Ryan, suggested they ditch their cargo immediately. The coffin was left in the wagon at the corner of Twenty-third and Pine, and the boys made their way on foot back to Bad Jack's.

The whole city was incensed by the ghoulish prank. Tough Bill Condon and Dutch Louie Fingerlin surrendered the next day after sobering up. Condon (while carefully omitting mention of John Ryan's presence) declared that they weren't body snatchers, and that the whole thing was done as a joke. The police failed to see the humor, as both men were charged. When Bad Jack Williams was questioned as to why he would want to steal Gam Lee's body, he snorted, "Hell, the chink was already dead. He wouldn't mind it a bit."

The Williams Gang's violent antics continued at the Irish Nationalists' picnic on August 11, 1901. Tough Bill Condon, well known as a tinhorn gambler, was operating a poker game. One player named Hugo Stang had the audacity to accuse Tough Bill of cheating and was shot for it. The bullet that passed through his leg did an encore number on an innocent bystander named George Maxwell.

Ten days later, the top Butler hoods were carousing and desired entrance to the Delmar racetrack. Not fazed by their drunken threats, gatekeeper Joseph Graham ran them off at the point of a shotgun. Later that night Bad Jack, Tough Bill, Dutch Louie, and "Oyster Jack" Seifort found Graham outside Louis Cella's saloon at Twenty-first and Washington. Twenty to thirty shots were fired, but Graham was able to jump up and sprint away from the scene. The gangsters had been drinking so heavily that hot summer day that only one of their shots hit Graham, and he soon recovered from the wound. Colonel Ed Butler now found himself in the position of being the primary alibi for his main goons.

Probably at Butler's behest, Williams conceived a scheme to get himself some good publicity by inviting renowned black preacher Mary McGee Hall to preach and pray at his saloon. On the evening of August 30, 1901, Hall and her choir performed in the rough dive. The Williams gangsters cleaned themselves up and refrained from alcohol and profanity while Hall preached a sermon and her choir performed several hymns. It was such a success that Hall returned for a repeat performance two months later. But despite his best efforts, Bad Jack Williams still found himself in the worst legal trouble of his short life.

On the night of December 22, 1901, John J. Ryan was shot in the back in front of a saloon at Twelfth and Clark. Ryan survived his wound and loudly declared that his assailant was Mike Kinney, Snake's younger brother.

Ryan declared that, although he had been shot in the back, he had chased Mike Kinney half a block before collapsing. "I haven't got any hard feeling toward Mike," he said later. "He and his brother Snake are dead ones in politics, and that's why they're sore on me. Their gang drew straws to see which one would kill me. I've got that straight from fellows that used to train with them."

Kinney ridiculed his charges, saying, "He just brought us into this trouble to make the public think that he cuts a little ice in politics up in the Fourth Ward and that he is my rival. It's good advertisement for his saloon business to tell the public that I think I must get him out of the way to keep my standing in the ward."

No matter what the public made of the tit-for-tat sniping in the paper, everyone could see that John "Baldy" Ryan was now running scared after two attempts on his life. Within a year, Snake Kinney's power would be established without a doubt and the Butler machine would be virtually destroyed.

George Williams (no relation to Bad Jack) was the smallest detective in the St. Louis Police Department. Standing five feet four and weighing about 130 pounds, he was nevertheless strong and fearless in the line of duty. The main reason the undersized man got on the force was because his father, William Williams, was a well-known detective and pulled enough strings to create the necessary opening for his son. George soon built a reputation as a cop who, some thought, resorted to his gun a bit more often than was necessary.

On the morning of April 23, 1898, he chased, shot, and killed William McBriarty, a derelict he had found in the 3900 block of Washington Avenue. Witnesses said the shooting was unprovoked, but Williams walked, probably due to his father's juice and the fact that the victim had no family in America. In November 1901, Detective Williams had assisted in the capture of the notorious outlaw Ben Kilpatrick, member of the Wild Bunch. A month later, while in Houston, Texas, on a case, Williams was involved in a shootout that left two detectives and a confidence man dead.

And it just so happened that Detective George Williams would face off against Tough Bill Condon in the early morning hours of January 6, 1902.

At 2 a.m. Williams was at the corner of Twenty-first and Chestnut with his partner, Detective James Burke, when they heard yelling, curses, and the sound of breaking glass. Rushing into the brothel of Belle Payton at 2032 Chestnut, the two learned that Condon had gotten into an argument with one of the girls and had physically worked her over. The two detectives bounded into the back alley and caught the intoxicated Condon before he had gone very far.

Detective Williams said later that he acted in self-defense, and a jury believed him. Condon claimed the attack was unprovoked and politically motivated. Whichever was telling the truth, Williams shot Tough Bill four times. Condon staggered out of the alley and south on Twenty-first Street. By the time he got to Market Street, he collapsed in a heap.

As doctors prepped the dying Tough Bill Condon for what turned out to be unsuccessful surgery, he murmured, "Tell Jack I'm still Butler's man."

Bad Jack's saloon at Nineteenth and Chestnut had been closed two days earlier when Williams lost his liquor license, probably due to all his notoriety. Two days after that, his assault trial began. He, Dutch Louie Fingerlin, and Oyster Jack Seifort were ultimately acquitted on the charges of shooting Joseph Graham. Williams would celebrate by attending a parade on St. Patrick's Day. Feeling confident and brash, Williams spent the day without an overcoat, despite cold temperatures and biting winds, which resulted in his catching a bad cold.

In 1902, there was a world of difference in treating illnesses. Williams remained up and about, spending time in smoky saloons. His cold turned into tuberculosis, and in the middle of the following summer, he journeyed to Arizona, thinking the dry air would relieve his lungs. However, triple-digit temperatures drove Williams back to St. Louis within a few weeks.

The formerly large man eventually wasted away to a shadow of his former self, although even in the face of death, Williams remained personable and chipper. On the morning of October 7, 1902, Bad Jack Williams died in his home at 2833 Bernard Street. He was only twenty-nine years old.

The Butler Machine

Colonel Ed Butler probably paid scant notice to the passing of his old protégé, because he was fighting for his political life.

Butler's nemesis came in the form of Joseph W. Folk, the son of a Baptist preacher who was born in Brownsville, Tennessee, in 1869. In his early twenties he left his rural background behind and migrated to St. Louis to practice law. Folk originally had hitched his career wagon to Harry Hawes, whose original attempt in 1900 to break up the Butler machine was unsuccessful. Almost all policemen were fanatically loyal to Hawes, having joined his political club, the Jefferson.

In 1900, St. Louis was rocked by labor troubles, the worst of which involved the new Amalgamated Association of Street Railway Employees union. More than a dozen men were killed in skirmishes throughout the spring and summer. Certain city Democrats, who had always smarted under Colonel Butler's heavy hand, had been grooming Joseph Folk for the circuit attorney slot, figuring the strikers certainly could be counted on to vote for him.

At first, Butler underestimated the bland, bespectacled country boy, but years later he recalled his fatal mistake:

> "I was going to nominate a man named Clark—good fellow, and all right, far's I know—when in comes Harry Hawes to my office one day an' says, 'Colonel, how bad do you want that man Clark?' An' I says, 'I dunno; I've promised it to him.' 'Well,' Harry says, 'I got a young feller named Folk who wants to have it.'
>
> "That was Harry's way. He wanted to be a leader, an' he knew he couldn't beat me fair, so he done it the other way. I said, 'Well, I'll see Clark and see what he says.' And I seen him, and he says he didn't need the office particularly, and I says, 'Well, if you don't, Harry Hawes's got a young feller named Folk that's been attorney for the union labor fellers and settled up their strike for 'em, and Harry kind o' wants to name him.'
>
> "So the next time I seen Harry I says, 'Bring your little man around,' and he done it and I looked him over and there

didn't seen to be anything the matter with him, so I says all right, and he was nominated. An' look what he done—spent four years tryin' to put me in the penitentiary—that's the kind of man Harry Hawes is. He's a leader and now I'm out. An' that's how he done it."

Actually, the episode had little to do with Hawes. The reason that Butler was so eager to please the police board director is that he wanted his son, James, to be elected to Congress as painlessly as possible. Jim Butler was indeed elected to Congress, and James Folk won the race for circuit attorney, because of a ton of "Indian" support at the polls that November.

In light of his personality and future actions, it seems that Joseph Folk wasn't necessarily in need of Colonel Butler's help. He just used a man he personally despised to get himself into a position where he could destroy him. Folk began seeking the details of every bribe Butler had ever paid, every contract that he had ever greased, and every "boodler" he'd had contact with. Many people were arrested as a result of Folk's investigations, including Butler himself, on March 14, 1902.

By the end of the year, Folk had obtained thirteen convictions against the Butler machine. The big man remained out of reach temporarily, but in 1903, he amassed five convictions, and the following year, the year of the World's Fair, he had tallied another five. Overall, Folk's investigations against the Butler machine resulted in sixty-one indictments, forty-three for bribery and eighteen for perjury.

Even Colonel Ed Butler's trial in Columbia, Missouri, resulted in a guilty verdict for the boss in early February 1904. The Missouri Supreme Court, however, threw out that conviction (as it had done earlier) on specious legal grounds. Many of the justices were Butler's friends and hated ambitious Circuit Attorney Joseph Folk. While Butler may have escaped prison, his political machine was shattered, and he was never again an important force in St. Louis politics.

3

ON THE RISE

AS THE BAD Jack Williams Gang split up and Colonel Ed Butler was preoccupied with his legal troubles in 1902, the war between the backers of Ed Butler and Harry Hawes cooled off.

Snake Kinney was becoming very well known among the city's business elite, especially the Lemp brewing family. He drew unwanted heat after a March incident in which he shot and wounded a Cuddy Mack supporter named Daniel Shea. Kinney's bond was posted by Charles Lemp. That same month, Tom Egan was charged with assault with intent to kill when he tried to gun down Barney Caples (a brother of Will and the late Jerry) outside a Franklin Avenue saloon. Egan easily beat the rap, as he did when he was charged, along with Guinea Mack McAuliffe, with brutally pistol-whipping and robbing a man on a deserted downtown street the night of November 14.

Cuddy Mack McGillicuddy had been elected as a constable of the Fifth District, in addition to running his saloon at Sixth and Franklin. For Christmas 1902, Cuddy Mack received a gold badge embroidered with diamonds, a gift from some of his well-connected friends. But like his predecessors, Cuddy Mack couldn't keep a low profile.

A month after receiving his fancy badge, in the early morning hours of January 20, 1903, Cuddy Mack got into an argument with two black men on a streetcar. At High and Franklin, all three men got off, hurling oaths and curses at each other. Cuddy whipped out his revolver and opened fire, killing an innocent bystander, J. H. Lahmer. The two blacks, as well as several witnesses, claimed Cuddy Mack had drunkenly hurled racial slurs at them and they responded in kind. At his two subsequent trials, Cuddy claimed that the black men had tried to steal his gold watch. Whoever was telling the truth, Cuddy Mack was acquitted of murder at his trial.

Cuddy Mack's fortunes began to decline after this embarrassing incident. John "Baldy" Ryan had been a partner in Cuddy's saloon, but they had a dispute in the fall of 1902 which led to the dissolution of that partnership. In the wee hours of May 3, 1903, that falling out came to a head. None of the witnesses ever admitted to seeing a thing, but Cuddy Mack and Baldy Ryan engaged in an epic bar fight at the former's saloon. During the scuffle, Cuddy got his pistol out but Ryan snatched it away from him and proceeded to fracture his skull with it. Ryan grazed him with a couple of bullets before he fled. Cuddy was taken to the police station by a corrupt beat cop.

Newspapers speculated over what had provoked the fight. Cuddy Mack was found, badly beaten, at his Morgan Street house, claiming it was nothing doing. He recovered from his wounds, but his reputation on the street did not. Baldy Ryan, under indictment for fraud charges, beat his cases and quit St. Louis forever, moving down to New Orleans.

Kinney, in other words, literally had to sit back and watch his rivals destroy themselves. The Kinney gang continued to gain members and satellite clubs sprung up all over St. Louis, after pledging allegiance to the Fourth Ward boss.

Snake himself submitted to an interview with a *Post-Dispatch* reporter in early May 1903. He claimed he didn't want to be referred to as "Snake" anymore, now that he was respectable, and expounded on the ins and outs of city politics: "There's only one way to get along, whether it's politics, business, or religion, an' that's to hustle. What's the use of goin' around the corner— jump the fence! It keeps me hustlin' all the time between business and politics. I make my livin' out of business. I'm in politics because I like it, just like some men get their fun out of bettin' on the races or goin' to a ball game or gettin' rich or goin' to church. Every man to his sport. Mine's politics."

What was left of the Butler political machine suffered another blow with the murder of Michael Churchill. Thirty-seven years old, Churchill had been a top Butler gangster from the mid-1880s until the early 1890s, mentoring such future gangsters as Bad Jack Williams and Tough Bill Condon. Eventually he opened a saloon and two popular dance halls in the Bad Lands. Churchill's bar, located at 2301 Chestnut Street, had been a popular hangout for Butler "Indians" for more than a decade. Ex-cop William Williams, father of George, served as the bouncer.

On May 30, 1903, the sixty-two-year-old Williams spent the whole day drinking and got into an argument with his boss in front of the Imperial Garden dance hall. Mike Churchill was fatally shot in the stomach, proving that itchy trigger fingers ran in the Williams family.

Snake Kinney re-opened his old saloon downtown at 211 North Ninth Street. His heart was still with the clubs and gangs, which was probably the reason for his re-entering the saloon business. He also mulled over the possibility of running for the state senate in 1904.

His best friend and brother-in-law, Tom Egan, was the undisputed leader of the Kinney gang on the street. The twenty-eight-year-old Egan was now married to Nellie Woelfel, a shapely brunette who was a sister of two members of the gang, Fred and George Woelfel. Tom's nineteen-year-old brother Willie had now thrown himself wholeheartedly into the mix, trying to emulate his big brother, who now operated his own saloon at the southwestern corner of Broadway and Carr, which would become home base for the gang.

In later years, a reporter offered this description of Egan's saloon:

> His boast that the saloon at Broadway and Carr streets is perhaps the quietest in St. Louis' appears well-founded to a casual visitor. Almost a hush, which becomes uncanny after a few minutes, seems to brood over the place. There is no clinking of glasses, no shouted toast, no laughter. The bartender steals about silently. Pallid young men, well-dressed, sit solitary at tables, or tiptoe across the floor to whisper to a comrade.

Just after midnight on the sweltering evening of August 20, 1903, two men robbed the St. Charles Hotel at Fourteenth and St. Charles. Patrolman Michael Cremins stumbled upon the robbers as they escaped. One shot him in the leg and ran off while the other fled in the opposite direction. Cremins hobbled after the second bandit, Richard Wright, wounding and capturing him a few blocks away. He would later identify the robber who got away as Deputy Constable John "Guinea Mack" McAuliffe.

Ten minutes after the robbery, Guinea Mack was spotted in a runabout buggy near the scene of the crime, accompanied by a man identified later as Frederick Becker. A patrolman ordered him to stop, but McAuliffe flashed his star and proceeded east along Washington Avenue. At Broadway, at 12:30 a.m., he met up with a fellow deputy sheriff, John Munson, in his buggy. The men, along with several others, had attended a funeral earlier in the day and had been at Egan's saloon most of the evening. The three childhood friends began racing their rigs, the finish line being Egan's saloon at Broadway and Carr, five blocks away.

The horse-drawn buggies clattered furiously north on Broadway, scaring passersby out of the way as the two men boozily laughed and shouted at each other. Guinea Mack won the first race. A bunch of the boys had spilled out of the saloon to watch, including Tom Egan's father, Martin. The deputies turned their buggies around and raced back to Washington. Police Sergeant

Ted Lally saw the pair speeding down the street and furiously ordered them to stop.

Instead, they wheeled around and headed back to Egan's at a dead gallop. By now the noise of the racing buggies had attracted considerable attention, and Guinea Mack had even run over a pedestrian. Two policemen, Michael Burke and James Kennedy, along with a private watchman named William Burke, were waiting by the saloon for the men to return.

Guinea Mack McAuliffe, in the lead, bore down on the saloon. Witnesses reported one of the cops saying, "Here he comes. Line up." The three peace officers opened fire on his buggy. One bullet struck McAuliffe in the head, while Becker jumped out in terror and bounced painfully along the street. The horses pulled the buggy another two blocks before Guinea Mack tumbled out dead at the intersection of Broadway and O'Fallon.

At the sound of the shots, John Munson immediately wheeled his rig west on Carr Street and escaped. Martin Egan stood on the sidewalk outside his son's saloon screaming that the police had murdered "Guinea," whom he had known since birth.

Just about everyone on the scene told conflicting stories about McAuliffe's death. The police at first denied they had shot him, even though witnesses stated they had deliberately lined up and fired. When arrested later, John Munson shed no light on what happened. A grand jury decided that Patrolman Burke had fired the fatal shot. Why the police shot Guinea Mack is open to question. No warnings were given. It's possible that the police were notified by telephone of the hotel robbery, went to Egan's saloon to look for suspects, and came upon the racing thugs. The wounded robber, Richard Wright, at first identified Guinea Mack as his partner but later recanted.

In the end, all that's certain is that twenty-six-year-old John "Guinea Mack" McAuliffe was fatally shot by police officers who escaped punishment—a prime example of how far civil rights have progressed in the last century. Whether they were acting forcibly toward a potential robbery suspect and attacker of a fellow officer, or were acting on someone's orders, will never be known. Guinea Mack was given a grand funeral with a huge cortege to Calvary Cemetery, his coffin resting in a white hearse pulled by a team of white horses.

The banner year of 1904 saw crime and politics in St. Louis in a state of flux. Since the collapse of the Butler machine, no one group controlled the city. The ward bosses in the House of Delegates ran their respective districts as their personal fiefdoms. Joseph Folk, fresh from his triumph against Colonel Ed Butler, announced his candidacy for the Democratic nomination for governor of the state of Missouri. Butler's old nemesis Harry Hawes was making his long-desired grab for power. Hawes could count of the support most Democrats, who were still smarting from the corruption investigations.

At the beginning of the year, Thomas Kinney declared his candidacy for the state senate, representing St. Louis's Fourth Ward. However, he jeopardized his career in the early morning hours of February 19, 1904, while partying with a group of friends at the Morgan Club at Jefferson and Chestnut as group of black musicians played onstage. Kinney, like most other white St. Louisans of the era, was prejudiced against blacks. In a drunken funk, he began to verbally abuse a singer named Walter Sloan, finishing his tirade by jerking out a pistol and firing a bullet into him. Kinney was hustled away and lucked out when Sloan eventually recovered.

The episode seems finally to have convinced Kinney that he would get nowhere in state politics if his kept getting arrested for shootings and fights. It was around this time that Tom Egan assumed all responsibility for the street gang. Thus, by the spring of 1904, the Kinney gang was now being referred to as the Egan gang.

Shortly after the Morgan Club shooting, Mike Kinney and Tom Egan served as the Fourth Ward's delegates to the St. Louis Democratic convention, supporting Harry Hawes. The head of the police board also could count on the fifty or sixty men who at times were under the banner of Egan. Their ranks had swelled quite a bit in the last ten years, since the days when they were a handful of delinquents who snatched purses and broke into houses.

Hawes also could count on support form various judges and aldermen throughout St. Louis, as well as most of the St. Louis Police Department, many of whose members belonged to Hawes's Jefferson Club.

The Egan gang wreaked serious havoc at the St. Louis County Democratic convention on March 1, 1904. Many of the boys headed for the courthouse in Clayton as fast as the streetcars could carry them. The hoods stormed the building, physically assaulting the Folk delegates and disrupting the convention. A murder trial in an adjacent courtroom was halted due to the ruckus. Two newspaper reporters who attempted to capture the melee on film were attacked, and their camera was smashed to pieces on the ground.

A few weeks later, Hawes carried the city of St. Louis by a 5-to-1 margin. The "Indians" were indeed on the warpath. Intimidation at the polls, repeat voting, and voting under other people's names were standard operating procedure.

Despite a poor showing in the city, Folk was carrying many counties across Missouri, as many people were encouraged by his anti-corruption platform. Judges and businessmen from around the region let it be known that they supported Folk for governor, and even President Theodore Roosevelt gave him a personal endorsement.

With the opening of the World's Fair in April, the eyes of the country, and perhaps the world, were on St. Louis like never before. With its awe-inspiring exhibits, fountains, and rides, it was an event for the ages, one that would be heralded even a century later. That August, athletes from around the world trekked to St. Louis to compete in the Summer Olympic Games, the first time the event had been held in the United States. There was a dark side, as well. Despite a strong police presence, members of the Egan gang worked the large throngs of visitors at the fair and in Forest Park itself. Their main crimes were pickpocketing and purse snatching, although con games and illicit gambling were not uncommon. Out and out robbery was discouraged by Tom Egan.

In all likelihood, Egan and his boys were exposed to the first wonders of the dawning twentieth century: X-rays, long-distance telephone service, the horseless carriage, and motion pictures, which were five- to eight-minute films whose flickering images were shown on sheets in darkened tents. Sixty-six automobiles completed a drive from New York to St. Louis, quite a feat at the time. More ominous for the Egan gang was a demonstration of the science of fingerprinting by a Scotland Yard detective. Billed as a revolutionary method in tracking down criminals, finger-printing was formally adopted by the St. Louis Police Department during the World's Fair.

After the Olympics ended and the crowds left, the Egans returned to doing what they did best: political terrorism. At two o'clock on the afternoon of September 19, 1904, nine members of the Egan gang aimed to do some repeat voting as well as put the fear of God into Oliver J. Beck, a local blacksmith and Republican judge of registration who had hated the Kinney-Egan gang for years. The polling place was located inside J. D. Stevens's painting business at the northwestern corner of Fourteenth and St. Charles streets.

The men barged up to the registration desk and crowded around Beck. He registered one of the men but then refused to sign up the other thugs. The judge accused the goons of fraudulently attempting to register, to which the Egans responded with loud curses and threats. Beck slipped away and armed himself with a large, blue-steel .41-caliber revolver. When he returned, he found that all the "Indians" had registered in his absence.

Soon it appeared that hell itself had ascended into downtown St. Louis. The weather suddenly turned nasty, and gray-black clouds brought a surreal darkness to the midday hours. The temperature quickly plunged twenty degrees, and winds gusting to thirty miles an hour swept the streets as a thunderstorm crackled and boomed overhead as the situation degenerated at the polling place.

The gangsters were still inside, and in a rage they chased Beck out into the street. The terrified election boss forgot about his gun and raced south toward Locust Street as a crowd of pedestrians gawked, oblivious to the raging storm. At least two of the Egans drew pistols and opened fire on the fleeing Republican judge. Beck made it to Locust and darted around the corner.

One of his pursuers stood in middle of Locust in front of the Crawford Theater and fired at least three shots at the fleeing Beck. Two of the rounds struck and killed Frederick Scheel, a postgraduate student at the St. Louis Law School who had emerged from class into a political riot. Beck disappeared into the pouring rain, as did the "Indians."

The youthful Scheel was a promising student and a member of one of the most prominent families in Belleville, Illinois. Public outrage at his slaying was tremendous Many people called for someone, *anyone*, to restore some semblance of order in city politics. The public furor was greater than the uproar five years earlier over Bad Jack Williams's antics in the Nineteenth Ward.

Witnesses to the slaying were generally confused and told conflicting stories. Oliver Beck added the interesting tidbit that a St. Louis detective named George Cosgrove had stood by and smiled as he watched the mob do its bloody work. The gunman on Locust who shot Scheel was described as being about five feet nine, 175 pounds, with red hair, a blue sack coat, and a black stiff hat.

Police knew exactly where to look for suspects. Nine members of the Egan gang were hauled out of Thomas Egan's saloon. It was duly noted that two of the suspects had red hair and the nicknames to match: Thomas "Red" Kane and William "Red" Giebe. The latter was identified as the main shooter; however, because of the con-

GETTING READY FOR THE FRAY.

COUNTY CONVENTION MARCH 1

When the Egan gang stormed the polls on Election Day, they were dubbed "Indians on the warpath," as this editorial cartoon shows.

fused accounts, a cloud of suspicion hovered over Oliver Beck. Despite cries for justice from many quarters, none was dispensed. Republicans in the city decried the shooting while accusing Harry Hawes of using both the police department and criminals to further Democratic supremacy at the polls.

During the grand jury investigation that followed, Giebe and the rest of the Egan goons disappeared, and Beck was accused of the shooting. The plucky blacksmith was soon exonerated; however, and Detective George Cosgrove quickly became the focus of the proceedings. Opinion was split over whether Cosgrove or Giebe had done the shooting. For a time, that was where the matter rested.

That fall, Joseph Folk was elected governor of Missouri and Theodore Roosevelt was elected U.S. president. In the most significant development for the Egan gang, Thomas "Snake" Kinney was elected to the state senate, giving the crew a personal representative in Jefferson City. Kinney's longtime ambitions had been realized. His was a classic American story: poor boy makes good and gives back to the community. Most people who trumpeted this version didn't mention all the blood that had been spilled for Kinney to attain that position.

As an added bonus, Sam Young beat out Cuddy Mack McGillicuddy for the constable position in Judge O'Halloran's court, gaining a foothold in the Fifteenth Ward for the Egans.

Given his new office, people finally stopped calling him "Snake"; now it was Senator Kinney. The Egan gang was now the single most powerful group in St. Louis, whether flexing its criminal or political muscle.

After the heat from the Scheel grand jury had died down, one of the original Ashley Street boys was embroiled in a crime that would remain a whispered mystery in St. Louis gangland. By this time, Eddie Kelleher had just about hit rock bottom; he was often ill and drinking heavily, living in a dingy room above a saloon at Eleventh and Chestnut. After midnight on January 29, 1905, Kelleher was standing at the bar in Mike Walsh's tavern at 2131

Pine Street with about six other people. The honored guest that night was a young lightweight boxer, "St. Louis Tommy" Sullivan, who was extremely popular among the city's gangsters and had amassed a modest record in the ring. By the end of the night, St. Louis Tommy would be shot to death and Eddie Kelleher would be accused of his murder. As usual, no one in the bar had seen a thing, but one stranger claimed that Sullivan had gasped on his deathbed that Kelleher was his assailant.

At his arraignment, Kelleher nearly fainted when he learned of the indictment and screamed his innocence up until the moment he was sentenced to twenty-five years in prison. No motive was given, and the only evidence the state presented was the testimony of one witness who claimed to have heard the alleged deathbed confession. The incident was branded yet another St. Louis saloon dispute that had ended in bloodshed. The investigating officer in the case, Detective Lee Killian, often hinted that he had an explosive clue regarding the Sullivan slaying.

By the summer of 1905, a new gang began to make itself heard in St. Louis.

The Bad Lands had been somewhat quiet in the years since the Bad Jack Williams gang had broken up. Since then the local hoods had been aimless, with no sense of purpose or direction. Into the void left by Williams stepped Frank Hussey, the only member of Bad Jack's inner circle who survived had Governor Folk's assault on the Butler machine in the early 1900s.

By the time Williams succumbed to consumption, Hussey had gone into city politics, representing the Twenty-second Ward in the House of Delegates. The twenty-six-year-old bruiser was one of the few gangsters in the city who had attended college, studying business and political science at St. Louis University. Despite his political gains, at heart Frank Hussey was still a tough guy. At one meeting of the House of Delegates, Hussey approached brewing bigwig August "Gussie" Busch to try to get him to quit holding up the passage of a bill. After a long, threatening speech before the delegates, Hussey finally had to be dragged out of the place by police. Gussie Busch was said to have admired his pluck.

Sometime during the first half of 1905, Hussey reorganized the local roughnecks into a new gang. Their home turf, known as the Bad Lands or Bottoms, gave them their name: the "Bottoms Gang."

The mob's leader on the street was seventeen-year-old Tony Foley, a short, heavily muscled kid who had lived his whole life on the rough streets of the Bad Lands. Others gang members included Beverly Brown, Cornelius "Connie" Sullivan, Edward "Red" McAuliffe, Edward Devine, John Murphy, Richard McLaughlin, Joe Swisher, John Bracken, Wesley "Red" Simons, John Cotty, Rex McDonald, and Pete, Eddie, and Emmett Carroll. They began terrorizing the rundown neighborhood in earnest, assaulting the residents and engaging in more serious crimes such as gang-rape and murder. Two of them, Richard McLaughlin and Red McAuliffe, would survive assassination attempts that winter.

Frank Hussey assumed his place as the political head of the Bottoms Gang, serving the same function that Snake Kinney did for the Egan gang. In pictures of the era, a broken-nosed Hussey gazes vacantly at the camera, a smug, bored look on his rough face. Frank dreamed of the day when he would be the overlord of all crime in St. Louis. To do this, he knew he eventually would have to unseat Tom Egan, a task Hussey considered himself up to. Ever since being shot by the Egans in a Bad Lands street brawl in 1900, he'd been itching to pay them back.

Hussey's partner was his half-brother, Lawrence "Lawler" Daly, a member of the city and state Democratic committees. Daly was also eager to topple the Egan mob, after losing to Sam Young in the constable's election. His political roost was the Hibernia Literary and Social Club at 2320 Olive Street. Daly also controlled most of St. Louis's "policy" games, or illegal lottery games. The games were prevalent in the city's black neighborhoods, and Daly controlled the racket with an iron fist. The most popular policy wheels in the city, the "Little Joe" and "Mobile," were run out of the Hibernia Club, with Daly's black runners collecting the bets and handling the payoffs. The policy game would remain the bread and butter of the Bottoms Gang for many years.

The grand jury in the Scheel case reconvened in October 1905. Circuit Attorney Joseph Sager asked for an indictment against Detective George Cosgrove. Sager also claimed that the police had totally botched the initial investigation by failing to locate and interview many potential witnesses. A secret indictment was soon issued for William "Red" Giebe, who was still in hiding while fighting a five-year sentence for robbery. After his arrest, Giebe's $30,000 bond eventually would be posted by Charles Lemp.

The Egan gang got word of the secret indictment, and Senator Kinney pulled some strings to get Giebe out of trouble. Red's robbery conviction had recently been upheld by the Missouri Supreme Court, and Kinney worked out a deal whereby Giebe would surrender to Supreme Court Marshal Finks on the robbery warrant, insulating him from the murder charge. At 1:30 p.m. on May 30, 1906, Red Giebe and Mike Kinney pulled up to the Chestnut Street entrance of the Laclede Hotel in an expensive coach. Within twenty minutes, Giebe and Finks were on their way to the state prison at Jefferson City. According to the deal struck, the only punishment Giebe received for killing Fred Scheel was a five-year sentence for the robbery.

This maneuver was child's play for Tom Kinney, who was proving himself a most able legislator. He constructed landmark legislation that curtailed child labor practices, spearheading one bill that forbade the employment of children under fourteen and another that limited women's work no more than eight hours a day. Kinney was also praised for his efforts to use state prisoners to repair Missouri's road system, providing cheap labor, smooth roads, as well as fresh air and exercise for the convicts. Despite his support for the alcohol industry, he passed a law forbidding the opening of saloons near the University of Missouri in Columbia, so students could concentrate on their classes.

A *Post-Dispatch* article in August 1906 detailed what happened the first time Kinney, who had spent almost all his life in Missouri, visited the East Coast, specifically Atlantic City, New Jersey:

> The Hon. Thomas E. Kinney of St. Louis and Missouri, who says he does not wish to be called "Snake" any more, is getting into trim for the Bryan reception in New York next week.

Incidentally he is having the time of his life in this gayest of coast resorts.

Senator Kinney came on from St. Louis with Louis Lemp and Joseph Hannauer. Mr. Lemp is attending a meeting of brewers. Saturday night the trio will go to New York, Kinney as a member of the Bryan Reception Committee and Lemp and Hannauer as spectators of the show.

So far, they have only touched the very highest places here. At first Kinney seemed bashful, and let Lemp, who has been here before, do all the leading. But soon the one-time "Snake" was leading the pace.

The resort is crowded as never before, but the party got rooms at the largest and fashionable hotel on the island.

When Kinney, hot, tired, and dusty, entered the hotel lobby, the first thing he noticed was a group of men loung-ing around in evening clothes. He grabbed Lemp by the arm and jerked his thumb toward the white shirt fronts. "Say," he exclaimed, "this is a new one on me. I thought they only wore them things in winter. It's up to you to pilot this junket. I thought I was coming to a summer resort."

In the dining room, finding several French dishes on the menu. Kinney studied the card for some time, then turned to the waiter and said, "O, just bring me something to eat."

It was not until they started out on the board walk that Kinney began to feel his stride.

"Why, this is as good as the Pike," he said, and puffing out his chest with the sea air, he took the lead.

There are several cafes in Atlantic City which have helped make the place famous. Lemp knew of them and gave the necessary directions, but Kinney led the way.

In one of the places the music of the orchestra pleased Kinney so much that he began waving an imaginary baton. When the brilliantly dressed women and men at the little round tables among the palms smiled at him he grinned back at them cheerfully.

But it was the Bowery section along the board walk that took Kinney's fancy most. There are no cafes in the Bowery, but there are several unique beer gardens, where you see no evening clothes and where there is a generally a fight every now and then to make things entertaining.

"Say now," said Kinney to Lemp and Hannauer, who were eyeing rather doubtfully the customers of these places, "this is just like home, ain't it?"

When the three finally got back to their hotel, Lemp and Hannauer were all but down and out, but Kinney was still full of life.

"Say, this is great," he said to a *Post-Dispatch* correspondent. "This air makes me feel like accepting the nomination for President myself. This is the first time I've been to the seashore, but it won't be the last. No more Creve Coeur Lake for me."

"Going in bathing?" he was asked.

"Well, what do you think I came here for? Say, when I get one of your regular seashore sunburns, those ducks out in St. Louis who are going to the reception next week won't know me, will they?"

By the summer of 1906, Tom Egan headed an organization that boasted well over a hundred men, and he himself served as a deputy constable to Mike Kinney, literally giving him a license to do whatever he pleased. All the men in the Egan gang adhered to a rigid code of silence. What happened or was said among them stayed among them. Egan would take care of his men and their families if they were sent away to prison.

Egan's inner circle consisted of about ten to twenty men, most of whom he had known for years and trusted implicitly. First and his foremost was his twenty-two-year-old brother, Willie; Sam Young, with Thomas "Red" Kane serving as his deputy constable; Fred Woelfel, Tom's brother-in-law; John Whelan; James Barry; Joseph Rosewell; Fred "The Yellow Kid" Mohrle; and Tony Garrity. Two original members of the old Ashley Street Gang were still around, Dave Hickey and Jimmy "The Rat" Collins.

Sam Young had special duties as one of Egan's most trusted lieutenants; he was the gang's representative in the hotly contested Fifteenth Ward. Thirty years old, of French descent, his given mame was Etienne. Young was a native of Cahokia, Illinois, and well built, with a round face and hard eyes that could turn dangerous without warning. Another in the long line of tough guys from the St. Louis ghettos, Sam ran a saloon at 1402 Franklin Avenue and bossed his own crew, being the Egan equivalent of a Mafia *caporegime*. Known as a crack shot, he packed a blue-steel .45-caliber revolver with a pearl handle in a shoulder holster. Young's men included Red Kane and his brother Michael, "Yellow Kid" Mohrle, Pat Clancy, Edward "Dutch" Hess, Harrison "Doc" Fitzgerald, and Walter Costello.

The boys still earned their income through robberies, extortion, burglaries, and pickpocketing. They began invading rail yards at night, rifling through the cars for whatever goods or valuables they could find. The gangsters would then sell the swag—tobacco, shoes, silk, gingham, leather, clothes, furs, and anything else of value they could find—to fences or trustworthy civilians. One of the gang's notable terror tactics was to severely beat saloonkeepers and wreck their bars for stocking Anheuser-Busch or other brands instead of Lemp beer. The Egans were also available for union-busting, or "slugging," as it was called. If the price was right, any corporation or businessman could have Egan muscle intimidate striking workers into signing a new contract. Some of the gang members also began operating legitimate businesses, saloons, or pool halls. Fred "The Yellow Kid" Mohrle owned a popular coal yard which did a brisk business.

The long-awaited confrontation between the Egans and the Bottoms Gang came during the Democratic primary on October 6, 1906, when Tony Foley led his crew into the Fifteenth Ward to carve out their own territory. The two opposing groups met at Twentieth and Morgan and began exchanging words and blows. Gunplay followed, with Foley and Egan gangster Charles Burns sustaining mild wounds. Notified of the Bottoms Gang's incursion by telephone, Tom Egan personally led eleven of his toughest minions into action. Brawls between the two groups highlighted a dramatic day at the polls. The rampage came to an end when a well-known ward politician named John Thomas Brady tried to stop the Egan gang and was beaten to within an inch of his life by the two Egan brothers.

Not everything was cherry for Tom Egan in 1906, however, as the Excise Commission finally succeeded in yanking his liquor license. Senator Tom Kinney spoke up loudly for his brother-in-law, complaining that Governor Folk and the Republicans were all out to get the city's Democratic saloonkeepers. Egan eventually got his license back and sidestepped any future problems by listing his headquarters at 1031A Broadway under the name of a law-abiding friend.

The Egans' chief rival in the mid-1900s was their old Democratic benefactor Harry Hawes, who still held sway over the police department and had powerful connections in city hall. Snake Kinney's ties to the Lemp brewing family made for a powerful combine.

Despite the power of his street gang and political faction, Tom Kinney's ticket lost to Harry Hawes at the Democratic city convention that year, as Hawes was able to marshal the tide of delegates in his favor. Kinney responded by keeping his gang, the most intimidating in the city, away from the polls on Election Day in November. As a result, the Republicans won enough delegate seats to take control of the city government. While Republican Party boss Jeptha Howe didn't specifically thank Tom Kinney in his victory speech, he might as well have. Once again, Harry Hawes found out the hard way that one didn't mess with the Kinney-Egan-Lemp faction.

CHANGING TIMES

O N THE NIGHT of January 15, 1907, members of the Egan and Bottoms gangs gathered in the Jolly Five Club at 1505 Morgan Street to try to peacefully mediate the dispute about which Democratic group should run the Fifteenth Ward. During the previous month, Tom Egan had used his connections in the police department to turn up the heat on the Bottoms Gang's policy racket. The ensuing pressure and possible grand jury action made Frank Hussey sue for peace. Both Egan and Tony Foley were present at the meeting that was arranged, and about thirty men in all stood by while their leaders talked. After the conference, which ended amicably, a more dramatic turn of events occurred.

Outside, in the chilly winter darkness, a man walked up Morgan Street toward the Jolly Five. He wore a coat with its collar turned up against the wind, a slouch cap, and his hands were jammed into his pockets, where he gave a reassuring caress to a pistol concealed there. The man's dark-brown hair was mowed into a crew cut, and his face was pasty white, the result of many years of incarceration in the state penitentiary at Jefferson City.

His brown eyes were hard yet quick, appraising the world up, down, and sideways without giving any hint of the man's opinion, having seen all the bad things that life has to offer. The man once again marveled at how much things had changed since he'd gone away. The first time he saw an automobile on the street, he froze in his tracks and watched in amazement as it sputtered down the avenue.

This man's name was Willie Gagel. He was an original member of the Ashley Street Gang and recently had been released from the state prison at Jefferson City after serving ten years for killing Jerry Caples during a drunken brawl at Senator Kinney's old saloon at Second and Carr on Thanksgiving Eve 1895. Gagel knew that Tom Egan had sworn to kill him, and had readily agreed to the prison term to get away from him. But now, more than a decade later, Gagel was free once again, and he didn't wish to live the rest of his days looking over his shoulder. Willie later said he had gone to the Jolly Five to formally apologize to Egan for his actions in the hope that all would be forgiven. The gang boss told it differently, saying his old pal had come there to kill him.

Gagel had a friend inform the doorman who he was, then walked into the club and ordered a large glass of beer to help calm his nerves. Tom Egan was sitting with two of his best men, Sam Young and James "Kid" Wilson. Gagel walked over to Egan's table, bringing the two men face to face for the first time in nearly eleven years. Gagel's hands were at his side, with his thumbs curled on the edges of his pockets, ready for anything. When Willie began to speak, Egan remained silent and glared at him with his glacial blue eyes—then, in a blur of motion, he raised a revolver and shot Jerry Caples's killer through the abdomen. Most of the men in the club stampeded for the exit, leaving the ex-convict writhing in pain on the floor.

Rushed to the hospital, Gagel refused to say who had shot him or why. Police officers responding to the scene rounded up a group of gang members who had been unable to escape from the club. When the hoods were locked in holding cells, men like Edward Giebe (possibly a cousin of Red Giebe) and John Bracken began shouting to the others, "Don't snitch! Don't be a louse!" The desk sergeant in charge of booking that night wearily noted the suspects were the same hoods as usual. A rookie cop asked the sergeant who the roughnecks were. "They're all a bunch of rats! That's who they are! These bums are with Egan!" he thundered.

Thus it was this frustrated desk sergeant, on the night of Willie Gagel's shooting, who gave the Egan gang its famous moniker: Egan's Rats.

Gagel clung painfully to life for eight days, finally dying without naming his killer. A few hours after Willie's final breath, Tom Egan was arrested at his home, where he was sleeping in bed with a revolver underneath his pillow. The gang boss was charged with first-degree murder but freed after paying a $5,000 bail.

The Jolly Five Club was Frank Hussey's outpost in the Fifteenth Ward, but after Gagel's murder, it was shuttered by police. The Bottoms Gang began to loaf about in saloons around Twenty-second Street and Franklin Avenue, causing nothing but trouble. A few weeks after the Jolly Five was closed, the gangsters started gathering in a bar at Jefferson and Franklin, and the police immediately began harassing the rowdy punks.

Tony Foley nursed a burning hatred of the police officers who walked the beat in the Bad Lands. His younger brother Tim had been shot to death on December 22, 1906, while trying to burglarize a newsstand. The shooter got off on a plea of self-defense, but Foley blamed the police for an allegedly slipshod investigation. Tony drank heavily throughout that winter and often fantasized about taking revenge against the St. Louis police.

Shortly after midnight on February 10, 1907, Tony Foley and more than a dozen of his followers were loitering at the corner of Twenty-third and Franklin. Patrolman Patrick Stapleton passed by on his beat, telling the men to move off the street and disperse. Stapleton was known throughout the neighborhood to be as tough as nails, more than able to handle a few unruly criminals. In defiance of his order, the Bottoms boys strutted across the street, loudly singing a popular melody. This enraged Stapleton, who stomped toward the hoods and was promptly slugged by Tony Foley. The Bottoms thugs rained fists and feet upon the patrolman, who finally managed to draw his service revolver, causing his assailants to flee. Firing two shots after them, Stapleton ran in pursuit, collaring Foley at Twenty-second Street.

With his pistol in Foley's neck, Stapleton roughly marched the criminal back to Twenty-third Street, where he was jumped by the remaining Bottoms boys. During the melee, Foley grabbed Stapleton's gun and opened fire, just missing the officer. Foley and his men disappeared into the darkness, hard laughter trailing in their wake.

This spectacular fight was heavily covered by the city's newspapers. Tony Foley surrendered to police two days later. He consented to an interview with a reporter for the *Post-Dispatch*, in an attempt to tell his side of the story. His contempt for Patrolman Stapleton dripped from the pages. Foley disingenuously claimed that they hadn't touched the police officer. "This Stapleton is the biggest four flusher on the force He's been trying to make a hero of himself. Now in the first place he says fifteen of us jumped on him and beat and kicked him. Well, I defy him to show a single bruise or cut. He deliberately lied when he said we jumped him. Why, we could have killed him."

The beating of Patrolman Stapleton garnered the Bottoms Gang more media coverage in three days than the Egan's Rats had received in the previous two and a half years. A picture of Tony Foley was featured with the article on the front page of the February 13, 1907, edition of the *Post-Dispatch*. The rough-and-tumble twenty-year-old leader of the Bottoms Gang had done something that even the feared Tom Egan had not: appear on the front page of a

Youthful Tony Foley seemed at war with the world, leading the Bottoms Gang against both the archrival Egan's Rats and the St. Louis Police Department.

major newspaper. Foley was convicted of assault with intent to kill, but he remained free during an appeal.

Just after the attack on Patrolman Patrick Stapleton, the Egan gang got some unexpected "good" news.

In the years during his slow downfall, John "Cuddy Mack" McGillicuddy had been keeping a low profile, running a saloon in the Fifth Ward at 208? North Eighth Street and attracting attention only for such misdeeds as public drunkenness and abusing Italian fruit vendors. The former Butler thug Louis "Dutch Louie" Fingerlin was the only major St. Louis gangster still in Cuddy Mack's corner. Fifth Ward boss John "Skinny" Golden got into a fistfight with Dutch Louie around Christmas. The massive Fingerlin cleaned Golden's clock and stole his diamond ring to boot.

At 8:30 on the evening on February 13, 1907, Golden shot Fingerlin three times in the back in the saloon at 1101 Chestnut Street. Lingering in the hospital for nine days, Dutch Louie refused to say who had shot him, although it was practically common knowledge that Golden was the culprit. Fingerlin remained adamant, saying, "If my time has come, why, all right, but I'm not telling anything. That's not my way of doing business."

Criminals throughout the city nodded approvingly at Fingerlin's final words. Not "snitching," or keeping your mouth shut about who killed you, was seen as the most honorable way possible for a gangster to check out.

With the murder of Dutch Louie Fingerlin, Cuddy Mack finally realized that he was completely washed up, and he retired just a few months later.

While St. Louis's underworld continued to rock and sway, something happened that would shock the city to its core and kick the gangsters clear off the radar.

The last three years had not been good ones for the St. Louis Police Department. Ever since the murder of Fred Scheel, various corruption probes had sought to clear out a generation's worth of bad cops. Many of the peace officers who were fired had acted as enforcers for police board head Harry Hawes. One such detective was the flamboyant, diamond ring-sporting Lee Killian. Just after he was canned in December 1905, Lee and his brother Don got into a public fistfight with Detectives George Williams and Tom McGrath, Lee's ex-partners, both of whom were fired as a result.

The bad blood between the former detectives came to a head at 7:30 on the evening of February 27, 1907, when the Killian brothers were attacked in McGrath and McMahon's saloon at 724 Olive Street. Lee was shot by George Williams, while Don Killian was pistol-whipped by proprietor Tom McGrath. Half the witnesses in the place would say the Killians were the aggressors, while the others supported Lee Killian's version, in which he was shot in "cold blood." Williams produced a note he said he wrote before shooting Killian, saying that he was acting in self-defense.

In the aftermath of the brawl, the two-year-old mystery behind the murder of St. Louis Tommy Sullivan began to unravel. While on his deathbed, Lee Killian sought to clear his conscience about George Williams, saying, "He got away with the Sullivan killing; don't let him get away with this one!" Killian's revelation that Williams had murdered Tommy Sullivan was, in simple terms, swept under the rug. Most witnesses from the murder scene had mysteriously disappeared; those who remained developed amnesia. The only evidence police had was Killian's statement; thus, there was nothing they could do. Eddie Kelleher managed to get a new trial, but he never was able to clear his name because he died soon after of natural causes.

An artist's rendering depicts Detective George Williams gunning down a derelict in 1898. The sleuth would gain several notches on his gun and ultimately be dismissed from the force.

Four months later, after intense grand jury and media scrutiny, George Williams went on trial for killing Lee Killian. The various witnesses recounted their tales, and Williams provided a tearful and vivid re-enactment of the night's events. It was either the confession of a tortured, remorseful man or the performance of a lifetime by an icy psychopath. The jury grappled with this dilemma for quite some time before acquitting the former detective, who was never charged in the murder of St. Louis Tommy Sullivan.

After the scandal in the wake of the fatal brawl among the ex-detectives had abated, the Bottoms Gang began to regroup. With the police constantly harassing them and watching their every move, the thugs needed a new clubhouse. The upper echelon of the gang decided to form their own political club, gathering in the back room of a saloon at 20 North Eleventh Street on the night of March 2, 1907. The Bottoms boys were far too volatile to discuss things democratically, and adding plenty of St. Louis's finest beer to the mix proved to be a recipe for disaster.

A huge brawl erupted among the gangsters just after midnight. Arthur Thompson chose this fight to exact revenge on Rex McDonald for a previous scrap and shot him three times. Even though Thompson admitted shooting Rex in self-defense, McDonald died without naming his killer. Police could only shake their heads.

Emboldened by their new reputation, the Bottoms Gang went on a violent reign of terror in the Twenty-second Ward. The diabolical attacks, robberies, and burglaries reached an all-time high, with the thugs beating shopkeepers, terrorizing women, harassing senior citizens, and engaging in countless other acts of violence. After accosting one mild-mannered orchestra musician on the street, one of the boys grabbed the man's violin and broke it over his head.

The Bad Lands became a war zone, with residents and merchants alike begging the police for help. However, Frank Hussey had quite a lot of pull with certain officers, who were very sympathetic to the Bottoms Gang, just as they were to the Egan gang. Hussey himself led the gangsters on a raid into the Twenty-second Ward in early April, terrorizing saloonkeepers and extorting money from them.

Throughout the summer of 1907 the Bottoms Gang cut a large swath through the Bad Lands. Tony Foley, Edward Carroll, Arthur Thompson, Richard McLaughlin, and T. S. Bentley were at the bar in the Hibernia Club at 3 a.m. on August 2, 1907, when the police barged in, suspecting the men had tried to kill a bartender earlier in the evening. The boys made a break for it, beginning a running pistol battle between them and the police that nearly turned into a riot.

Countless pedestrians were endangered by the gunplay. Three bullets shattered windows of the nearby Bell Telephone headquarters, scaring the dickens out of some female operators, and Bentley wounded one of the pursing cops and an innocent bystander. But once again, the Bottoms Gang escaped punishment. Chief of Police Creecy loudly declared that "the Bottoms Gang has to go," but unfortunately, the Bottoms boys weren't going anywhere.

Tom Egan had been found not guilty of the killing of Willie Gagel in June 1907, successfully pleading self-defense. Egan may well have still been angry with Gagel for killing Jerry Caples, but given the tension of the gang conference, Tom had every right to think that Gagel was there to kill him. In retrospect, it seems that the ex-convict couldn't have picked a worse time to confront Tom Egan; it was a final bad choice in a lifetime of bad choices. Meanwhile, Egan was soon swamped with domestic problems as well.

The domestic problem was in the form of James "Kid" Wilson. One of his closest aides, Wilson had been by Egan's side in January at the Jolly Five Club when Gagel was fatally shot. Wilson also happened to be a cousin of Egan's wife, Nellie. The gang boss eventually began to suspect that Nellie was having an affair behind his back, with her cousin, no less. Egan concocted a ruse to see if Nellie was cheating. After leaving their home at 814 Wash Street in the early part of the evening on October 22, 1907, he hid in an alleyway and from a distance saw Nellie leave.

After several hours of waiting, Tom saw his wife come into view shortly after midnight. She was walking with Kid Wilson and the two stopped under a bright street lamp at Ninth and Wash streets to talk. As silent as a snake, Egan emerged from the shadows, very close to where Nellie and Wilson stood under the light. Wilson began babbling, perhaps trying to plead his case. The youthful hood was suddenly face to face not with a friend and relative, but with the most ruthless gangster in St. Louis. Two bullets crashed into Wilson's chest, dropping him to the pavement. Tom and Nellie ran into their house. Neighbors quickly summoned the police, who bagged Tom as he calmly strode out the front door to make his escape. Nellie was found sobbing in the back yard.

Nellie Egan never implicated her husband. Neither did Kid Wilson for that matter. Just before he died, he spat, "I won't tell who he was. I'll get him myself." We will never know for certain if Nellie was indeed having an affair with her cousin. If so, James "Kid" Wilson was playing a very foolish and dangerous game by calling on her. He, of all people, should have known better. Egan was eventually acquitted of murder, his lawyer successfully arguing the unwritten law of the jilted husband. Despite whatever headlines Frank Hussey and the Bottoms Gang grabbed, Tom Egan was still the powerful gangster in St. Louis.

Egan realized that with all the head-turning the Bottoms Gang was causing, they drew even more attention to themselves and away from the Egan gang. They and their lunatic rampages were bad for business. If he engaged the Bottoms boys in open combat, it would be an overpublicized bloodbath. Just as Egan figured it, the gang's reckless activities hastened their downfall.

An editorial cartoon shows James "Kid" Wilson, his cousin Nellie, and his boss and killer, Tom Egan.

At 5:30 on the morning of April 14, 1908, Eddie Carroll, one of three brothers in the crew, led six members of the Bottoms Gang to the Jefferson Club, still a roost for many members of the police force. All men brandished pistols and snake whips. Alas, at that early hour of the morning, the club was empty. The hooligans succeeded in only breaking some windows and terrorizing the doorman. The boys repaired to a nearby tavern, drinking heavily and hungry for action. They set their sights on the large building at Twelfth and Market.

Just after 9 a.m. the placid calm of City Hall was shattered. Driving up to the Market Street entrance in an expensive coach, the six Bottoms boys charged into the building, cursing and whooping. Eddie Carroll was on point as the thugs pointed their revolvers at passersby and violently cracked their snake whips with their other hands. They made a beeline for the office of Lewis Marks, Superintendent of the Water Tap and Motor Department, who had recently fired Carroll from his cushy job. Eddie was frustrated that Marks was not there. As they left, Carroll cracked his whip against the ceiling and growled to the secretary, "De guy wot we wuz looking for ain't here." Carroll and his merry crew were collared a short while later boozily celebrating their raid in a beer joint at Eighth and Market.

After the latest outrage by the Bottoms Gang, their chief rival began using his contacts in the St. Louis Police Department. Tom Egan started his own campaign of harassment against his rivals, the very same one the chief of police had promised the previous summer. The Bottoms boys were rousted at every turn. Tony Foley was sent to prison on a robbery charge, and several others joined him at Jeff City, including a particularly formidable gangster named Wesley "Red" Simons.

And the city's residents, especially in the Bad Lands, were growing less tolerant of the wild, haggard thugs. One of the original Bottoms boys, Edward "Red" McAuliffe, was "canning" beer in the alley behind a females-only rooming house at 2114 Lucas Avenue around midnight on September 1, 1908. The woman of the house, Lena Sales, came outside and told the men to stop drinking beer in back of her place and making noise. Red jumped up, slapped the woman, and told her to mind her own business. Miss Sales pulled a pistol and fatally shot McAuliffe through the head.

By time of the elections in November, a heavy Egan presence was felt at the polls and virtually nothing was heard from the Bottoms forces. Tom Egan had prevailed without killing anyone or losing any of his men to the police or rivals.

With the Hibernia Club closed, the gangsters moved into the West End Athletic Club, an old church at the corner of Twenty-second and Washington they had converted into their new head-quarters. In a strange counterpoint to the drab criminality of the place, a cross graced a stained-glass window of the former sanc-tuary, and when the sun shined through, the image of the cross took up most of the center of the floor. And it was here that the Bottoms Gang's Waterloo would occur, almost exactly two years after it first rose to citywide prominence.

Just as the gang's meteoric rise to notoriety had begun with an attempt to kill a police officer, its downfall would start with one, as well. The West End Athletic Club was a sore spot for the neighborhood, whose denizens knew full well who occupied it. Patrolman John Hutton passed it every night on his beat; he would often tell the boys to keep the noise down, but his warn-ings never did any good. On the night of January 17, 1909, Hutton got into it again with the Bottoms Gang.

The crew was throwing a loud party, featuring two neighbor-hood kids singing on stage to the accompaniment of a piano. Frank Hussey and the club's manager, Charles Haughton, snarled at the police officer and told the youngsters to continue singing as loudly they wanted while the twenty men on hand shouted the chorus. As Hutton stomped toward the Washington Avenue exit, the men began whooping even louder, banging their chairs and tables on the floor.

Two gunshots rang out. Hutton whirled around but couldn't tell who the shooter was. What he did see was Hussey and Haughton walking through a partition to the barroom, which faced Twenty-second Street, followed closely by Danny Hogan, Jere Reardon, and Connie Sullivan. Hutton approached the group and saw Sullivan spin around with a drawn revolver as Hogan and Reardon unsuccessfully attempted to pinion the officer's arms. Hutton was shot in the abdomen and left arm, and as the Bottoms boys fled through the Twenty-second Street exit, he staggered out the Washington exit, emptying his gun at the fleeing Sullivan, who was soon collared at Twenty-second and Lucas.

Patrolman John Hutton was permanently disabled by his wounds, and the St. Louis Police Department launched a campaign to smash the Bottoms Gang. Frank Hussey, Charles Haughton, and Beverly Brown fled to Springfield, Illinois, where they were arrested. Hussey drew even more heat when it was discovered that he had pulled strings with Governor Joseph Folk to get thirteen members of the gang—including would-be cop killer Connie Sullivan—early paroles from prison. Nearly all of the goons involved in the fracas at the gang's headquarters were sent to prison, as was "Kid" Gleason, who, two weeks after the shooting, went on a crime rampage that left one man dead and a score terrorized.

The Bottoms Gang as a large, connected criminal enterprise was destroyed; it would survive only as an ineffectual shell of what it once was. And like Colonel Ed Butler before him, Frank Hussey escaped prison but was finished in city politics.

Things around the country and in the city of St. Louis had changed rapidly over the last decade. The Egan's Rats had now been in existence for nearly twenty years in some form or another, and their home town was a far different place in 1909 than when the Ashley Street boys first got their start in the early 1890s. Tom Egan was virtually the only original Egan Rat still in St. Louis. Many of the others, like Willie Gagel, Guinea Mack McAuliffe, and Eddie Kelleher, were dead, and some were locked up, like William "Skippy" Rohan, who languished for years in New York's Sing Sing Prison. Mickey Mack McNamara reportedly was killed in a 1903 train crash, but he soon turned up as a common thief in New York City. Others simply disappeared into obscurity, never to be heard from again.

St. Louis now had a population of over 600,000, making it the fourth largest city in the country. It was also the nation's leading producer of beer, bricks, stoves, and shoes. Many more immigrants began to pour into the city, and a new Italian neighborhood rapidly sprouted on the large hill west of Kingshighway in southwestern St. Louis. It was derisively referred to by longtime residents as "Dago Hill." An older Italian colony was downtown, bounded on the east by Broadway, north by Cass Avenue, south by Franklin Avenue, and on the west by Twelfth Street.

The ragtime craze was at its peak, with piano players across the city enthralling saloon patrons with the lively tunes, many of them written by St. Louisan Scott Joplin. Old-style song-and-dance theaters and nickelodeons began showing films, becoming the first movie theaters in St. Louis. Telephone usage in the city had reached an all-time high, and automobiles were becoming more common on the streets by 1909, especially after Henry Ford had introduced the Model A the previous year. While most people still used horse-drawn carriages to get around, cars were catching up fast. Auto registrations would skyrocket, and within four short years, motorcars would outnumber buggies.

By the end of March, one of Sam Young's men was to the point of defecting. Fred "The Yellow Kid" Mohrle and his sidekick William Wright were intending to switch to the Republican Party for the upcoming city primary election. Young tried to curb the mutiny with threats and stories about what Mohrle could expect if he deserted the Egan gang. Mohrle, fearing for his life, holed up in his coal yard at 822 North Twenty-first Street.

On the afternoon of April 4, 1909, a cool, clear, spring Sunday, The Yellow Kid and several of the boys were in the yard sipping on bottles of beer that Mohrle had produced from a trapdoor in a "lid club" (after-hours drinking establishment) on the premises. The men were playing "quoits," a game similar to horseshoes.

The coal yard was surrounded by a six-foot-high wooden fence, and the southern gate opened onto a small alleyway, down which Constable Sam Young, Thomas O'Brien, and Joseph Byrnes walked. They banged hard on the gate and called out for The Yellow Kid, putting emphasis on "Yellow." Mohrle and Wright fled on nerveless legs into the lid club and grabbed pistols. What happened next has never been satisfactorily determined. Mohrle said Young drew his pistol and fired through the gate at him; however, O'Brien and Byrnes claimed that Sam never discharged his weapon. For his part, Mohrle pumped five shots through the gate, one of which struck Young squarely in the heart.

The Yellow Kid promptly surrendered to police, claiming that Young had fired first. The constable's pistol was found under his body, with one empty chamber. Mohrle claimed that was evidence of self-defense, but the Egans scoffed at the notion.

When informed of Sam Young's death, delegates attending a joint meeting of Fifteenth and Sixteenth Ward Republicans burst into cheers. Fred Mohrle was likely in a jolly mood over the crooked constable's demise, but he also was fearful for his life. The husky gangster told police that the Egan gang wouldn't rest until they killed him. He told a *Post-Dispatch* reporter two days after the shooting, "Now they're going to get me. I've had word that I didn't have but three days to live. The time's up tomorrow. I am not afraid of them. I won't run. I won't leave town. I was born and raised here, and I'm going to live and die here. But they may shoot me in the back. I've got my eyes open. They can't get me from the front."

Some remarked on Mohrle's courage in deciding to buck the Egan gang. Others, however, whispered that The Yellow Kid would be "burned" before he reached the supposed safety of prison.

Mohrle's trial was set to begin in early June, and Fred, his wife, and William Wright found themselves living in a constant state of fear, continually harassed and threatened by various members of the Egan's Rats. When the Mohrles moved out of the neighborhood to a house at 2319 Sullivan Avenue, their moving van was followed all the way by an Egan spy. Pat Clancy and Harry Exnicious often loitered near Mohrle's house brandishing revolvers. Rumor had it that Mike Kinney himself had picked Clancy to avenge Sam Young.

As the trial approached, Tom Egan was an prominent spectator during jury selection. He spent most of the time glaring at the two defendants with a stare that could have caused hell to freeze over.

William Wright was so unnerved by his eyeball duel with the gang boss that he flipped out a few days later while standing on a street corner, jerking a pistol and wounding an innocent bystander whom he mistook for an Egan gunman. Not long after that, Mohrle's wife, Marie, finally had enough of the hoods menacing her home and loudly complained to a neighborhood beat cop about Pat Clancy. The officer just laughed and told her to leave him alone. The cop's indifference to her plight filled Mrs. Mohrle with despair and a sense of rapidly approaching doom.

The day of the trial arrived. Monday, June 4, 1909, was a warm, muggy late-spring day, with temperatures reaching the upper seventies by 8 a.m. Fred Mohrle left his home for the Four Courts Building at Twelfth and Clark streets downtown without his gun, ignoring a bad premonition Marie said she'd had. The Yellow Kid contemptuously believed the Egan gang was too cowardly to shoot him from the front, so as long as he kept his back to the wall, he felt he was safe. Mohrle and Wright arrived at the courts building about 9 o'clock, and seeing no Egan's Rats lurking in the hallways, they began to relax.

The trial was set begin at 10 a.m. in the building's eastern main courtroom. Once the proceedings were underway, Mohrle's attorney, former Missouri Lieutenant Governor Charles P. Johnson, asked that the charges of second-degree murder against his client be continued until June 21, a motion the judge granted. About fifteen minutes later, Mohrle was tapped on the shoulder by his second remaining friend in the world, Elmer Holmes, who indicated that he desperately wanted to talk to The Yellow Kid in the hallway. "Whatever you do, don't leave the courtroom," his attorney whispered. "You know that gang. You know you're in grave danger."

Nonetheless, Mohrle followed Holmes out into the hallway, walking past the circuit clerk's and city marshal's offices as they weaved through corridors clogged with lawyers, spectators, and police officers. The front doors were chocked open to allow whatever cool air there was to enter, and while passing the main entrance, Mohrle briefly caught a glimpse of people walking up and down the building's wide stairs and the morning traffic on Twelfth Street.

The two men found a quiet nook near the entrance to the western courtroom, in front of the door to the jailer's office. The gangster calmly rolled a cigarette and puffed it as Holmes jabbered away. Something, no one is sure what, caused Mohrle to turn slightly to the left, just before a loud noise erupted and The Yellow Kid felt his head explode.

Fred Mohrle died just as he had predicted he would: shot from behind by an Egan's Rat. The agent of death was Thomas "Red" Kane, deputy constable to Sam Young. Nattily attired in a blue pinstripe suit, red bowtie, and matching bowler, Kane had been waiting for Elmer Holmes to lure Mohrle out of the courtroom to the spot in front of the jailer's office. He stalked through the crowd, adrenaline pumping, with nothing less than Young's pearl-handled, blue-steel .45 revolver in his pocket.

When he had closed to within three feet of his quarry, and just as Mohrle began to turn, Kane pulled out his gun and fired a shot into the back of The Yellow Kid's head. He then quickly pumped four more shots into his back and chest as Mohrle fell in a lifeless left-hand turn. The gunshots echoed noisily off the walls, and people in the corridor began yelling and screaming, most of them either hitting the deck or dashing out the front door.

Kane ran out of the building with the crowd and jogged across the street to police headquarters. Running into Detective John Schmidt, Kane calmly declared that he had "just shot The Yellow Kid" and then surrendered his cordite-stinking hand cannon.

Pandemonium reigned inside the Four Courts Building. Everyone staggered about excited and dazed. At the sound of the shots, William Wright jumped up from his chair in terror, clasped his hands in prayer, and begged to be arrested and put in jail. People gawked at the area where Mohrle had been shot, and more than a few spectators left with ashen faces and glazed eyes after seeing the bullet holes, pools of blood, and brain matter that stained walls and floors.

Constable Mike Kinney, who happened to be on the second floor of the Four Courts at the time of the shooting, sauntered downstairs (glancing indifferently at the gore as he walked past) bound for the police station across the street. When the assistant circuit attorney cornered Kinney, he groaned, "Mike, what's the matter with you fellows?" Kinney smirked, "You mean what's the matter with the other fellows. I guess it's the hot weather." Just five days before, Kinney had named Red Kane as his deputy, thereby securing Kane a spot in the building and giving him a permit to carry a firearm.

The entire city was abuzz about the stunning assassination of Fred "The Yellow Kid" Mohrle. Until then, the majority of those who had known about the Egan's Rats were police and other criminals, but now the whole city had been rudely introduced to the gang. People were astounded by the sheer audacity of the murder plot, that Tom Egan could have a man killed while surrounded by police officers and court officials on a Monday morning in a crowded hallway of a courthouse in the nation's fourth-largest city.

The shooting sent the most powerful message yet that the Egan gang, after years of dogfighting with various crews around town, was now the most powerful gang in St. Louis. The city's newspapers devoted days of coverage to the shooting, and it was during this time that the name Egan's Rats was used for the first time in print. Even the *Post-Dispatch*'s Weatherbird, a cartoon character that expressed comic or wry sentiments on the weather or a current event, got in on the act.

Co-defendant William Wright eventually calmed down and met with the press. "Those fellows are a cowardly set of cold-blooded assassins," he said. "They can't get a man unless they do it from behind. They will only attack you in the dark, when you can't see them.

"Mohrle came to me in the courtroom this morning while waiting for the trial to open and asked me if I had a gun. I told him I didn't have one, and he said he didn't either, and he was not going to carry [one] hereafter. He said he thought that gang was [too] cowardly to shoot unless they shot a man from behind his back."

Fred Mohrle's widow, Marie, was shattered. The interview she gave to a local newspaper reflected her frustration:

> This thing never would have happened if the police had had the courage to proceed against the gang that was bent on murdering my husband. ... The gang has killed a lot of men, and they always get away with it. They have gone in men's houses, cut them to pieces with knives, and no one is arrested for it. The wounded men go to the hospital and refuse to tell who attacked them.

At the coroner's inquest, she gave a detailed narrative of the threats that she and her husband had endured.

Chief of Police Creecy was proving himself tragically inept at handling the city's gang problem. Cynical souls sneered that Creecy was on the take. Too late to help Fred Mohrle, the police chief announced that all known gang members would be kept out of the Four Courts and people would be randomly searched. As he had done with the Bottoms Gang, Chief Creecy declared war on the Egan's Rats.

After things had finally calmed down, William Wright was tried and acquitted of the second-degree murder of Sam Young. The night of his acquittal, June 30, he attended a small celebration at the Mohrle home at 808 N. Jefferson Avenue. A friend named Charlie Tozer walked onto the front porch where Wright was dozing in a recliner. Wright, who would later claim he was having a nightmare about the Egan's Rats, jumped up with a gun in his hand and shot Tozer in the stomach. Tozer would pull through, but after his second non-fatal shooting of an innocent bystander in a month, William Wright was bundled off to a mental hospital.

Marie Mohrle had been grappling with anxiety and depression since the murder of her husband, and the shooting on her front porch apparently pushed the poor woman over the edge. In the early hours of July 10, 1909, with the same pistol her husband had used to kill Sam Young, Marie Mohrle shot herself in the chest. Her aim was poor and she missed her heart, but she told police she had attempted suicide to "cheat Egan's Rats."

She had been keeping a journal for many months, and its anguished entries cast a bright light on what it was like to be victimized by a gang. The entries, like her suicide note, bashed all of the Republican leaders who had abandoned her husband even though he had risked his life for their party by leaving the Egan gang. In one, she wrote":

> I have nothing to live for but my baby, and I will not be able
> to give him the education I would like to. I have lost all hope.

I thought some one would help me and advise me, but I am as much alone as if on a desert island.

If any insurance is ever collected on Yellow's life by Donohue, who is bringing suit, I want it held for the baby boy, Willie. My insurance, if anything is left after burying me, the same. My clothes and Yellow's, also jewelry and furniture, to be the property of Mrs. Con Ryan, 806 North Jefferson.

When I lost my sweetheart I lost my best friend. Bill will find friends, but don't ever let him know our experiences with friends; it would only serve to harden his heart against all mankind.

"'Vengeance is mine, I will repay,' saith the Lord." But against my enemies I am powerless. If they can persecute Jep Howe, what can they do to me, a lone defenseless woman?

This Post-Dispatch *Weatherbird was one of the first times the name Egan's Rats appeared in print.*

A June 22 entry:

Tonight they left me word as to what I may expect when they broke into my house and took two revolvers. Nothing else was touched; only the house upset looking for more guns. What can I do? I don't know, we were accorded no special protection until we moved in Captain Pickel's district.

I realize better than anyone in the world that I know too much about several murders. I only hope God will punish every man in any way connected with Yellow's death. I have prayed and tried to reason, but O, my love. I may be adjudged insane. If I am, we are all insane. If loving is a sign of insanity then I plead guilty. Young can cry who he fed and gave shelter to.

O, my head. I think I may have lost my mind, but only in one way. He might have been yellow to the world, but he was my love. Life without him is unbearable.

From June 26:

> If anything should happen to me don't let the detective force waste time looking for the why and wherefore. There is an old saying and a true one that an ounce of prevention is worth a pound of cure.

Finally, a poem called "The Creed," which was under the sofa on which she tried to take her life:

> I believe if I were dead
> And you upon my lifeless heart
> should tread
> Not knowing what the poor clod
> chanced to be
> It would find sudden pulse beneath
> the touch
> Of him it ever loved in life so much
> And throb again, warm, tender,
> true to thee.
>
> I believe if on my grave
> Hidden is woody deeps or by the
> wave
> Your eyes should drop some warm
> tears of regret
> From out the salty seed of your
> dear grief
> Some fair, sweet blossom, would
> leap into leaf
> To prove death could not make my
> love forget.

Marie Mohrle initially survived her self-inflicted gunshot, but the wound refused to heal properly and eventually blood poisoning set in. Several months later, after much suffering, Marie died in Muskogee, Oklahoma.

"WE DON'T SHOOT UNLESS WE KNOW WHO IS PRESENT"

THOMAS "RED" KANE went on trial October 13, 1909, for killing Fred Mohrle. He had been mostly quiet and indifferent since the shooting, claiming only that it was a case of "him or me." His defense centered on the theory that he had acted on impulse and in self-defense, as well. Most court spectators snickered at that because Mohrle had been unarmed and shot in the back of the head. A large police contingent was present at the Four Courts to prevent a reprise of the events of June 4.

As the trial began, Kane finally betrayed a little emotion when he became apprehensive after receiving death threats at the Four Courts. The proceedings began in the same courtroom Mohrle had been standing outside back in June, and many members of the Egan gang were in attendance. There was little doubt of his guilt; the main question was how to punish him. While on the stand the next day, the stocky gangster shed some crocodile tears as he haltingly testified how he had shot Fred Mohrle in self-defense, and he ended his testimony by demanding the jury either sentence him to life in prison or acquit him.

Thomas "Red" Kane was the closed-mouth assassin who rubbed out Fred "The Yellow Kid" Mohrle in the bowels of the Four Courts Building in the spring of 1909.

Kane was convicted of the slaying but remained free on a $12,000 bond until sentencing. Controversy erupted the day after Kane was handed a twelve-year term when the seventy-year-old mother of jury foreman Thomas Satterfield was found drowned in Harlem Creek, near the North Side nursing home at Taylor and Lee streets. Police ruled the drowning accidental, and Satterfield concurred.

However, rumors swirled that perhaps Satterfield had promised the Egan's Rats he would deliver an acquittal for Red Kane. When the twelve-year sentence came down, some theorized that the gang had taken its revenge on Satterfield's senile mother, which would attract less attention than if the foreman himself had been eliminated. It was also rumored that James Satterfield got the message and accordingly had agreed with the accidental-death verdict.

Although no evidence ever surfaced to lend credence to the theory that the Egan's Rats had killed the jury foreman's mother when he failed to prevent Red Kane's conviction, the story was told and retold for years afterward.

The month after he was convicted of Mohrle's killing, Red Kane went on trial for election fraud. On November 23, a bizarre incident involving his bondsman hit the news. It was announced that Kane was ill with rheumatic gout and confined to a bed at Alexian Brothers Hospital. Kane's lawyer, C. Orrick Bishop (who had been in the Four Courts corridor when Kane shot Mohrle), asked for a continuance, but it was discovered that the man in the hospital had-dark brown hair instead of red. Apparently, someone had impersonated Kane and lounged in a hospital bed long enough to buy Bishop some time in the courtroom.

Red Kane had notably left his boarding house, complaining of being sick, and saying he was going to the hospital. Records indicated that Thomas Kane had entered the hospital that night, with his bills paid in full by Constable Mike Kinney. For a week the ruse worked, until the stand-in blew it by not responding to the name of Thomas. It wasn't the first time the Egan's Rats had pulled the wool over the eyes of justice, recalling when they hustled Red Giebe off to prison to avoid prosecution for the murder of Fred Scheel.

Thomas "Red" Kane was hit with another two and a half years for election fraud to go along with the murder charge, but he would not serve his full sentence because he became ill for real and died of kidney trouble in the prison hospital on December 22, 1910. The trick of the previous year was duly recalled, so police officers armed with Kane's photograph journeyed to Jeff City to make sure another body switch had not been made. Tom Egan and Mike Kinney dutifully took care of Kane's widow.

With the start of the new decade, the Egan gang now numbered well over 250 men, operating in just about every ward of St. Louis. Tom's twenty-six-year-old brother, Willie, had taken over Sam Young's Franklin Avenue saloon and home base for the gang in the Fifteenth Ward. The political surprise of the year came during the November 1910 city elections when, despite the best efforts of the Egan's Rats, Thomas E. Kinney failed to win a major election for the first time his career. Kinney was defeated by Republican Leonidas C. Dyer in the race for the Twelfth District Congressional seat. The Egan organization was totally floored, as it had had expected to win easily and soon have a representative in Washington.

Kinney cried foul and immediately sued to stall Dyer's swearing in, taking the fight to save his political career a long way. One of the other issues on the ballot in 1910 was Prohibition. The temperance movement was gaining a good head of steam and gradually winning people over. The beer-guzzling city of St. Louis had handily tossed out local Prohibition, but the issue struck a large chord with rural voters.

Looking ahead, Tom Egan could sense that Prohibition eventually would become the law of the land, and realized that the man who prepared accordingly would be more powerful than any other. Egan was confident that, when booze was finally outlawed, he could corner the bootlegging racket in St. Louis and further cement his position as the city's most powerful gangster, and he began planning a smuggling network as soon as the early 1910s.

Tom Egan's visionary ideas took a backseat to gang warfare in 1911. A mildly resurgent Bottoms Gang was acting up again, despite the fact its members had become just a pack of hoods since the attempted murder of Patrolman John Hutton. Frank Hussey was no longer a factor, having died suddenly from a series of hemorrhages on August 3. A bloc of the old Bottoms Gang now known as the Nixie Fighters (a term which would endure in local slang as "one who fights the police") was the source of the trouble, loitering in saloons in the Bad Lands, picking fights with Egan men, robbing, and burglarizing. Instead of enlisting the police, Egan decided to handle the upstarts himself.

The recognized leader of the Nixie Fighters was Edward Devine, who, in true Bottoms Gang tradition, was charged with assaulting a police officer in the fall of 1911. At 9:45 on Halloween night of that year, a dapperly dressed Devine was seen chatting with two short, stocky men in an alley near Twenty-second and Morgan streets. At the end of the conversation, Devine was fatally shot in the back of the head. A woman nearby heard the shot and someone say, "Throw the revolver over the fence." The comment suggests this may have been the first time Devine's killer had taken a life, while his more experienced partner showed him the ropes.

Two weeks later, another member of the Nixie Fighters had his ticket punched. Charles Von der Ahe was in the back room of a saloon at Twenty-first and Lucas streets on the night of November 14, 1911. The bartender heard a gunshot then Von der Ahe scream, "Oh, Doc, you shot me!" One witness said a short, well-dressed man dragged the gutshot Von der Ahe out of the bar to a Twenty-second Street poolroom. Von der Ahe adhered to the gangster code of silence before he died. Police guessed that his killer had been Egan gang member Harrison "Doc" Fitzgerald, who had been charged with threatening Fred Mohrle's brother after the Four Courts shooting two years before. Doc Fitzgerald never was charged with Charles Von der Ahe's murder.

Thomas "Fingers" Regan was a well-known pickpocket and sneak thief. Regan ran into a whole bar full of Egan's Rats on Christmas afternoon, 1911. The Egans were having their Christmas party inside the O'Fallon Pleasure Club at 517 O'Fallon Street when Fingers Regan barged in uninvited. With him came booze and machismo, the lethal combination that took many lives in St. Louis's gangland. Words flew, then insults, glasses, fists, and soon bullets.

Regan and an undetermined number of men were shot in the fast and furious battle. The gangsters at first went to private doctors to avoid the police, but the pain became too great for Fingers, who soon wound up in the hospital. When questioned as to who shot him, the dying man said, "We were down at the club, and I was kidding a guy and he pulled his gun and let loose at me." When asked, "You know who shot you don't you?" Regan replied, "Of course I do."

Fingers Regan kept his mouth shut for the time being, "What's the use telling on him," he said. "We don't want to help out those cops. I wouldn't even tell the priest who came to see me who shot me, and I won't tell anyone else. But I'll tell you this much, Maggie. I wasn't the only one who got it. There were others who got it, too, but they'll have a hot time finding them."

Regan had a change of heart just before he died and whispered that his killer was Fred Woelfel, brother-in-law of Tom Egan. Woelfel was never charged with the murder, because there was no other evidence aside from the whispered confession.

The Christmas brawl involving the Egan's Rats once more got the public and police paying attention to the mysterious gang that could kill and get away with it, whose members never told who shot them even as they painfully bled. At the time, this code of silence was unfamiliar to most St. Louisans.

In the aftermath of the Regan homicide, Tom Egan saw an opportunity to flaunt his power. He was riding high after his successes in the criminal underworld and soon had an chance to show the world how far he'd come.

In all probability, Egan sent an emissary to the *St. Louis Post-Dispatch* to arrange an interview, which appeared in the newspaper's January 21, 1912, edition. A reporter took down what Egan said as an artist sketched the gang boss's portrait. Egan read the transcript of the interview and signed off on the results. Following is Tom Egan's statement as it appeared in the newspaper:

> Capt. Joseph Schoppe, in command of the Carr Street District, is known as one of the severest officers in the Police Department. He showed what he was when he knocked out the "Jolly Five Club." But neither Capt. Schoppe nor any other policeman can find out anything about the troubles that happen among my friends.
>
> The police do not know who killed Edward Devine and Charles Von der Ahe, and I do not think they will ever know. They do not even know why they were killed. The police do not know who killed Thomas "Fingers" Regan or why he was shot; and they know as much about it now as they will ever.
>
> In the last eight years I have built up a following of from to 300 to 400 men, not all of whom live in the Carr Street District. I bound them to myself by signing bonds without fees whenever they, or their relatives, appear in police court. I gave them a turkey dinner on Christmas Day. On the same day I dispersed several hundreds of dollars among friends of mine who are in the penitentiary.
>
> In return, the boys come to me at the Democratic primaries—I am a Democrat—and ask me how they shall vote. I tell them.
>
> Some of these men work, although some do not. They are steamfitters, bartenders, laborers, and factory workers. A few of them formerly held official positions at the city hall.
>
> I protest strongly against the nickname of "Egan's Rats," which the newspapers invented. If a man spoke this phrase in certain parts of St. Louis he would get his block knocked off. My friends are not rats, but men of principle, having more honor among themselves than there is among the best gentlemen of St. Louis.
>
> It takes a strong man not to tattle to the police. My boys have a principle never to tell the police anything. They

wouldn't "snitch" if they were arrested. They won't tell a priest when they are dying who shot them, so how can a detective expect to learn anything?

When a policeman asks them for information they laugh at him. "That's what you are paid to find out," they tell him. "I don't know anything about it and wouldn't tell you if I did."

I have been told that after a man was killed in the "Jolly Five Club," about twenty-five men who were supposed to have seen the shooting were witnesses before the grand jury. But they wouldn't tell a thing. Several were indicted for perjury. But what good did that do? The perjury could not be proved. If it had, they would have taken their medicine and gone to the penitentiary rather than "snitch."

The boys hate a "snitch" so that he has to get out of the neighborhood, or something would happen to him. There have been a few informants, but they left never to return. If they had come back, a way would have been found to get rid of them.

The only way a policeman could get evidence in a murder would be for him to happen to be present when it occurred. But we never shoot unless we know who is present. If some outsider were there, not bound by the rule of silence, he might tell the police what he saw.

The boys dislike the police and the courts because they have given them the worst of it. Many of them have been to the workhouse for some little thing like fighting, or their brothers have. We want nothing to do with the police or the courts. We don't want to prosecute or be prosecuted. If we have any wrongs to redress, we do it ourselves.

I do not remember that in the last several years any outsider has been injured. A stranger is perfectly safe to come among us. If he gets in trouble it is his own fault. Our affairs are all among ourselves, and we regard them as our own business.

We look at it this way. Supposing a man is killed; he is dead. What good would it do us to help send the man who shot him to the penitentiary? His work there would do us no good, and would not lower our taxes, but would help make some rich prison contractor still richer. In the meantime, the prisoner's wife and children might starve. It wouldn't help us out a bit to send any man to the penitentiary. If the dead man's friends want to take that matter, that is their business.

I have headquarters in a saloon at Broadway and Carr street, of which I had the license in my own name for several years. It is now in the name of John Ryan, a former commission man. It is a strict rule that their must be no disorder in the saloon. It is true that men have been arrested there, but not for offenses committed on the premises.

It is probably the quietest and most orderly saloon in St. Louis. This fact was proved on two occasions, when I was summoned before the Excise Commissioner to show why my license should not be revoked. Merchants from Franklin Avenue to O'Fallon Street, and from Third to Eighth streets, went to the front for me and the license was saved.

No policeman has ever been attacked by one of our men. On the contrary, we absolutely avoid any actual collision with the police. A plain clothes man can go among 50 of the boys and arrest five or all of them without trouble. They will go without resistance. If Capt. Schoppe telephones that he wants one of the boys, he will go at once to the police station without a police escort. Even the special policemen investigating so-called "gang murders" go unmolested among us and will admit it.

My following is not a formal organization. There are no elected officers, no constitution and no by-laws. They are mostly men who were raised in the same neighborhood, who have the same politics, and who have the same unwillingness to give the police the slightest information on any subject"

This interview still amazes nearly a century later. Latter-day crime bosses like Al Capone and John Gotti usually called themselves bootleggers or construction consultants or claimed to hold some other legal job. Tom Egan, on the other hand, sat down with the city's main newspaper and basically said, "Yeah, I'm a gangster. Not only that, I'm the boss. And what are you going to about it?"

Captain Joseph Schoppe, mentioned by Egan in the interview, went on to corroborate much of what the gang leader said.

He described questioning potential witnesses of the Christmas Day brawl, saying that not even an eleven-year-old boy could be coaxed into talking to the police.

Police Chief William Young was less than pleased. He sneered, "I see by his statement that Thomas Egan objects to the name 'Egan's Rats.' But he runs a 'ratty' place at Broadway and Carr street, and the name fits.

"He boasts that his men do not 'snitch.' That is nothing extraordinary. Thieves and pickpockets do not usually 'snitch' on each other.

"He says his following consists of 300 to 400 men. He is evidently suffering from exaggerated ego.

This sketch of a dapper-looking Tom Egan appeared in conjunction with his famous and candid 1912 interview in the St. Louis Post-Dispatch.

"The only good thing about 'Egan's Rats' is that they murder no one but themselves."

By the time Tom Egan gave his interview in January 1912, his brother-in-law Senator Thomas Kinney had fallen ill with tuberculosis and rarely left his home at 1720 Carr Street. Brother Mike began tending to his downtown saloon at 716 Pine Street. Growing weaker throughout the spring, Tom Kinney attempted to remain positive, but he knew the end was near after forty-four years and a remarkable career.

Kinney was removed to a hilltop bungalow near Kirkwood, Missouri, the logic being that the country air would help his lungs. It didn't, and within two weeks, the family gathered at his bedside and summoned two priests. One of them was Father Timothy Dempsey of St. Patrick's Catholic Church in the Kerry Patch, who had known the Kinneys and Egans for many years. After the last rites were performed, the family leaned in closer to say goodbye. They included wife Catherine, daughter Florence, siblings Mike, William, and Julia and brothers-in-law Tom and Willie Egan.

At 8 o'clock on the morning of May 15, 1912, Thomas Kinney, known to the cognoscenti as "Snake" and then "Senator," uttered his last words: "I am not afraid to die. I want to thank my friends."

The former senator, saloonkeeper, and "godfather" of the Egan's Rats was given one of the most impressive funerals in St. Louis's history. Thousands of people attended, rich, poor, white and black, a noticeable instance of integration in 1912 St. Louis. A huge procession of more than 200 carriages and dozens of automobiles made its way from the Church of the Blessed Sacrament to Calvary Cemetery, escorted by a 100-piece band. In a touching moment, a delegation of newsboys dedicated a floral wreath, acknowledging Kinney's days as a newsboy and his efforts to improve child-labor laws. There were more than 500 honorary pallbearers; two of the actual pallbearers were Mike Kinney and brewing magnate Louis Lemp. They stood by silently with other members of the Kinney-Egan family as the casket was lowered into to an airtight concrete vault.

Tom Egan eventually got some measure of revenge on behalf of his brother-in-law and best friend. He had accused a fellow Democrat, Michael J. Gill, of sabotaging Kinney's congressional bid in 1910 to further his own personal aspirations. As a result, when Gill ran for Congress in 1912, Egan squashed like him a bug, compiling such a large tally for his Republican opponent that Gill was literally speechless upon defeat.

The Egan's Rats were at the height of their power, and they never again would have as many members as they did in the early 1910s. Two of the newer members were a pair of Jewish hoodlums named Sam Mintz and Max Greenberg. The latter was originally from New York and quite familiar with organized crime there. One of his best friends was gang leader Irving Wexler, better known as Waxey Gordon. Mintz and Greenberg began hanging out at Willie Egan's joint on Franklin Avenue.

Also now full-fledged members of the gang were Ben Milner, Frank "Gutter" Newman, Beatty Babbitt, Willie Heeney, Lee Turner, William "Whitey" Doering, and a stocky, easygoing guy in his early twenties who worked occasionally as a plumber when he wasn't gangstering. The man was William "Dint" Colbeck, who was destined to run the Egan's Rats one day.

Another pair of hard cases at Willie Egan's were the Dunn brothers, Harry and John. Born and raised in the rough neighborhood north of Franklin on Dickson Street, they were little more than kids, but they more than compensated for their lack of age with daring nerve and merciless brutality.

Standing a little over medium height, twenty-year-old Harry was known as "Cherries" and had a reputation as a ladykiller. Pictures reveal him to look like a full-faced Colin Farrell. Dunn's stock in the gang would soar after he pulled off a daring escape from the city workhouse in the spring of 1913.

Younger brother John, age seventeen, was known as "Pudgy" because of the 240 pounds he carried on his five-foot-eleven frame. He was a brawler of citywide repute and wasn't as quick to use a gun as his brother was. The Dunns were inseparable, whether drinking, shooting pool, or committing crimes. They were close friends with Edward Schoenborn, a member of the Bottoms Gang and a bartender at Beverly Brown's saloon.

When they weren't robbing or stealing or hanging around the gang's headquarters saloon, they loved to carouse in the city's bars and niteries, dressed to the nines, cutting a noticeable swath wherever they went.

The Bottoms Gang was still around but posed no challenge to the Egan gang. The Bottoms' home base was Tony Foley's saloon at Twenty-third and Olive streets. The gang also spent a lot of time across the river in East St. Louis, in the raunchy entertainment district called "The Valley," and continued to self-destruct during the early part of the decade.

John Cotty was known as a killer and crack shot, but his reputation would prove painfully exaggerated on September 28, 1912, when he got into a fight in the middle of Jefferson and Olive streets with William Shinnick. The two men faced off about fifty paces apart. Cotty, the alleged crack shot, fired first and scored only one minor hit out of six shots. Shinnick scored four fatal hits out of five shots. The wild gun battle was witnessed by dozens of people, including a police officer.

While Tony Foley technically may have run the Bottoms Gang, he no longer accompanied the boys on robberies, having mellowed since his flaming youth. On the street, the gang was led by Wesley "Red" Simons, recently released from prison after five years. Simons was a large, imposing man, standing six feet tall and weighing 215 pounds in an era when the average St. Louis gangster stood about five feet seven. Simons was one of the most feared men in the city and, depending on who one talked to, may have had as many as seven notches on his gun. Despite his bulk and violent ways, Simons was noted as being a bit more intelligent than the average goon—at least he was smart enough to not attract the attention of the police or the Egan's Rats.

Not all members of the Bottoms Gang cottoned to Red Simons. Emmett Carroll hated the hulking gangster, suspecting Red of stealing his girlfriend. The feud between the two came to a head in Tony Foley's dive bar on the night of March 31, 1913, when Carroll was afflicted with a fatal case of lead poisoning. Simons and his friends attempted to conceal the crime by washing the bloodstains away, lugging Carroll's corpse to their automobile, and dumping it in a vacant lot blocks away. Their efforts were for naught when the police discovered that a murder had taken place in Tony Foley's saloon.

Red Simons confessed to the killing, stating that it had been a case of self-defense. Excise Commissioner Thomas Anderson swooped in to yank Foley's liquor license. A witness to the killing, John MacDonald, was shot and wounded a few days later, an effective message that everybody should keep their mouths shut.

A bartender/pickpocket named Henry Zang was subpoenaed and testified that Emmett Carroll's killing was premeditated murder, not self-defense on Simons's part. Bottoms goons terrorized him relentlessly and were so persistent that Zang took a long trip to Canada to get away from them. Sneeringly referred to as the "Dutch snitch" by Simons and his friends, Zang was a basket case by the time the trial came around.

Yet another ex-member of the Bottoms Gang, Albert Kapp, bought the farm in the early morning hours of August 16, 1913, when he was shot in the head by his girlfriend Rosa Powell as he slept in their stifling Division Street flat. The most gratifying detail in his murder was when Ms. Powell requested that her Sunday clothes be brought to the jail so she could wear them to her arraignment.

During that summer, the Egan's Rats put the squeeze on local bookmakers. Men like Henry "Kid" Becker, Sam and Will Pesch, and others were required to kick back a percentage of their daily takes. The gamblers and their numerous runners would roam the stands at whichever St. Louis baseball stadium had a game that day, either Sportsman's Park or Robison Field. Since both the Cardinals and Browns were struggling through dreadful seasons in 1913, the few people who went to the games had little else to do but gamble—on which team would win and by how much, or whether the next batter would get a hit or strike out. The bookies would give odds on just about anything or anyone. At the end of the day, they would retreat to their handbooks and tally the proceeds, always making sure to set aside Tom Egan's share.

A month before Red Simons's trial St. Louis saw another mystifying gang murder. The Friendly Ten Club occupied one of the lowest rungs on the Egan ladder. The ironically named group's headquarters at 1816 Division Street was an old, rickety two-room house that lacked electricity. Its only amenities were a table, a few chairs, and a beat-up piano. Ex-convicts and thieves of the worst order, most of the Friendly Ten boys lived right there in the neighborhood.

No one outside that area likely ever would have heard of the Friendly Ten Club until two dead bodies were discovered in the spartanly furnished house at 9:30 on the morning of February 10, 1914. Peter White and John "Pudgy" Burns lay tangled together on the floor with a half-full whiskey bottle nearby. The name of the gang's leader, John Harris, had been shakily scratched in chalk on a board near the bodies. Resting on the cellar windowsill outside by the back door was a loaded revolver, two cartridges of which bore strike marks. Police put the time of death at about 8:30 the previous evening. A steady stream of footprints in the snow leading to the house indicated that several people had visited during the night to see the bodies. Searching for a motive, police looked into the victims' background.

Peter White was thirty-five years old and had served seven years in prison for killing James Nolan in a bar fight during the Folk primaries in March 1904. Pudgy Burns was twenty-four and recently had been paroled after serving two years for robbery. At first, police thought the two men had killed each other in a duel. White had been shot once, the bullet entering his neck and ranging downwards, indicating he may have been sleeping when shot. Burns had been shot four times, and White lay at his feet.

The closest police ever got to solving the mystery was determining that White's brother had learned of the killings and gone to the Friendly Ten armed to avenge his brother's death. He found the place deserted save for the bodies on the floor. The brother's revolver was the one found on the outside windowsill, which he'd set there so he could avoid a weapons charge. The cops guessed that White had been killed in revenge for James Nolan, and Burns had died because he was in the wrong place at the wrong time. The prime suspect was a mysterious character named James "Short Sport" Kennedy. Needless to say, he was never arrested.

In an ironic footnote, the Friendly Ten clubhouse on Division Street was the very same house where one of the dead men, John "Pudgy" Burns, had been born.

Red Simons went on trial for the murder of Emmett Carroll on the morning of March 2, 1914. The trial was held at the new Municipal Courts Building, and four detectives were assigned to safeguard him from any Yellow Kid-style reprisal. The chief witness against him, Henry Zang, did not have the luxury of professional protection, but he did have an ace in the hole in the form of a .38-caliber revolver. The cops were so focused on watching Simons that they didn't bother to search Zang.

When the court broke for lunch at about 1:50 p.m., Simons walked down the block for a quick beer in James Mooney's bar at 1233 Chestnut Street, where he encountered Henry Zang. The two men were seen talking in low tones by the cigar counter. The sounds of gunshots shattered the early afternoon quiet of the place, and Simons fell to the floor fatally wounded, with two bullets in his stomach. Business inside the saloon continued uninterrupted, with customers stepping over Simons's body and claiming not to have seen a thing. When Mooney was hauled off for questioning, none other than former gang boss John "Cuddy Mack" McGillicuddy donned an apron and began serving patrons, ignoring the crowds of policemen working the crime scene.

Zang readily admitted killing Simons, saying, "He went to kick for his rod, and I let him have it." Simons was found to be unarmed, and it was loudly wondered what had happened to the detectives who were supposed to be protecting him. One of them, Detective Kelly, stated that it was only the policemen's responsibility to ensure Simons's safety in the Municipal Courts Building, and once he left the building he was on his own.

After a few days of detailing his long months of terror at the hands of Simons and his friends, Henry Zang walked out of the station house free as a bird.

By the summer of 1914, Tom Egan's smuggling network was in place. He had dispatched men to Chicago, Detroit, Terre Haute, Cincinnati, and New Orleans, and they made sure that secret shipments of liquor arrived safely on a regular basis. These out-of-town cells also ensured plenty of Democratic votes in their respective cities.

In the mid-1910s, the forty-year-old Egan was looked upon as one of the most powerful gangsters in the Midwest. During this period of expansion, the Egan gang ventured into narcotics sales. Drugs were rampant during the early years of the 20th century, and many addicts and transients would gather to sleep on the steps of the old city courthouse on hot summer nights. Dope peddlers would work the crowds, injecting them with morphine and offering other substances. With passage of the Harrison Narcotics Tax Act in December 1914, hard drug sales were officially outlawed, making Tom Egan's dope sideline all the more profitable.

One downtown neighborhood was known as a particular hotbed of drug use. Nicknamed the "Cocaine Bottoms," it was centered around Poplar Street, about where the southern edge of present-day Jefferson National Expansion Memorial Park is. The number-one hood in the area was a gaunt, high strung man named Thomas "King Coke-Head" Tremaine.

Bordering the Cocaine Bottoms was Filipino Row, whose Asian population was routinely terrorized by Tremaine's coked-up ruffians. Opium dens in "Hop Alley" drew people from throughout the city, as well as gangsters seeking something more exotic. By and large, the drug of choice of the Egan gang was alcohol.

Trouble flared again among the boys when Sam Mintz was suspected of snitching to the police and was killed in a fight on December 5, 1914. His murderers were suspected to be Ben Milner and Max Greenberg. Three months later, on March 12, 1915, the Egan's Rats clipped yet another informant. Daniel Sweeney paid the ultimate price for deciding to testify at an upcoming trial about numerous instances of Egan-inspired election fraud.

In 1915, an old face and a new one appeared among the Egan's Rats. The old face was a legend in St. Louis's gangland, and the Egan thugs still told yarns about his daring robberies, prison escapes, and assaults on police officers. But by the beginning of the year, William "Skippy" Rohan was nowhere near the fearsome Tasmanian Devil-like crook he had once been. Time had not been kind to Rohan, who had spent the last seventeen years in and out of prison, and he looked every year of his age of forty-six.

After he finished his latest term in the joint, Rohan dropped by the Egan headquarters at Broadway and Carr to visit his old pal Tom Egan, who was one of the few gang members that had been close to Rohan. During the next few months, the two men were seen sitting alone at a table in the saloon, sipping cold beer, and talking in hushed tones. Other gang members were deferential to the broken thief, showing him respect they usually didn't accord to others. Egan especially was glad to have Rohan back, since by this point he was probably the last surviving member of the old Ashley Street Gang, the original Egan's Rats.

Skippy Rohan was determined to finally go straight, having promised his wife that he would stay out of trouble. Rohan kept his word, and Egan seems to have respected his wishes. Skippy worked in a shoe repair shop and hung around the old neighborhood in his spare time, probably enjoying freedom with a clean conscience for the first time in decades. He would go to Egan's bar, drink with his old pal, and otherwise hang out with the boys, but Skippy Rohan's days of crime were done forever.

Sometime around the fall of 1915, a new recruit began to appear at Tom Egan's joint and at Willie Egan's place on Franklin Avenue. In his early twenties, he stood an inch shy of six feet tall and was built like a prizefighter. The man was a heavy drinker, volunteered little about his past, and was well known to be much smarter than he looked. The hard-drinking, close-mouthed newcomer would be the primary reason the name Egan's Rats would endure in the lexicon of American criminal history, for he was destined one day to become America's most wanted man under the alias of Fred "Killer" Burke.

He was born Thomas Camp on May 29, 1893, on a farm near Mapleton, Kansas. One of eight children, Thomas was known as a quiet, hardworking, and respectful boy. According to one of his descendants, his downward spiral began at the age of seventeen, when a traveling salesman from Texas passed through the region and came to stay at the Camp farm. The taciturn teenager became fast friends with the smooth-talking salesman, who secretly specialized in selling phony land deeds to gullible real estate agents and recruited the naïve Thomas to join the scheme. The slick glad-hander pitched the deeds, while the hulking boy stood by silently as a "heavy closer," his mere presence giving the suckers extra initiative to sign on the dotted line.

Soon enough the law closed in, but the mysterious salesman disappeared without a trace and left Camp holding the bag. Filled with anger, despair, and resentment, Thomas left his family for good before his trial, saying he was going off on his own.

He spent his formative years in Kansas City, drinking and fighting, and eventually graduating into burglary and armed robbery. Somewhere along the line, he started calling himself Frederick Burke. With a solid reputation among K. C. hoods, he turned up in St. Louis for the first time near the end of 1915. Living modestly at the downtown YMCA, he was known as a ladies man and for his ability to pose as an honest businessman.

Although it's unknown just how Burke hooked up with the Rats, it's possible that he was introduced to the gang by Tony Ortell. Born around 1884, Ortell was an alcoholic robber and safe-blower who pulled jobs with the Egan gang. Vouched for by Ortell (whose intelligence he vastly exceeded), Burke was soon a regular in the two saloons and probably participating in crimes with the Egans.

Later that fall the police came within a whisker of solving Sam Mintz's murder, when Morris and Max Greenberg, Michael "Heavy" Connors, and Ben Milner were picked up for doing "torch jobs"—burning down buildings so the owner could collect a bundle on insurance, with the boys usually muscling their way in for a sizable chunk of the settlement. Mintz was murdered for allegedly providing information that led to their arrests. The gangsters were never charged with the killing, a familiar refrain when dealing with the Egan's Rats.

6

ROTTEN CHERRIES

THE HANDSOME, VOLATILE gangster Harry "Cherries" Dunn was under a lot of pressure in late 1915, primarily because of his growing dissatisfaction with the Egan's Rats. His good friend Edward Schoenborn constantly asked him to join up full time with the Bottoms Gang, the leadership of which Schoenborn had assumed after Red Simons's death. Cherries' frustration was that his brother, John "Pudgy" Dunn, was rotting in an Illinois prison cell.

On November 5, 1914, the Dunn brothers had gotten into a street fight in Chicago, and Pudgy ended up killing a hood named Robert Koch, whom the Dunns were convinced had been sent specifically to assassinate them. Pudgy was sentenced to prison and had received little or no help from Tom Egan, which infuriated Cherries, but not enough that he spoke out about it.

Although details would remain hazy, it was rumored that Cherries Dunn in December 1915 made a visit to police headquarters at Twelfth and Clark, offering to share his considerable knowledge of Egan gang crimes with police if doing so would get his brother out of prison. Police rejected his offer, and as Dunn quickly made his way out of the building, he reportedly ran into

Skippy Rohan. The two men traveled in different circles and barely knew each other, but the fact remained that someone in the Egan's Rats now knew that Cherries Dunn had tried to talk to the cops. And Dunn knew full well that if Tom Egan suspected he was a snitch, his life wouldn't be worth two cents.

Later that month, Cherries Dunn became a central figure in a yearlong murder spree that would spark long-lasting changes in the St. Louis underworld.

The killings began with a private quarrel among Egan gang members. Late on December 16, 1915, the men were in a lid club at 1420 North Seventh Street when Bart O'Donnell, James "Fats" Feeney, John O'Hara, and John and Spud Murphy got into it. Both O'Donnell and O'Hara had been shot in previous months, and ex-Bottoms Gang member John Murphy was accused of being the shooter. In this dingy barroom, the Egan gang court of law was convened and Murphy was found guilty. Sentence was passed in the form of seven bullets. His body was left in a vacant lot several blocks away.

At midnight on December 21, Cherries Dunn was sitting in the wine room of Harry Parcher's saloon at Goodfellow and Cote Brilliante with a tough guy named Fred Beumer and two girls. The four were having a great time and minding their own business when three boisterous carpenters on the other side of a partition separating the saloon from the wine room began flipping matches over the divider onto the men. Either Dunn or Beumer complained to the bartender, "Are those fellows out there trying to boob us?" The partition was thin and both groups could clearly hear each other.

When Dunn and his friends ordered limburger cheese sandwiches, the carpenters made loud sarcastic remarks about them. Dunn and Beumer snarled back, then gulped more beer, attempting to hold their tempers in check. One of them growled again at the barman, telling him to get the workmen to "cut it out." One of the women tried to calm her date down by saying, "Don't kick. You were a bartender once."

After about an hour of tension, the four in the wine room asked to leave by the side door and walked south on Goodfellow

Avenue. The carpenters quickly trotted outside and around the corner after them, thinking fistfight. Finally losing his temper, Cherries spun around and began shooting, fatally wounding one of the carpenters, John Groenwald, in the abdomen.

Four nights after Christmas, Cherries Dunn, Fred Beumer, and Eddie Schoenborn sought to rob saloonkeeper Charles Reutilinger. They invaded his place at 1447 North Broadway, not far from Tom Egan's joint, and found the bar deserted. Somehow their plan went awry and Reutilinger was plugged just above his lip. Two passing patrolmen came up to the robbers as they exited the place, but since they were unaware of the murder, the cops let the three go. The lethal trio ended up hiding in the three rooms above Egan's saloon.

By the next day, the police had learned that Harry "Cherries" Dunn had been the ringleader in the shootings, and warrants were issued for his arrest. Dunn was growing more paranoid by the day, about the killings and his visit to the police station a few days earlier.

William "Skippy" Rohan went with his friend August Hartmann to a meeting of the shoemakers union early on the evening of January 7, 1916. At 8 o'clock the meeting broke up, and the two went barhopping across the city. At midnight, Rohan and Hartmann dropped by Tom Egan's saloon. Only four or five others were in the place, and the two friends stood at the bar drinking and talking with bartender John Laker.

At 12:30 a.m., Cherries Dunn swaggered into the saloon and told Laker to set up everyone in the house with drinks—expect Rohan. Skippy frowned, "What's the matter with me?" Curling his handsome face into a sneer, the young Dunn snarled, "Go on, you snitch." Rohan heatedly began to respond, perhaps thinking to spill Dunn's big secret right there in Egan's joint, when Cherries jerked out his .38 and shot Rohan squarely on the tip of his nose. He shot Skippy once in the heart and once in the arm before the latter fell over dead, and then fired two more rounds that missed before tossing his revolver to the floor and stalked out the door.

John Laker immediately had Rohan's shocked friend cart his body outside, so police wouldn't think the murder had occurred inside the bar. When the ambulance arrived, police were shocked to see who the victim was. Despite his reformation, William "Skippy" Rohan had still died violently. Police knew who the killer was, but since any witnesses were silent as usual, they were at a loss for a motive, other than Dunn calling Rohan a snitch. Cherries most likely shot Skippy in a rage because he suspected Rohan had told police about his December shooting spree, or perhaps, as the police would later suggest, Rohan knew something that Dunn couldn't afford to have his partners find out.

But Harry Dunn was finished in the gang anyway, having violated a cardinal rule of the Egan's Rats. In fourteen years, no one had committed a crime on the premises of Tom Egan's saloon. It was a sacrilege in the Egan universe, and all the boys knew not to do it. Making things worse was that Cherries had not only killed someone in Egan's joint, he'd cut down a lifelong friend of the boss. The police, in the aftermath of Rohan's murder, permanently padlocked Egan's saloon, ending an era.

Tom Egan wanted Dunn dead, but his brother Willie, a good friend of Cherries, successfully argued for his life. While the younger Egan was sorry to see Rohan dead, Skippy probably didn't mean a whole lot to him. After all, Willie had not grown up with Rohan as Tom had, and both brothers apparently were still in the dark about Dunn's offer to become a snitch to secure his brother Pudgy's freedom. Thanks to Willie Egan's efforts, Harry Dunn continued to be vertical, and the two often got together for drinks at a neutral location.

After his banishment from the Egan's Rats, Cherries Dunn signed on full time with the Bottoms Gang. After killing a living legend in Skippy Rohan, he was accorded quite a lot of respect in some gang circles and as a result became more trigger-happy than ever.

Dunn and his pal Eddie Schoenborn were nearly inseparable. Schoenborn was known as a somewhat disreputable roughneck, having skated on a murder charge in 1912 after sneaking up behind a guy and clubbing him to death with a pool cue. During the spring and summer of 1916, Dunn spent most of his nights at Charles "Cap" Troll's lid club, the Typo Press Club. Troll was a longtime Republican politician who had claimed what was left of the Bottoms Gang as his own. The bar was located at the rear of 712 Pine Street, facing an alley that ran north-south midway down the southern block.

Another favorite hangout of the Bottoms Gang was a saloon owned by Beverly Brown at 1233 Chestnut. Other members of the inner circle were Dave Creely, Harry Greiser, and a deadly pair of brothers known as the "Heavenly Twins," David and Tom Rowe.

Dunn and his new pals pulled stickups and engaged in other crimes throughout the hot summer. Sometime in late July, Willie Egan introduced Cherries Dunn and Eddie Schoenborn to two recently arrived crooks from New York, Harry Romani and Arthur Fineburg. A semipro boxer who fought under the name "Jack O'Brien," Romani had made fast friends in the Egan's Rats, and the New Yorkers used Willie's saloon as their headquarters. The quartet pulled a caper together, but a dispute soon arose over the spoils.

The four men agreed to meet at midnight on August 21, 1916, to settle the dispute. The site was the Fifth Precinct Democratic Club at 107 North Twelfth Street, and Bev Brown was on hand to serve as mediator. Harry Romani arrived first; Eddie Schoenborn showed at 12:30, accompanied by Arthur Fineburg. The three were sitting at a table drinking beer and talking in hushed tones when Cherries Dunn showed up about 12:45 and made a beeline for them. A loud argument arose, and soon the Bottoms boys and the New Yorkers were swinging on one another. Romani and Fineburg were badly beaten, and Dunn and Schoenborn finished off the ex-boxer with four bullets. While Romani was being shot, Fineburg dashed out the door and ran for his life.

The egg was nearly visible on Willie Egan's face. He had saved Dunn's life several months earlier, but now his pal had finally passed the point of no return.

Cherries holed up at the Typo Press Club, while Schoenborn rarely ventured from his home and Bev Brown's saloon. In his fearful state, Dunn managed to finagle the murder of Joseph Toomey in early September, having discovered that it was Toomey, not Skippy Rohan, who was the informant that had made his life so miserable in December. A burly crook named

Gus Dietmeyer did the deed, telling the cops he'd shot Toomey when the latter tried to pick his pocket.

At three o'clock on the morning of September 19, 1916, a seven-passenger touring car glided along deserted Pine Street. The vehicle had its side curtains drawn, so even if pedestrians had been on the sidewalk they could not have seen the five men inside. Halfway between Eighth and Seventh streets, the automobile pulled soundlessly into the alley that ran south toward Chestnut. After parking the car at the mouth of the passageway, Arthur Fineburg slipped from behind the wheel and stepped into the cool, late-summer night. From the backseat emerged a dapperly dressed Willie Egan, who walked down the alley flanked by Walter Costello and Frank "Gutter" Newman, two of the Egan's Rats' most dangerous gunmen. On point was another Egan triggerman, Edward "Dutch" Hess; Fineburg wordlessly trailed a step or two behind the group.

Four of the men strode into the Typo Press Club, while Fineburg stood guard outside. There were only four or five people inside, including Cherries Dunn, who was standing alone at the far end of the bar. Egan stepped in front of him and ordered a round of drinks, while Costello and Newman took up positions on either side of Dunn and Hess stood off to the side. The gang boss and his trigger-happy former friend talked quietly, no doubt about the murder of Harry Romani. Their conversation was so subdued that none of the other patrons could hear what they were saying clearly. The only other sounds in the bar were coming from a strange character sitting at a table near the group, wrapped in an Indian blanket and twanging a tune on a Jew's harp.

Suddenly, right in the middle of the conversation, Costello and Newman shoved revolvers under both of Dunn's ears and fired three times apiece. The twenty-three-year-old Dunn fell to the floor as the four Egan's Rats dashed out of the place and Cap Troll immediately got on the telephone to the cops.

The police and media correctly suspected that the victim had been killed for shooting Harry Romani, but Dunn's other crimes escaped the public's attention at the time.

The other guy on the scene when Romani was rubbed out, Eddie Schoenborn, knew what soon awaited him and told his wife that he was next on the gang's hit parade.

Schoenborn was behind the bar at Bev Brown's joint on Chestnut Street on the evening of October 4, 1916. At 11:30, none other than Walter Costello and Gutter Newman walked in, followed by Arthur Fineburg and Dutch Hess. The four walked from the barroom into the wine room, the same area where Red Simons had been killed by Henry Zang two years before. The saloon's porter overheard two of them say, "We ought to start the fight now."

At that point, the four men began shouting and swinging at one another in a fake brawl intended to attract management's attention. Sure enough, Schoenborn and Bev Brown came charging in to break up the fight, and the former was immediately hit by three bullets fired by one of the faux brawlers. The deadly quartet ran outside and got into a waiting Ford sedan that was driven by Evelyn Palmer, Gutter Newman's girlfriend.

Arthur Fineburg had come to St. Louis to pull some choice jobs, but he instead found himself in the midst of a blood feud. Fineburg surrendered to the police just after Dunn's killing, but they inexplicably turned him loose. The shaken jewel thief was frantic and clearly apprehensive, as he probably had been included in the Schoenborn hit against his will. Fineburg got out of the North Side and spent his nights at a saloon at 1421 Chouteau Avenue on the city's South Side. Unfortunately for Fineburg, he had picked a bar in a neighborhood where Harry Dunn had plenty of friends.

On a lively Friday night, October 20, 1916, Fineburg was in the bar along with dozen others, drinking to calm his nerves. As he leaned against a piano while its player cranked out a popular tune, two men barged through the saloon's sliding doors and shouted, "There he is, now!" The pair pumped at least seven slugs into Fineburg, who spun around like a top before crumpling into a chair. The New York thief spent his last minutes in the hospital begging for his mother to forgive him for his life of crime.

Dunn's avengers struck again within twenty-four hours. John Carmody had come from Chicago to join the Egan's Rats, but his membership was terminated when Joe Swisher shot him to death at Twenty-third and Olive. The next night, Edward Biegunski, one of the last remaining Bottoms boys on the North Side, unknowingly wandered into a new Egan roost, the Mullanphy Pleasure Club at 818 Mullanphy Street, with a friend. A gun battle erupted, and the outnumbered gangsters put up a good fight at first, but Biegunski eventually succumbed to superior firepower.

Three gangland killings in one weekend, coming on the heels of two previous homicides, jolted the police to life. They raided saloons and clubhouses, making life as miserable as they could for the hoods.

That winter there was a lull in the gang war, but tensions were rekindled on March 11, 1917, when police chalked up the double murder of Pete Carroll and Dennis Fennell to the Egan's Rats. Fennell and Carroll, the latter part of the large Carroll clan in the Bottoms Gang, were shot at the Auburn Social Club at 1507 Cass Avenue. At 3 a.m. a taxi driver named "Skinny" Hempstead received a phone call at his stand telling him to drive north on Blair Avenue in the direction of Cass. A man then stepped into the street and flagged him down, and three or four others materialized from the shadows, saying they were going to pick up a couple of drunks. As the cab pulled into an alley leading to the back door of the Auburn Club, the group's leader drew a pistol and ordered Hempstead to kill the headlights. Two groaning and bleeding men were shoved into the vehicle and held upright by two men while another stood on the running board.

Hempstead was ordered to drive a zigzag route southeast. When he passed a group of policemen on the sidewalk at High and Biddle, the leader put the gun to the cabbie's temple and told him to drive fast. Making his way to the Free Bridge approach on Gratiot Avenue, Hempstead overhead someone say, "We'll have to dump 'em in the river." As the car headed up the approach to the bridge, three pedestrians appeared and the gangster in charge made the terrified cabbie pull a u-turn. The killers left the bodies of Carroll and Fennell underneath the bridge approach at

Sixth and Gratiot, then released Skinny Hempstead after he dropped them off at Eighteenth and Franklin, just four blocks from Willie Egan's saloon.

The Bottoms Gang's response to the dramatic double killing came at 1 a.m. on April 14, when The Heavenly Twins cornered Dutch Hess in a saloon at 3149 Olive Street, chased him into the bathroom, and then filled him and his pal Charles Nelson full of holes. The Egans retaliated in the wee hours of May 31, when Bryan Walsh was shot to death at Leffingwell and Locust by triggerman Beatty Babbitt.

A month after Dutch Hess's murder, John "Pudgy" Dunn was released from the Joilet Penitentiary on parole. One of the conditions of his parole was that he leave Illinois and return to St. Louis. Dunn immediately put the word out that he would personally kill every man involved in the murder of his brother Cherries. That meant the two triggermen, Walter Costello and Gutter Newman, and instigator Willie Egan.

Frank "Gutter" Newman's girlfriend Evelyn Palmer lived in a house at 3323 Lucas Avenue. Palmer had showed no qualms about mixing in her boyfriend's business when she drove the getaway car in the Eddie Schoenborn murder; however, their relationship wasn't always a good one. The previous summer, Miss Palmer had strayed from Newman with the more dashing Harry Dunn, and jealously over the cuckolding had made Newman eager to be included in the Dunn hit. Now, with Cherries gone, Evelyn was back with Newman.

Toward the end of May 1917, with their relationship once again in trouble, Newman showed up drunk at Palmer's house and demanded admittance. Evelyn refused, and Newman responded by shooting several holes in the glass panel of her front door. Gutter's pal Dave Creely, another hood who moved freely between gangs, had a potential solution. Since the slaying of Cherries Dunn, the two men had had little to say to each other, but now Creely agreed to help Newman by talking to Evelyn Palmer.

Despite confused accounts of what occurred, forensic evidence found at the Lucas Avenue house confirmed what happened there on June 8, 1917: At 8 p.m., Frank Newman pulled up across the street from Evelyn Palmer's place. Dave Creely bounded out the front door, telling Newman that all had been squared with Evelyn. Gutter jogged up the walk as Creely began cranking his auto in front of the house.

When Newman approached the door, he saw that a large piece of white cloth covered holes he had shot in the glass a couple of weeks earlier. The gangster then noticed that the person staring at him through the glass panes wasn't Evelyn Palmer but Pudgy Dunn, who proceeded to fire five shots through the white cloth into the man who had killed his brother. Gutter Newman bucked backwards off the porch and collapsed on the front lawn. Pudgy Dunn bolted out the door and ran to where Creely was waiting in his automobile.

It turns out that Evelyn Palmer's feelings for Cherries Dunn were much stronger than anticipated, and she helped his brother Pudgy avenge his murder. Evelyn confessed to police that she had killed Newman, but the cops didn't buy her story. The case became totally moot because of a lack of evidence, and Frank "Gutter" Newman's file was relegated to the permanent "unsolved" bin.

By now Willie Egan had learned of Pudgy Dunn's oath, and he and his men went on high alert, venturing out only as a well-armed group. The tension was palpable on the streets that summer, as the city waited for Egan to get Dunn, or vice versa. The evening of July 24, 1917, found the gang boss in the Falstaff Café at 11 North Sixth Street. He was accompanied by his right-hand man and fellow target, Walter Costello. The latter was a deputy constable in Justice Andy Gazzolo's court, which entitled him to carry the two pistols he sported in holsters on his waist and shoulder. Also in the party were Ben Milner, Max Greenberg, James Durant, Elmer Norman, and William "Red" Giebe, the fabled Egan's Rat who had escaped serious punishment for the murder of Fred Scheel in September 1904.

The men had been drinking heavily all night, growing louder and more belligerent as time passed. Closing time came at 1 a.m., but the Egan boys refused to leave. While Costello demanded more drinks, the barkeep slipped away and called the police. Fifteen minutes later Patrolmen Frederick Egenreither and John Sipple arrived. Egan and his crew went outside to their automobile, with Egenreither and Sipple physically dragging Costello out of the place.

As the boys began to get into their car, Costello whipped out one of his guns and drew down on Sipple. Growling, "Here, you fool, we're not killing policemen!" Egan grabbed his pal and yanked him backward just as Egenreither shot Costello through the heart. Giebe howled in rage and jumped out with his pistol drawn. Egan knocked the gat out of his hand and Giebe took off running. Willie Egan would later state, "I've saved a policemen's life tonight."

With Walter Costello's slaying, the two killers of Cherries Dunn were now dead and the war between the Egan and Bottoms gangs petered out. Willie Egan holed up in his saloon, while Pudgy Dunn was relentlessly hounded by police. What was left of the Bottoms Gang disintegrated while the Egans got back into business.

Tom Egan was out of the saloon trade by now but still ruled the city's underworld with an iron fist. His brother Willie was the main street boss of the Egans, running the show from the Franklin Avenue saloon. Although the two men were brothers, they were a study in opposites. Forty-three-year-old Tom was a gregarious, direct man who wouldn't hesitate to maim or kill to achieve his goals. His outgoing manner greatly assisted him in reaching out to other gangs and politicians. His brother-in-law, Mike Kinney, had succeeded Tom Kinney as state

St. Louis Post-Dispatch

Rogue Egan gangster John "Pudgy" Dunn swore vengeance against his old pals for the murder of his brother Harry.

senator upon the latter's death, reestablishing the gang's connection in Jefferson City.

Thirty-three-year-old Willie was Mike's opposite. Quiet and unassuming, he didn't like to socialize except with his personal cadre of gangsters at the Franklin saloon. He didn't have Tom's ambition or passion, and it was often a sore point between the two, as the Cherries Dunn situation illustrated. Also unlike his brother, Willie never settled down and raised a family. A lifelong bachelor, the younger Egan preferred to play the field and live unattached in his luxury suite at the Holland Hotel.

By the end of summer 1917, the gargantuan Egan gang began to fragment a bit. Among those noticeably absent were Fred Burke and his two closest buddies in the crew, John Reid and Robert Carey, who both had grown up in the North Side neighborhood surrounding St. Louis Place Park. Reid, born January 4, 1891, was slender and slightly built, his frail frame concealing a tough attitude and demeanor. Born in August 1894, Carey was of above-average height, with brown hair, a muscular build, and a handsome Irish face. Both he and Reid had typically rough childhoods, and both quickly turned to crime and the gangs. Like Fred Burke, the two probably were ushered into the Egan's Rats by Tony Ortell.

Burke, who was dodging an indictment for forgery, suggested a trip to Detroit, but he and Carey soon wore out their welcome and were sought on burglary and robbery charges. The two were back in St. Louis by the New Year. The more enterprising Reid decided to stay in Detroit and opened a saloon in the city's Cass Corridor.

Other gangs in the city had long since made deals with Tom Egan and his crew about criminal enterprises such as bootlegging, gambling, robberies, and other illicit activities. Egan for the most part was very generous; his main stipulation was that other gangs could do what they wanted as long as they didn't infringe on the Egans or their business.

One of the biggest gangs in the city was the local branch of the Sicilian Mafia, headquartered in the Italian neighborhood just north of downtown and bossed by Dominick Giambrone. The boss had cemented his control of the city's immigrants through extortion and terror tactics, as well as gruesome murders (one witness in a murder trial was abducted on a winter's night and had his head sawed off while still alive). Giambrone had also built an extensive network of moonshiners in both the downtown Italian district and The Hill. But the don knew enough to leave Tom Egan alone.

What was left of Cherries Dunn's old crew, the Bottoms Gang, had by and large relocated to the Soulard district. There they fell in with a group of neighborhood crooks led by Jack Lyons, and by 1917, the new gang was committing crimes on the South Side. Although no one remembers why, this rabble soon became known as the Cuckoo Gang.

Tom Egan's main political rival these days was a Democratic state representative named Edward J. Hogan Jr. Born on the North Side in 1886, Hogan was the son of a policeman who had gone first into the saloon business and then city politics. Hogan owned a popular tavern at 3201 Park Avenue. Because of his pudgy build, somewhere along the line he unwittingly picked up the nickname "Jelly Roll." Hogan's only sore spot was his kid brother James.

At the age of eighteen, Jimmy Hogan had fatally shot a man named Michael Lynam during a bar fight at Jefferson and Cass avenues, but his brother had managed to pull strings in the governor's mansion to get him out of trouble. At this time, during World War I, the last thing Jelly Roll Hogan wanted was a fight with Tom Egan. But things would soon change.

In the fall of 1917, the main news about the Egan's Rats, as usual, revolved around murder. Eighteen-year-old Joseph "Green Onions" Cipolla, a gang hanger-on and vegetable peddler who dabbled in petty crime, gained citywide recognition for putting an end to a notorious rapist. He and his girlfriend were held up by a black man who had been tying up women with rope and assaulting them after running off any male escorts. Green Onions and two others tracked down the man on the night of October 3,

1917, and after gaining his confidence, Cipolla invited the rapist into his car and shot him dead.

Cipolla told police that the man, Haywood Wilson, had said he was raping white women as revenge for the horrific race riot in East St. Louis on July 2 that claimed the lives of dozens of blacks. Property that had been stolen from the female victims was recovered at Wilson's home, and the police, believing that Cipolla had eliminated a dangerous menace, were grateful.

Gang member James McNulty was assassinated as he exited a poolroom at 2141 Cass Avenue on October 14. McNulty was denied a Catholic funeral by Archbishop Glennon, while his alleged murderer, Arthur Reidy, who was killed a few days later in retaliation, was granted a funeral mass.

With America's entry into World War I earlier that year, on April 6, many of the nation's able-bodied men had been going into uniform. Not all of them were enthusiastic about serving their country, and many took to crime while they dodged the draft. The number of armed robberies and burglaries in St. Louis skyrocketed during the war, and many of the draft-dodging crooks who committed those crimes found their way into the Egan gang.

But not all members of the Egan's Rats were avoiding the war in Europe. William "Dint" Colbeck joined the Army in late April 1918. Assigned to the infantry, he served with Company K, 354th Regiment of the 89th Infantry Division, a unit primarily composed of Missourians. Colbeck would fight in every major engagement of the 354th and eventually would attain the rank of corporal.

Born in Union, Missouri, in 1892, Louis Smith was a large, quiet man with a permanent scowl and a thick shock of wavy red hair. During the war, "Red" Smith served with Company M, 356th Regiment of the 89th Infantry Division. After his discharge, he resumed his place with the Egans.

Fred Burke was dodging several indictments in different states, as was his pal Bob Carey. Since both had used aliases while committing their respective crimes, they were able to join the Army under their real names and thus elude the authorities. Burke and Carey enlisted on the same day, in different cities.

Fagin-like Tony Ortell tried to follow their lead but was rejected because of his prison record (he even went so far as to offer a $25 reward for anyone who could get him signed up).

Burke landed in the U.S. Army's fledgling tank corps, shipping out to France with Company C of the 302nd Tank Battalion. His eventual fascination with machine guns in all probability stemmed from his wartime service, and he would be discharged after the war's end as a sergeant.

Carey wound up stateside in the ambulance corps, which was probably not what he had in mind when he joined up. When he finally was sent overseas, Carey landed in France on the very day the armistice was signed, November 11, 1918. During his service in Europe after the fighting had ended, Carey sustained an injury of an unknown nature that resulted in the Army awarding him a 50 percent disability. In later years, the nickname "Gimpy" would be added to his file by various law-enforcement agencies.

Ortell proved tragically incapable of carrying on during his pals' absence. When he led a disastrous burglary attempt on the Baden Garage at Halls Ferry Road and Walter Avenue in the dead of night on August 18, 1918, watchman Charles Hoffman surprised the crew and shot Ortell's youthful partner, David "Chippy" Robinson, before Tony blew him away. Both robbers escaped but found themselves hunted by the police, and broke to boot.

By war's end, another member of the Egan's Rats had been murdered for reasons that have remained a mystery. After killing Bryan Walsh in May 1917, Beatty Babbitt (real name William J. Werth) had taken up with Walsh's girl, Nellie Trudell. The only problem was that Nellie was already married. Her husband was infuriated by the murder of his friend and his wife's cheating, but he didn't dare move against the dangerous Babbitt. Just before New Year's, Babbitt and Nellie had a quarrel, and Nellie and a girlfriend ended up with their throats cut. Both women survived and eventually would have their revenge.

When a highly intoxicated Babbitt and *his* wife, Marie, walked into Ben Heckemeyer's saloon at the corner of Nineteenth and Cass at two o'clock on the morning of November 21, 1918, the gangster was forcibly removed from the Egans by six bullets, fired by an unknown assailant whom he apparently trusted.

In the late 1910s, a newer, younger generation of hoods started gravitating toward the Egan's Rats, providing them with a fresh infusion of manpower in the wake of the 1916-17 gang war.

Two of them were brothers whose stocky builds, pale skin, and flaming red hair made them almost look like twins. The eldest, Edward Powers, was known as "Big Red"; the younger was Clarence "Little Red" Powers.

Big Red Powers, Ben Milner, and Max Greenberg were soon sent to Leavenworth Federal Penitentiary in Kansas for robbing freight train cars in Danville, Illinois. Longtime associate William "Whitey" Doering was sprung from Jefferson City in 1918 when Tom Egan called in a favor and got Governor Frederick Gardner to issue him a parole. The thirty-three-year-old Oliver "Ol" Dougherty was perhaps the oldest of Willie Egan's hoods.

Also on board was a short, smooth-faced fellow with clear blue eyes, a square jaw, and a Roman nose. David "Chippy" Robinson was twenty-one years old when he was shot during the Baden Garage heist in 1918, and he was already establishing a name for himself as one of the most dangerous crooks in St. Louis.

Another recruit was Steve Ryan, a tall, well-built dude with an easy grin and a reputation as a formidable hand-to-hand combatant. Eddie Linehan was a feisty, hard-drinking kid in his early twenties whose specialty was armed robbery and extortion, and who preferred jobs that were both fast-paced and violent.

Joseph "Green Onions" Cipolla had signed on full-time with the Egans, becoming one of the few Italian members of the gang. Rounding out the inner circle were George Ruloff (who replaced Walter Costello as Willie Egan's bodyguard), Louis "Red" Smith, and Lee Turner.

Some members of the gang were merely hangers-on, never trusted with important jobs; they were the "punks" who stole cars, intimidated witnesses, set fires, and performed similar menial tasks. Their recognized leader was twenty-three-year-old ex-convict Andrew "Big Boy" Kane, a lumbering brute who was a throwback to the days of Snake Kinney and Baldy Higgins, when street gangs brawled bare-knuckled in the streets. Noted for his prodigious strength, Kane had killed at least two men either with his fists or an iron bar. Big Boy was also a bully, smacking around the younger punks, but despite his status among the gang's lowest tier, Kane himself remained an insignificant punk.

By the beginning of 1919, the Egan gang was considered to be by far the worst of St. Louis's underworld element. Willie Egan finally got off the hook with John "Pudgy" Dunn when Dunn was collared for another murder and had his Illinois parole revoked.

Tom Egan, chairman of the Democratic City Committee and leader of the Egan's Rats, saw a decade-long dream come true on January 16, when Prohibition became the law of the land, with enforcement to start in exactly one year. The Eighteenth Amendment's ban on the manufacture, transportation, and sale of beverages containing more than 0.5 percent alcohol meant that Egan's well-established bootlegging business would bring in more money than he could ever dream of.

But, as fate would have it, the gang boss would not reap the rewards of Prohibition. He had been diagnosed with Bright's disease, a kidney disorder, in November and was growing worse with each passing day. Willie Egan, for all intents and purposes, took over the gang as his older brother lay dying.

With Tom bedridden, the crew branched out into other states to commit crimes. In March 1919, George Ruloff and three of the boys invaded one of the swankiest hotels in the resort town of Hot Springs, Arkansas, and robbed some New York bookmakers of $8,000. Ruloff was captured and sentenced to fifteen years in the state penitentiary, but Willie Egan managed to pull strings and wrangle a parole for his pal after just ninety days.

The Egans ventured into bank robbery for the first known time at 10 o'clock on the morning of April 10, 1919. Eight of the boys pulled up in front of the Baden Bank at 8200 North Broadway in a blue-black 1915 Hudson Super 6 sedan lacking license plates. All were dressed in matching long raincoats with plaid caps and carried Army-issue .45-caliber Colt automatic pistols, which would become the sidearm of choice for most of the gang's members. Two men remained in the idling car, while one stood guard outside the bank and four rushed inside, brandishing their pistols and barging behind the counter.

Quickly scooping cash off the counter and out of the drawers, they forced cashier M. W. Muntzel into the vault for more. As the robbers made their getaway, the suddenly plucky cashier grabbed a hidden pistol and fired three shots at the Egans as they drove off. Three policemen heard the shots, commandeered a car, and chased after the Hudson. The robbers headed west on Calvary Avenue, threading between Bellefontaine and Calvary cemeteries, and lost the detectives on West Florissant Avenue. The overall take was $59,310.15—not bad for a morning's work.

The police never got a conviction in what was at the time the biggest bank robbery in St. Louis's history, but there's no doubt the boys at Willie Egan's saloon were high rollers for quite some time after the heist.

Just ten days later, on April 20, 1919, forty-four-year-old Tom Egan passed away at his home at 4551 Arlington Avenue. By gangland standards, his funeral was a very low-key affair. The namesake of the Egan's Rats was lowered into the Kinney-Egan vault at Calvary Cemetery, joining his brother-in-law and sister Catherine, who had passed away the previous summer. Egan's parents and other deceased siblings were also reinterred with him.

Dawn of a New Era

W ITH THE BADEN bank job and the death of Tom Egan, April 1919 marked a turning point in the fortunes of the Egan's Rats. The gang still focused primarily on bootlegging, but the bank robbery had given the boys an adrenaline-pumping taste of quick, easy money. Although some of the gang members preferred the fast money of robberies to the methodical business of rumrunning, Willie Egan, now at the head of the entire Egan empire, at first strove to run the business the same way Tom had.

The gang got a big boost when William "Dint" Colbeck returned from France in May. When Dint strutted into the Egan saloon in his dress uniform and began regaling its denizens with anecdotes of his combat experiences, the boys immediately gravitated to the charismatic veteran.

Fred Burke, another gang member returning from the war, detoured to Detroit on his way back to Missouri and was slapped with a five-year sentence for a land-fraud scheme that was very similar to one that had gotten him trouble in Kansas. Burke's pal Bob Carey occasionally hung around Egan's saloon, but whatever crimes he may have committed during this period didn't attract any attention from the police.

One Egan crime did attract attention: Burly, likeable hood Louis Mulconry led two of the boys on a safecracking expedition near Compton and Olive avenues at 3:30 on the morning of May 20. Mulconry used nitroglycerine (called "midnight julep" by the gangsters) to open the safe, but the resulting explosion only awakened the neighborhood and attracted the cops. Police saw the safe blowers hop into their car and speed off, but the boys soon crashed into a tow truck owned by Gus Buselaki, whose gas station just happened to be a popular hangout of the Hogan Gang.

On January 16, 1920, gangsters across America hit the jackpot as national Prohibition went into effect. Many of the country's older organized criminal gangs had been dying off, but the new booze laws gave them new life. The flood of illegal booze into St. Louis continued, with the Egan's Rats supplying many of the taverns in the city. While major brewing empires such as Anheuser-Busch went into the soft-drink business, others, such as longtime Egan ally Louis Lemp, decided to close up shop forever.

Despite the potential for unlimited profits from bootlegging, however, the Egan boys were busy planning another bank robbery. At 9:50 a.m. on January 21, gang members targeted the Water Tower Bank at 2100 East Grand Boulevard. In a virtual replay of the Baden heist, five or six masked men dressed in tan raincoats and caps barged inside, waving .45 automatics and commanding employees to open the vault.

Across the street, Patrolman Harry Shea noticed the gang's lookout on the sidewalk while walking his beat and correctly deduced that a bank robbery was in progress. Inside, the boys had gotten their hands on $2,000 in cash and bonds and were trying to get into the vault when they saw the big policeman lumbering across the street. "There goes a copper!" one of them shouted.

The lookout instantly opened fire with his .45, grazing Shea in the left hand and hip. Quickly drawing his .38, the officer ignored his wounds and shot back, hitting the lookout five times. Two of the robbers opened fire through the bank's windows, causing Shea to dive behind a parked car for cover as he reloaded. The thieves inside evidently panicked, as they dashed out the door and jumped into their car, leaving behind both the loot and their dying comrade.

When his mask was taken off, the dead lookout was identified as twenty-five-year-old Walter Fischer, an Egan associate and armed robber who had received an early parole from Governor Frederick Gardner in December 1917. Patrolman Shea recovered from his wounds and was awarded $1,000 plus a gold medal.

Undeterred by the disastrous job, the Egans quickly set their sights on another target, the Lowell Bank located at the southeastern corner of Warne and West Florissant avenues. At 9:15 a.m. on April 9, six men, outfitted in the same manner as the two previous robberies, entered the bank and cleaned out the teller cages, netting a total of $11,877. They were scared away from the vault when a courageous teller triggered the bank's outside alarm, forcing the Egans to make a speedy getaway.

While the gang's liquor-smuggling network was in full swing, it was not the foremost item on Willie Egan's agenda. Despite the flood of money to be made from Prohibition, Egan preferred to run his saloon and collect the proceeds while his minions did the robbing and stealing. His kin Snake Kinney and Tom Egan may have been natural leaders, but Willie was not. As a result of his inattention, the Egan gang cells in other cities, such as Chicago, Detroit, Cincinnati, Kansas City, and New Orleans, began to go their own way. They didn't report to St. Louis as often as in years past, and their respective leaders increasingly began to create their own empires.

The most noticeable example of this was in Cincinnati, where what was left of the old Egan group became a large bootlegging mob headed by longtime local gangster George Remus. In Detroit, Johnny Reid had moved on to New York City while dodging a murder indictment. Reid eventually would gain fame throughout the underworld after surviving four gunshot wounds to the head administered by notorious con man "Dapper Don" Collins on May 15, 1921, in a beef over a woman.

In St. Louis, the Egan's Rats were enjoying the high life: nightclubs, showgirls, big-money robberies, rail car thefts. Dint Colbeck by now was firmly established as Willie Egan's right-hand man and always led heists with the same bulldog courage that had kept him alive while fighting the "Huns" on the Western Front. Colbeck also had gained a political title. just like his boss, Willie Egan. Egan was a constable under Judge Andy Gazzolo and member of the Democratic City Committee, while Colbeck served as the DCC's sergeant-at-arms.

Colbeck led four of the men on a newsworthy caper in the dead of night on July 24, 1920, posing as Prohibition agents and forcing their way into the Pine Lawn home of Ward Ireland. They were looking for whiskey certificates, and right in the middle of the robbery Colbeck stopped and got on the phone and called the chief of the St. Louis Police Department, flaunting his clout before the terrified victim. The boys finally set their sights on Ireland's safe, and one of them, later identified as Chippy Robinson, was especially rough with Ireland. The take was minimal, and the caper is known today only because Colbeck and Robinson were eventually arrested for it.

Other gangs throughout the city, which had maintained peace with the Egans since the Cherries Dunn-inspired war of 1916-17, were also busy at the start of Prohibition.

Dominick Giambrone, leader of the St. Louis branch of the Mafia, faced a challenge from John and Vito Giannola, brothers from Balestrate, Sicily. The Giannolas, accompanied by their best friend and most dangerous killer Alphonse Palazzolo, began trying to wrest control of the extortion and moonshining rackets from Giambrone. After an on-and-off gang war that lasted four years, the brothers would depose the longtime mob boss.

The Cuckoo Gang, based primarily in Soulard and off of Chouteau Avenue, grew more powerful as its reputation spread. In April 1919, the gang gained city-wide notoriety after three members killed the best-known gambler in St. Louis, Henry "Kid" Becker, during a botched holdup attempt. However, all was not well in the Cuckoos' universe, as Benjamin "Red" Allen led a *coup de etat* against the boss, Jack Lyons. Said boss was eliminated with a few .38 slugs in the outdoor seating area of Allen's speakeasy at Tenth and Hickory streets on June 13, 1920, by two homicidal brothers named Robert and Thomas Creed.

Edward "Jelly Roll" Hogan was kicked out of the state legislature as the result of a fistfight he had with an opposing lawmaker.

Hogan was now deputy state beverage inspector, giving him leverage over the booze trade. The previous deputy inspector was thirty-two-year-old attorney Jacob H. Mackler, who took Hogan's place as chief consul and advisor to the mob. The Hogan Gang, while not as feared as the Egan's Rats, had built up a good head of steam in the bootlegging business and had proved it was more than capable of brutal murders when its members killed suspected informant Edward Ambs on December 15, 1918. Hogan's headquarters was a saloon at Jefferson and Cass avenues.

This artist's rendering shows William "Dint" Colbeck as he appeared in 1919 when he became Willie Egan's second in command.

James Hogan, at age twenty-three, was young and impulsive. With his hair shaved close to his skull and his sharply defined facial features, he certainly looked like a gangster. Rounding out the Hogan crew were Luke Kennedy, Humbert Costello, Pat Scanlon, Tim Lotsey, James Traynor, "Alibi" Charley Vance, and a massive, sneering gangster named John "Kink" Connell.

Since the Hogans didn't inspire the same sense of fear that the Egan's Rats did, some criminals didn't think twice about double-crossing the gang. Enter a tough ex-con named Charlie Cody, who held out on the Hogans in the aftermath of a payroll heist at the Yellow Checker Cab Company. In a double whammy, he was also marked for death by the Egans, because Dint Colbeck was a shareholder in the taxi company. Cody was summarily executed in a saloon at 2745 Cass Avenue on September 3, 1920.

The Egan's Rats had gained some new, even younger recruits by 1920. James "Sticky" Hennessey was short and stocky, with crew-cut blonde hair and blue eyes, looking like a tough choir boy in pictures. Isadore Londe was a nineteen-year-old Jewish kid who was noted as one of the toughest young hoods in the city. He had been arrested for armed robbery at the age of twelve and had once stolen the entire life savings of an aunt. Londe was estranged from his family because of his lawlessness and the fact that he had married a Gentile girl (Hennessey's sister.) "Izzy" Londe originally had been introduced into the Egan's Rats by Green Onions Cipolla.

Also tagging along were two violent, hyperkinetic kids, Harry Londo and Elmer Runge. The eighteen-year-old Runge eventually would marry the niece of Willie Egan, seventeen-year-old Mary Woelfel. Runge was an impeccable dresser, so much so that his mother nicknamed him "Astor." These young kids would become the foremost leaders of the "red hots," a faction of Egan's Rats that specialized in high-risk robberies.

Another popular member of the gang was Bernard Deaver, known as "Oklahoma Red." A safecracker who always had a kind word, a joke, and was friends with everybody, Deaver literally laughed his way into the Egan's Rats. When Dint Colbeck sized him up for the first time, he asked Okie Red what his line was. "Safes," Deaver replied. Colbeck frowned, "Is that all?" Red said with a perfectly straight face, "I can drink." Dint roared with laughter and told Deaver he could come around anytime he wanted.

In the dog days of the long summer of 1920, the seeds of war between the Egans and Hogans were sown. The trouble had actually begun in April 1919, on the same weekend Tom Egan passed away. Edward Georgan was an unemployed alcoholic who was a friend of certain Egan gangsters, foremost the Crowe brothers, Patrick and William. A Hogan Gang member named Thomas Horan was suspected of shooting Georgan in the back of the head as he urinated in the bathroom of a saloon at Garrison and Easton avenues. Horan skated on the charges, and after that no one much cared. Yet another bloody bar fight in St. Louis. After a year, however, the Crowes finally decided to wreak their vengeance.

On August 3, 1920, the day of the Democratic primary election, Thomas Horan was shot and severely wounded in front of the same saloon where he had killed Georgan. Three days later, three men tried to kill Horan again by shooting up his house at

1017A North Leffingwell Avenue. Patrick Crowe was nabbed by police running away from the scene.

Jelly Roll Hogan decided these offenses would not be tolerated and sent killers after the Crowe brothers. On August 22, two thugs were sent to rub out Pat Crowe. They spent the whole day drinking to prepare themselves for the task, and at 4:35 that afternoon the gunmen staggered into a tavern run by Clarence Hammond at Vandeventer and Fairfax, looking for their quarry. The two were so inebriated that one of them dropped his pistol on the floor as he entered. When they loudly demanded to know the whereabouts of Patrick Crowe, twenty-five-year-old crippled handyman Leo Looney asked them to leave. He should have kept his mouth shut, as they dragged him outside and fatally shot him in the stomach.

Hogan's men continued their stakeout of Hammond's saloon, convinced the Crowes would show up eventually. Just after midnight on September 1, Egan associates James and John Sweeney were grazed by gunfire at the same joint, the only noteworthy detail being that James kicked a policeman in the eye as he was lifted into an ambulance.

The sordid series of events between the rival thugs would heighten tension between the two gangs. Twenty-nine-year-old John P. Sweeney was a lawyer in the circuit attorney's office who served as the gang's liaison to the circuit attorney. Sweeney's father at one time had been a political ally of Snake Kinney, and he and his brother wanted a measure of revenge for their wounds and were angered when Willie Egan decided to cut his losses and quit the useless sniping.

Around this time, Ben Milner, Max Greenberg, and Big Red Powers were released from Leavenworth after Willie Egan and Senator Mike Kinney exerted their considerable influence and got none other than President Woodrow Wilson to issue them pardons. Milner and Greenberg would show their gratitude by conspiring against Egan.

Max Greenberg entertained notions of breaking away from the Egans and forming his own gang. At thirty-seven years old, he wasn't a young man any more, and it galled him to see his old friend

Waxey Gordon doing so well at the heel of gambler Arnold Rothstein in New York while Maxie was scraping by on robbing rail cars in the Midwest. While in prison he had learned much about the liquor smuggling business and made contacts with gangsters from other cities who were serving time there. In September 1920, Willie Egan entrusted Greenberg with $2,000 to make a deal with a Mexican smuggler for a load of whiskey. Max paid the smuggler but kept the booze for himself and his new gang.

Egan had no intention of letting Greenberg go quietly. Long after midnight on October 16, 1920, the Franklin Avenue headquarters were rocked by a large drunken brawl. Every stick of furniture in the place was smashed to bits and several men were severely injured. One also sustained a gunshot wound to the arm. Another victim of the melee was the hapless John Sweeney, who would soon resign his post and cut his ties to the Egans because of the fight.

It was later suspected by police that the brawl may have come about when Max Greenberg was confronted about the missing whiskey shipment.

After the bar fight, Max Greenberg cut out for Detroit, where he briefly smuggled whiskey across the Detroit River from Canada at the behest of Waxey Gordon and Arnold Rothstein. After establishing his contacts, he began shipping booze south to St. Louis and east to New York. Ben Milner distributed the Canadian whiskey, and the group had just started to turn big profits when it was ripped apart.

Ben Milner was carousing with Ben "Cotton" Funke, Danny O'Neil, and Milford Jones on the night of November 21, 1920, when he picked a fight with members of the Russo Gang at a popular cabaret called Jazzland, located at North Grand and Easton avenues. The Russo mob was composed of American-born Italian bootleggers headed by the three Russo brothers—William; Anthony, known as "Shorty"; and Vincenzo, who was universally called Jimmy.

The brawl grew in ferocity, and the Italians wound up chasing Milner's group down Clayton Road and popping shots at them as they sped along. Many witnesses saw the gun battle along the darkened road as the men headed west out into St. Louis County.

At 2 a.m., the fight re-ignited when the four Milner men

walked into the Rigoletto Inn, a roadhouse in Richmond Heights off the North and South Road. Catching sight of the party of Italians inside, Jones immediately snarled, "There go the dagoes!" Willie Russo shook his head and growled, "You oughta stop chewing the rag!"

A gunshot rang out, and the owner killed the lights, plunging the roadhouse into total blackness. The Milner group attempted to find their way to the door, all the while trading shots with the Russos. Ben Milner was nailed right on the chin, while Cotton Funke was mortally wounded in the neck. Danny O'Neil was hit as well, but Milford Jones managed to drag him to safety. There was only one casualty among the Russos, as Charles Lombardo sustained a slight wound.

John Sweeney's law office was located in the Title Guaranty Building, but he would often conduct his business meetings one block over on the southwestern corner of Sixth and Chestnut. Sweeney was having yet another meeting there at 9:30 on the night of March 11, 1921, with the recently returned Max Greenberg, Willie Egan, and an unknown man, possibly a policeman or politician. A cold rain was falling as the men conversed, and they stepped under the awning of a barbershop for shelter. The subject of this meeting was Greenberg's failure to compensate the gang boss for the missing whiskey. It soon became apparent that Egan would not be getting his money back, as Greenberg clung to his cover story of the whiskey barge sinking in the river.

The meeting broke up at 10 p.m., and Greenberg walked to the corner. A signal was transmitted, perhaps by Egan lighting a cigarette, and a man materialized out of the rainy darkness, firing a .38 Smith and Wesson revolver. Max Greenberg was shot through the right side of his face, and John Sweeney sustained a fatal head wound. Willie Egan was struck in the left arm by a stray bullet. Greenberg, his face gushing blood, staggered in a northwesterly direction, collapsing into a speakeasy at Eighth and Pine.

The shooting earned multiple headlines in the city's newspapers. Once Max Greenberg's condition had stabilized and he regained the use of his jaws, he said he didn't know who had shot him and denied that Egan was even at the meeting. The gang boss said the bullet that wounded him had been fired from a passing car. Police couldn't yet see the battle lines being drawn, but they would soon realize this was the beginning of a new gang war.

Willie Egan couldn't capitalize on his attempt to kill Greenberg because he left town to recuperate. Both the Egan and Hogan gangs spent the spring and summer robbing with great abandon. The Egan bootlegging business began to suffer as the boys opted to pursue the quick cash of violent heists.

A police crackdown during the Christmas season of 1920 resulted in many St. Louis gangsters hanging out in saloons and roadhouses in towns such as Collinsville, Madison, Edwardsville, and similar places in Illinois. It was during one of these jaunts that the boys learned that companies involved in the booming Southern Illinois coal industry shipped their payrolls in lightly guarded mail trucks. Egan began sending men into Southern Illinois in 1921 to inquire about potential capers. They reached out to both the Shelton Gang and the Birger Gang, two bootlegging mobs from the Williamson County area that in later years would turn on each other in a brutal gang war that would astound the region.

Willie Egan was received with mostly indifference by Carl Shelton and Charlie Birger, who didn't take kindly to the Missouri gangster and his minions poaching in what they saw as their private preserve. This was an indication of how much the gang's influence had eroded in the two years since Tom Egan's death, with the outfit degenerating from a national organization back to what it had been at the start: a local gang.

The Hogan Gang began the spring of 1921 with two mail robberies, one in St. Charles and the other in Jefferson City. In both cases, when the perpetrators attempted to fence the bonds they had stolen, the police moved in to bust them. The Hogans correctly suspected there were informants in the gang. Despite this, James Hogan green-lighted another job and on April 4 led a group of thugs who accosted a bank messenger for the North St. Louis Savings Trust Company at Jefferson and Wash streets, wrestled him into their car, and sped away. Near the intersection of Compton and Adams streets, the hoods crashed into a truck, forcing them to abandon their disabled vehicle and flee on foot with the messenger's satchel.

Combing through mug-shot books later, the bank messenger, a black man named Erris Pillow, identified James Hogan as the man who had hit him over the head and made off with the loot. A furor was raised over the fact that someone who had been pardoned by former Missouri Governor Gardner had returned to robbing and stealing. Hogan was arrested and bound over for trial.

The Hogan crew spent the new few weeks trying to extricate themselves from their legal troubles. Just after the North St. Louis heist, gang members permanently closed the mouth of Michael "Shamrock" McNamara, who had snitched to police about the St. Charles caper. McNamara was low-level Egan's Rat who had joined the Hogan Gang after being shot in the leg by one of the Rats during an argument on September 21, 1920, in front of the Egan saloon. When the Hogan boys discovered Shamrock was moonlighting as a police informant, two thugs paid a visit to a rundown flat at 2529 Glasgow Avenue on April 11, 1921, and shot him dead.

Several men, including Jelly Roll Hogan himself, also visited Erris Pillow at his home at 4056A Fairfax Avenue to try to bribe or intimidate him into not testifying. Jelly Roll, whom neighbors later identified as a "fat white man," had given a friend of Pillow $2 to tell the messenger to "stay away," and the gangsters that day offered Pillow $300 not to identify Jimmy Hogan. But Pillow remained unmoved; he wanted some measure of revenge for being robbed, socked over the head, and subjected to numerous racial slurs that were undoubtedly hurled at him during the robbery.

With his steadfast intention to testify, the messenger's fate was sealed. Pillow was shot dead by two men as he entered his home after work on the evening of May 9. Governor Arthur Hyde offered a $200 reward for the apprehension of his killers. Two Hogan goons, Dewey McAuliffe and Leo Casey, were soon arrested and charged with the murder. Just three days after Pillow's death, a second St. Charles snitch was rubbed out; Allen Morris was shot and left at a lonely spot near the river outside

Newport, Illinois. The prime suspect in the murders of McNamara and Norris was later identified as Tommy Hayes, who in later years would make a name for himself as a killer for the Cuckoo Gang.

The Egan's Rats were not idle during this period; they spent their time sizing up hoods to see if they stood in their corner against the Hogans. William "Shorty" Regan was a forty-two-year-old bartender who had been running with the gangs since the days of Bad Jack Williams and Tough Bill Condon, and always seemed to be in the wrong place in the wrong time. He had witnessed several gang murders during his long and colorful career, including a January 1918 shootout at the Market Street saloon of bail bondsman Joe Mount that left three men dead, including Mount.

A violent thunderstorm was in progress at 10:15 p.m. on April 25, 1921, when five Egan gangsters walked into Regan's beer joint at 2900 Olive Street to ask whether Shorty sided with Willie Egan or Jelly Roll Hogan. It was a loaded question, and when Regan failed the quiz, he was expelled by the Egans with five bullets.

Summer came and went, but the expected gang war did not materialize. The Egan's Rats pulled a number of capers early in the fall, including one that was an audacious display of bravado. On September 23, six gang members stole $3,400 from a National Biscuit Company messenger at one o'clock in the afternoon right downtown at the corner of Eighth and Pine, in front of dozens of witnesses. No one was ever arrested.

The Egans struck again on the morning of October 24, 1921, when four men marched into the Hodiamont Bank at 6145 Bartmer Avenue in Wellston and left a couple of minutes later $7,189 richer. The boys were now accomplished robbers and hijackers and loved the thrill of the heist. Life for them was one big party, punctuated by the occasional job when they ran low on funds. They had no inkling, as they sped from the Hodiamont Bank back into St. Louis, that their whole world was about to change.

8

COMBAT

DAYS OF GREAT change often start unremarkably, and that was the case on October 31, 1921. It was an overcast, cool day in St. Louis. A slow news day, the main item was the local American Legion convention where the heralded General John "Black Jack" Pershing discussed the Great War and rebuilding efforts in Europe. As evening approached, children dressed in Halloween costumes and began making their trick-or-treating rounds with their parents. Most adults in the Fifteenth Ward knew better than to take their kids to Fourteenth and Franklin.

Willie Egan's saloon at 1400 Franklin was dead at nine o'clock that night. The boss himself was on the premises, looking dapper as usual. Willie had $431 in his pocket, a gold watch dangling on a chain, diamond rings on his fingers, and an expensive sedan parked outside. Money was definitely around.

Whitey Doering was at his normal place behind the bar, while Dint Colbeck, Little Red Powers, George Ruloff, and John Dougherty talked with Egan. The boss took a stroll outside for some fresh air, returning at 9:10 after making a quick trip to the Palace Theater up the street. At the front door, Willie stopped to talk to a roughly dressed man, evidently a panhandler.

As Egan spoke to the derelict, with his back to the street, a dark sedan approached rapidly from the west, slowing as it passed the saloon. Two men opened fire with a shotgun and a pistol. A .45 slug tore into Egan's back, piercing his left lung, barely missing his heart, and exiting to do an encore on the glass pane of his saloon's front door. A shotgun blast landed some buckshot in his left arm for good measure. The dark sedan skidded off into the night.

George Ruloff immediately dashed to his boss's side, and Egan reportedly gasped out the names of the shooters. Dint Colbeck and Little Red Powers ran outside with their drawn pistols, and Ruloff disappeared in the commotion that followed. A patrolman rushed over from across the street. Egan groaned, "I've been shot. Get me to the hospital as quick as you can." Dougherty hoisted his wounded boss into Egan's car and was joined by Patrolman Dolan, while Colbeck and Powers jumped into a second car for the trip to the hospital. Cleverly, just short of their destination, Dougherty pretended that Egan's car had run out of gas, and while Dolan dragged Willie to the front door of the hospital, John discreetly slipped away.

By 9:40, Father Timothy Dempsey of St. Patrick's Catholic Church had been summoned to Egan's bedside. Father Tim had known the Egan family for years and had administered the last rites to both Snake Kinney and Tom Egan. And he had come to the hospital to do the same for Willie. The gang boss gasped that he knew who had shot him, but he never spoke their names. At ten o'clock, fifty minutes after he had been shot, thirty-seven-year-old William Egan died. A few days later, after an elegant funeral, he was interred in the Kinney-Egan vault at Calvary Cemetery.

The press had a field day, reviewing Egan's colorful career and that of the Egan's Rats. It was suspected that Egan's killer may well have been John "Pudgy" Dunn, who had recently been paroled again and was seen back in town. Max Greenberg was also suspected, but he had ostentatiously boarded a New York-bound train earlier in the day, so it was unlikely that he pulled the trigger.

The police interviewed Mike Kinney and asked the state senator to put pressure on the gangsters who had spoken with Egan before he died, so they could learn the identities of the killers. But senator or no senator, Kinney was still a product of the streets, and the police got no more out of him than they did the red hots. Willie Egan died without a will and had left an estate estimated at $200,000. It was soon discovered that he had fathered a boy named James, now sixteen, out of wedlock, and after a lengthy paternity suit, the boy was ruled to be a joint heir to Egan's fortune.

William "Dint" Colbeck was now boss of the Egan's Rats. Although the gang's numbers had greatly diminished since its heyday, Colbeck had built a good relationship with Mike Kinney and thus maintained the Rats' political clout.

A few days after Egan's funeral, a fateful meeting occurred. Izzy Londe brought a potential new recruit before the boys at the Bartling Tire Company, 3024 Locust Avenue, which was run by Little Red Powers. Ray Renard was a car thief and burglar in his early twenties and was known as the Beau Brummell of the city's underworld. Many hoods didn't trust him, saying Renard cared more about the ladies than the money.

Looking him over, Colbeck joked to Oliver Dougherty, "Say, Ol … is this guy a red hot or Rudolph Valentino?"

A miffed Renard retorted, "Say, big boy, are you a red hot or a comedian?"

Colbeck laughed and asked, "Can you shoot?"

"Good as the next one."

"Can you take care of yourself?"

"I'm still alive, aren't I?"

"Well, there's going to be some trouble before long, and I can take care of a few guys with guts. Be careful who you talk to. Guys that talk get killed. If you get in a jam, keep your trap closed. If you get a slug in your belly, don't squeal about it." And with that, Ray Renard became a member of the Egan's Rats.

Willie Egan's suspected murderers were preoccupied with getting two of their number, Dewey McAuliffe and Leo Casey, off the hook for killing bank messenger Erris Pillow back in May. Although there was considerable evidence pointing to his guilt, McAuliffe was acquitted a few days before Thanksgiving. Both men were released, which caused outrage among the city's black community.

The Egan crew had made no drastic moves after Willie's murder, aside from some quiet conferences where Dint Colbeck consolidated his power. The boys did manage to pull off a heist at the St. Louis Refining Company at 1005 Pine Street on November 26 which netted them $60,000 in diamonds. The next day, a group of red hots was arrested in Madison, Illinois, for taking part in the robbery, including Harry Londo, Thomas Skinner, new member Ray Renard, and Hogan gangster Alibi Charley Vance. Skinner eventually would be sentenced to two years for his part in the crime.

Shortly thereafter, the Egans suffered another loss, and a baffling one at that. George Ruloff, Willie Egan's personal bodyguard, had been very vocal in saying that he and the boys had a good idea who had killed their boss. Ruloff had shown up at the funeral, telling anyone who would listen, "We may not know who killed Willie Egan, but we know whose money got him killed."

Up the street from Egan's saloon, at $1318\frac{1}{2}$ Franklin Avenue, was the Allies Restaurant, a small lunch counter that was a favorite hangout of the gang. Proprietor Joseph Cavasino left Ruloff in charge while he went to run an errand before lunchtime on December 2, 1921. Ruloff was alone in the place when a visitor walked in at noon, placed a .32 automatic against Ruloff's stomach, and pulled the trigger. George staggered to the back of the restaurant, where he futilely tried to hide in the coal storage room. He was shot once in the back as he ran, and the killer pumped three more slugs into Ruloff's head as he lay half in and half out of the coal room doorway.

The most the police could discover during their investigation was that George Ruloff was killed to close his mouth. If the Hogans had killed Willie Egan, as was widely believed, would Ruloff have let a Hogan gangster get close enough to put a gun against his stomach? The forensic evidence suggested that he had known his killer. Had it been one of the Egans? Was Dint Colbeck responsible for killing Ruloff, and possibly his boss? In light of subsequent events, this seems unlikely. Whoever did the crime accomplished his mission: George Ruloff was silenced forever.

The heat generated by Ruloff's murder caused Colbeck to move the Egan gang's headquarters to an old union hall on Sixth Street between Chestnut and Market. The Egans also began meeting at "Belvedere Joe" Gonella's Country Club roadhouse in Olivette.

A few days after the killing at the Allies, Ray Renard and Oliver Dougherty ran into Max Greenberg and Hogan gunsel John Doyle at the crowded corner of Broadway and Chestnut. The Hogans were in a playful mood.

The way Renard told it, Doyle asked, "Looking for us?"

"No. Why?" Dougherty replied.

"Well, Greenberg just went out and threw a couple of slugs at Whitey Doering."

"Kill him?" Renard inquired.

"Don't know," Greenberg shrugged.

Doyle hooked a thumb at his partner, saying, "Greenberg is too smart for that bunch; they'll have to get up early in the morning to get him!"

Later, at the Locust Avenue tire store, Colbeck was enraged that Doering hadn't killed Max Greenberg when he'd had the chance, and coerced him into driving around and looking for him. Dint then announced to the gang that Willie Egan's killers were John Doyle, Luke Kennedy, and James Hogan. Colbeck also intimated that Greenberg had paid each man $10,000 for the hit. The boys immediately cleaned and oiled their weapons and began looking for the Hogans.

Realizing that the gang's new downtown headquarters was far too close to the police station, Colbeck bought a large roadhouse out on St. Charles Rock Road, bordering the eastern edge of Valhalla Cemetery. Formerly a racetrack, the Maxwelton Club was an ideal hideout since it was outside the city limits and somewhat isolated, the only neighbors being a couple of farmers.

Before the Egans could begin to avenge their fallen leader, they had to attend to some gruesome internal affairs.

Joseph "Green Onions" Cipolla had prospered in the years

since he joined the Egan's Rats. He was widely feared in the downtown Italian neighborhood and had added at least one more notch to his gun since killing rope bandit Heywood Wilson in 1917. Also, Green Onions had introduced a few of his friends into the Egan ranks—Pete, Anthony, and Thomas "Yonnie" Licavoli—brothers who, like Cipolla, were tough American-born Italian kids barely out of their teens, and their cousins Jimmy, Pete, and Thomas, whose large family originally came from Terrasini, Sicily.

Since the murder of George Ruloff, Green Onions and his main partner, a cadaverous twenty-six-year-old burglar and heroin addict named Everett Summers, had stopped hanging around the Allies Restaurant. While the two were drinking at a roadhouse in Madison, Illinois, they bumped into new Egan gang member Ray Renard. The twenty-two-year-old Cipolla told the dapper crook that he and Summers had a terrific score lined up, a fat bank in Dupo, Illinois, that was just begging to be robbed. Renard agreed to help. Cipolla went back across the river and bought a Grant Six sedan from a used car lot owned by Little Red Powers and Whitey Doering.

Cipolla, Summers, Renard, and two unidentified red hots from Chicago plucked $10,000 dollars from the State Bank of Dupo on the afternoon of December 23, 1921. It was a nice little score that left the boys flush for the holidays.

A day or so after Christmas, Little Red Powers sent word to Cipolla that he had a job lined up for him. Green Onions and Summers asked Renard to come along, but the latter decided to sit this one out, a move that saved his life.

Around 5:30 a.m. on December 27, 1921, Cipolla and Summers drove to the Country Club roadhouse in Olivette where they met Dint Colbeck, Little Red Powers, Sticky Hennessey, Steve Ryan, Chippy Robinson, and Oliver Dougherty. The mood was far from jovial as the police had found the Grant sedan used in the Dupo bank job and traced it back to the Egan car dealership. The enraged Rats demanded to know why Cipolla had used a car from their lot in the robbery and allowed it to be traced back to them. Green Onions attempted to talk his way out of the jam, basically by pleading stupidity.

The Egans stalked out, leaving Cipolla and Summers in the

deserted barroom clutching their drinks in stony silence. Powers and Hennessey re-appeared holding a .45-caliber handgun and a sawed-off shotgun. Green Onions Cipolla caught the first load from the shotgun, a mixture of steel ball bearings, nails, and bolts that tore his face to shreds. Summers took the second blast from the shotgun flush in his chest. The other gunman moved in and finished off Cipolla with four pistol shots and put two more into Summers's head. The corpses were dumped on Shaftsbury Lane in University City.

In one of the cruel ironies that often surround organized crime, five men eventually were convicted of pulling the Dupo bank job, even though they were innocent and the actual perpetrators were killed just a few days after the caper, before they'd even had a chance to spend much of their loot.

Their blood up after the double murder, the Egans went gunning for the Hogans. Throwing caution to the wind, their attack was chancy and done in public, and would come to typify the coming gang war.

Picked up in a general sweep after the murders of Cipolla and Summers, James Hogan, Luke Kennedy, and Abe Goldfeder were detained for the maximum twenty hours before being released. The latter gangster was a former member of the Egan mob and a close friend of Max Greenberg. Hogan lawyer Jacob Mackler produced writs of *habeas corpus* for the three men.

At noon on December 30, 1921, the three gangsters and their attorney left police headquarters in Mackler's car. As they turned west into Market Street from Eleventh, a Premier touring car glided alongside and its occupants opened fire with "a rain of bullets," as Mackler put it. Five Egan mobsters blazed away with pistols and pump-action shotguns. Kennedy was struck in the left leg and hand, while a shotgun blast ripped through Mackler's derby, miraculously missing his head. Hogan ducked down and was unscathed, while Goldfeder was cut by flying glass. Amazingly, there were no fatalities.

Rattled by the shooting, Mackler drove into a wagon. The driver of the Premier attempted to make a right turn north onto Twelfth Street at a high rate of speed, and the car swerved wildly, bouncing off parked cars lining the street. A block later, the driver ran down a tourist from Hartford, Connecticut, breaking his nose. When a policeman attempted to stop the careening vehicle, one of the gangsters aimed a shotgun at him, but another of the shooters, Little Red Powers, pushed the barrel aside, saying "Never shoot a copper."

The Egans abandoned the Premier in an alley at Sixteenth and Olive, leaving behind two pistols and a pair of shotguns. The only confirmed shooters were Powers and Whitey Doering, but the other three were undoubtedly members of Dint Colbeck's inner circle. When questioned by police, the Hogan mobsters predictably refused to say who had tried to kill them and snarled about being detained again while the gunmen escaped.

Dint Colbeck laid low at the Maxwelton Club, reading about the aborted hit in the newspapers, while just about everyone else in the city was outraged by the shootings. While gang murders were nothing new in St. Louis, a full-blown shootout in the middle of downtown at high noon was too much for people to bear. A general alert went out for police to detain all members of the Egan and Hogan gangs they could find.

The Hogans responded to the Market Street attack at 5:30 p.m. on January 5, 1922, when one of the gangsters caught Isadore "Izzy" Londe at Tenth and Franklin and shot him three times in the back. The bleeding Londe staggered into a nearby jewelry store and had the proprietor hide his pistol before the ambulance showed up. Londe spent many weeks recovering from his wounds.

A little over eighteen hours after Izzy Londe's shooting, one of Willie Egan's accused killers was violently—and permanently—removed from the city.

The St. Louis Police Department had been sweeping the town since the Market Street shootings. At noon on January 6, Lieutenant Dudley McDonald was leading Detectives Fierce, Moellring, and Egenreither on a patrol, and as the four "dicks" drove west on Locust Avenue near Twentieth, one of them saw an Essex sedan belonging to Hogan gangster John Doyle heading in the opposite direction. Since the street was too narrow to pull a U-turn, the cops hurried up Twenty-first to St. Charles, hoping to zoom around the block and cut off Doyle. The Hogan thug and an unidentified passenger had seen the detectives, and they cut north on Twentieth to St. Charles. McDonald managed to turn around and speed after Doyle but lost him at Twenty-second and Washington.

The detectives picked up the Essex again at Jefferson and Cass, in the heart of Hogan territory. They noticed that Doyle was now alone in the car and opened fire on the Essex, which rolled on for four blocks before veering to the curb and crashing at Cass and Garrison avenues. John Doyle had been shot once through the head. The detectives reported they found a revolver with one empty chamber in the dead man's hand. It was later discovered that Doyle had a game warden badge, which allowed to him to carry a gun.

The sleuths who did the shooting were exonerated, although the circumstances they described were quite peculiar. Perhaps this is yet another example of how differently police enforced the law in years past, much like the shooting of Egan lieutenant John "Guinea Mack" McAuliffe nineteen years earlier.

Gang war or no, the Egan gang was still robbing and stealing with utter abandon. Two of the Rats cold-cocked a messenger for the Bank of Maplewood in a dry goods store at Manchester and Sutton avenues on the morning of January 17, 1922, making off with $4,500 in cash and $100 in bond coupons. Needless to say, the perpetrators were never arrested.

Just after the killing of John Doyle, the Egans received some formidable reinforcement when Fred Burke returned to the city after serving two years in prison, one in Michigan for land fraud and another in Jeff City for his 1917 forgery conviction. Burke and his pal Bob Carey began hanging out at the Maxwelton Club on a somewhat regular basis. The two were joined by a mysterious, violent hood whom Carey had befriended while Burke was locked up.

Raymond Nugent had come to St. Louis from Cincinnati and talked his way into the gang. Born around 1895, Nugent, a war veteran, was heavily built, with a strong jaw, no neck, and a dangerous gaze. For reasons no one knows, he was nicknamed "Crane-Neck." Although no one actually called him that, the moniker followed him on police records for the rest of his life.

Ray also occasionally used the alias "Gander." Nugent and Carey shared similar appetites for booze and mayhem.

Some members of the gang didn't like Fred Burke because he was quiet and didn't brag about his crimes, preferring to socialize within a small clique. While Burke was answerable to Dint Colbeck, unlike the others, he didn't sit around the roadhouse and wait for orders or ideas. Two cabins along both Creve Coeur Lake and the Meramec River served as his primary hideouts.

Burke also reached out to hoods in other gangs, including twenty-six-year-old Milford Jones, a new member of the Cuckoo Gang and survivor of the 1920 Rigoletto Inn shootout. Around the same time, Burke met a man who would become his best friend.

August Henry Winkeler was born March 28, 1900. In later years, the police and subsequently the media would drop an *e* from his name, and he went by Gus Winkler in the underworld. He grew up in Lemay, just south of the St. Louis city limits. A large, gangly youth, he fell in with the wrong crowd as an adolescent. Contrary to popular legend, Winkler didn't get his start with the Egan's Rats; he first fell in with the Cuckoo Gang, which operated a roadhouse on Lemay Ferry Road not far from his family's house. The Sharpshooters Club was a carbon copy of the Maxwelton Club, and it was here that young Gus met the mob. As a boy, he had been fascinated by automobiles, and he learned at an early age how to drive and to repair cars inside and out.

In September 1917, the tall, overgrown Winkler padded his age by two years and joined the Army, heading to France in July 1918 with the 562nd Ambulance Company, 316th Sanitary Train Battalion, 91st Infantry Division. Gus perfected his driving skills by piloting ambulance vans through the chaos of combat on the Western Front.

After returning to St. Louis, Gus Winkler was regarded as one of the best getaway drivers in the city. Because of his wartime service, he made fast friends with fellow veterans Fred Burke, Bob Carey, and Ray Nugent. All four frequented the Maxwelton and Sharpshooters clubs, but with the possible exception of Burke, they weren't members of Dint Colbeck's inner circle.

Edward "Jelly Roll" Hogan was, at heart, nowhere near the same caliber of gangster as was his rival Dint Colbeck. Colbeck was a product of the streets, having been involved with gangs all his life and returning from hellish combat in Europe unscathed, while Hogan was a soft-handed bootlegger who truly had earned his nickname. Hogan clearly had been unnerved by John Doyle's death at the hands of the police as well as the very public attempt to snuff out his brother and associates. His men persuaded him to target Colbeck again. What few details are known about this attack, which occurred sometime in late February or early March 1922, exist only because of Ray Renard.

According to Renard, the hit happened late at night, after Dint Colbeck had left the Maxwelton Club to drive back into the city. As he motored along the St. Charles Rock Road, he was overtaken by a carload of Hogan gangsters who opened fire on him. Struck in the left arm by a bullet, Colbeck managed to escape and retreated to the roadhouse, where he gulped whiskey to ease his pain and loudly cursed a blue streak against Hogan and his mob. The fact that Colbeck had actually been shot by the *Hogans*, a gang he considered to be a joke, was the biggest insult of all, and Dint immediately composed a list of sixteen Hogan mobsters to be eliminated:

- Edward J. "Jelly Roll" Hogan
- James Hogan
- Max Greenberg
- Harry Greenberg
- Jacob Mackler
- Frank Mercurio
- Luke Kennedy
- "Alibi" Charley Vance
- Buddy Knox
- Pete Flanigan
- Humbert Costello
- Pat Scanlon
- John "Kink" Connell
- Jimmy Toomer
- Abe Goldfeder
- Tony Russo

Colbeck continued to storm around the club that night, extracting promises from his men to kill any of these men on sight, regardless of the consequences. (Ray Renard would later claim that he stood up to Colbeck and refused to kill anyone, but that seems unlikely. Renard, who had become a police informant by the time he made that assertion, was probably trying to make himself look good to his police handlers, because it's extremely

unlikely that Colbeck would have allowed him to remain among the Rats' inner circle had he refused to kill any of the gang's enemies.)

Their preoccupation with retaliating against the Hogan mob led the Egans to neglect their business. Needing to come up with some quick cash for their war chest, some of the boys robbed a messenger for the Chouteau Trust Company in front of the Vandeventer Avenue bank on March 3, 1922. They easily relieved the messenger of his satchel and got away clean, only to discover they had just stolen $36,000 worth of checks, which they

War veterans and buddies, clockwise from top left, Fred Burke, Bob Carey, Ray Nugent, and Gus Winkler were all members of the Egan mob during its Prohibition-era heyday. All were also members of Al Capone's "American boys" who took part in Chicago's St. Valentine's Day Massacre in 1929.

would be unable to cash. More successful was their holdup of the Gravois Bank at 6301 Gravois Road in Affton on March 6. Six men entered, scaled a seven-foot wooden partition, and cleaned out the teller cages, making off with about $3,500 in cash.

The first name on Colbeck's hit list was crossed off by someone outside the gang. John "Kink" Connell got into a beef with his brother-in-law "Alibi" Charley Vance and shot him to death in front of Vance's Division Street house on March 20, 1922. Some two weeks after Vance's untimely demise, the Egan boys were at it again. This time they finally succeeded in victimizing the Water

Tower Bank by stealing $7,200 from one of its messengers on a Bellefontaine streetcar near Hyde Park on April 4.

Luke Kennedy, the most dangerous man in the Hogan Gang and the alleged architect of Willie Egan's murder, had been laid up all winter after being wounded and was feeling quite cocky about the Hogans' recent scores against the Rats. Kennedy would often call the Maxwelton Club and curse out any gang member who answered the phone, going out of his way to pick fights with the Egans' number-one sharpshooter, David "Chippy" Robinson.

Colbeck and his boys fumed, but there was nothing anyone could do. Kennedy was still off the grid, and systematic searches of the Hogan hideouts turned up nothing. Early in April 1922, Kennedy called the Maxwelton Club again, saying that his leg was nearly healed and that he would be "coming in a few days to shoot up that dump you hang out in!"

A mild-mannered gang hanger-on was detailed to follow Kennedy and get a line on his habits. On April 16, the unobtrusive spy sent the word: "I've got the dope. ... Kennedy visits a woman on Sacramento Avenue. He lives with his father at 4409 Greer Avenue." A hit squad was immediately dispatched to Greer Avenue, but after a fruitless five-hour stakeout, the frustrated and tired gangsters gave up. Their luck improved the next day, however, when their quarry kept a rendezvous with his girlfriend at four o'clock that afternoon.

Edith Gersbach met Luke Kennedy at the corner of Kienlen and Hamburger avenues in Wellston. Dressed in pajamas and slippers and still recovering from his wounds, Kennedy was not armed. Accompanied by Edith's five-year-old daughter, the couple drove to up Hamburger and turned onto Rosebud , where at 4:30 p.m., their car was cut off by a high-powered Essex and forced to stop. One man stepped in front of Kennedy's car and aimed a .38 at the passengers, while two men kept them covered through the open windows on the right side of the vehicle with a .32 pistol and a sawed-off, double-barreled 12-gauge shotgun.

The twenty-eight-year-old Kennedy must have realized his dangerous game had finally come to an end on the peaceful residential street. As he slowly raised his hands, he asked in a shaky voice, "How about a chance?" Behind him, one of the gunmen growled, "Here it is!" then simultaneously emptied both barrels of the shotgun into Kennedy's back, while his two partners added three pistol bullets for good measure.

The terrified Gersbach related the facts as she saw them to the police and the press, and soon everyone in the city knew that the Egan's Rats had struck again, erasing the second of Willie Egan's accused killers. Once again, the police vowed to find the shooters, but gangsters lounged unmolested inside the Maxwelton Club, smirking over Kennedy's cowardice in the face of death.

The murder of Luke Kennedy had shaken the Hogan Gang's morale, for they now finally realized they were out of their league trying to go toe to toe with their enemies. James Hogan, the third accused killer of Willie Egan, enlisted the help of his brother's friend, a member of the Missouri legislature who ran a blacksmith shop at 2430 Cass Avenue. Jimmy holed up in an apartment above the shop with a shotgun and a supply of whiskey and would not emerge for almost a year.

For Edward "Jelly Roll" Hogan, it was business as usual, although he increasingly stopped going out at night, preferring to stay at home with his parents. Jelly Roll visited his brother often and took elaborate precautions to keep Jimmy's location secret.

Dint Colbeck and his crew kept to the Maxwelton Club, and when they were in the city their headquarters was now Colbeck's plumbing store at 2215 Washington Avenue. The Hogans knew this, and after shadowing Colbeck and Charles "Red" Smith for a week, they set up and ambush for them there.

After attending a downtown meeting with Senator Mike Kinney on the afternoon of May 18, 1922, Colbeck and Smith returned to the plumbing store. Just after they arrived, a westbound black touring car pulled up in front of the store. Three members of the Hogan Gang leaped out and opened fire with pistols and a shotgun through the store windows, jumping back into their vehicle when their guns were empty. Colbeck and Smith were unharmed, but sixteen-year-old secretary May Redman was cut by flying glass, and a few bathtubs and toilets were chipped.

Colbeck was enraged, and he and the boys immediately began invading the Hogan Gang's North Side hangouts. Although they were unable to find their enemies anywhere in the bars, pool halls, and clubs, the Rats left plenty of nervous people in their wake. Finally, after a long night of hunting, Chippy Robinson groaned, "We gotta get *somebody!*" Steve Ryan suggested, "Maybe they're at Jelly Roll's house." Dint Colbeck decided to go for the source, declaring, "They shot up my store; let's shoot up their house."

The scene at Hogan's large red-brick house at 3035 Cass Avenue was one of springtime tranquillity at 11:20 on the morning of May 19 as three automobiles—a Hudson touring car, a Hupmobile, and a cream-colored sedan—approached rapidly from the east. The vehicles slowed in front of the house, and their occupants unleashed a deafening volley of pistol and shotgun blasts, riddling the building's walls and windows and forcing Jelly Roll's parents to dive for cover. Despite being pursued by a detective squad whose occupants had witnessed the shooting, the Egan cars quickly disappeared down different streets.

Public outrage over the attack on Hogan's home was palpable, but no seemed to know how to get the gangsters to stop their feuding. Probably the only person who could broker a truce, Father Timothy Dempsey of St. Patrick's Catholic Church, claimed to have a solution. Father Tim secretly began to meet with members of both camps, trying to get them to stop killing each other. The priest's efforts paid off on June 5, when the gangs agreed to a cease-fire. But the end to the violence almost came too late for Chippy Robinson, who the day before the agreement was reached had a potentially lethal domestic dispute with his wife, Mabel, when she caught him walking along the 1100 block of DeSoto Avenue with another woman and shot him in the leg. Chippy recovered in time to enjoy a new era of peace and prosperity in St. Louis's gangland.

Father Dempsey declared to the *St. Louis Post-Dispatch* that he had convinced the hoods to stop the violence. As he explained to a reporter:

> "I have interviewed 34 members of the two factions in the last two weeks, and they have promised me they will quit shooting at each other. Of course, it remains to be seen

whether they will keep their word or not, but I feel safe in predicting that there will be no more murders, so far as those two crowds are concerned.

"There is no religion in this. I have talked to Catholics and non-Catholics, and they have all agreed to give up the feud and attend to their own affairs in a peaceful manner. It is all very well for the police to say that gang killings result in good riddance of bad rubbish, and that the gangsters are subnormal, but I do not look at it that way. They are human, and can be dealt with just as other people are dealt with.

"I summoned the boys to the parochial house at various times. Sometimes they came alone and at times in groups of three or four. I told them they had no right to be taking lives, and that their endless war was a bad thing for themselves as well as the community. I asked them to forget their grievances and try to be decent citizens.

"From each one I exacted a solemn promise that he would no longer harbor the thought of murder, and I believe they will keep their word. I knew some of them personally. Others I had never seen before, but I had known them by reputation. None of them lives in this parish.

"I do not know who killed Willie Egan, and if I did know I would not tell. I was with him when he died at the city hospital. We were alone and he was conscious. I asked him who killed him and he told me he did not know. I had known Egan since his infancy. He was born here in my parish. I did not know the Hogan crowd personally, but now that I have talked with them I feel assured that they will no longer bother the Egan followers and that the Egan followers will let them alone."

The police were naturally skeptical of the truce, especially when a week later they caught Jelly Roll Hogan with a concealed weapon. However, it seemed that peace finally had returned to the city in the summer of 1922 as Hogan and his gang retreated to their usual haunts along Cass Avenue and the Egan's Rats remained close to the Maxwelton Club. Max Greenberg left St. Louis for good, with several armed Hogan gangsters escorting him to Union Station and onto a New York-bound train.

Dint Colbeck claimed victory in the gang war with the June truce, and he never again would regard the Hogan Gang as a serious threat. That summer, the Egans refocused their efforts on criminal enterprises, which had been sorely neglected thus far that year. Once again putting bootlegging on the back burner, the Egans opted for the quick buck, robbing a Tower Grove Bank messenger on the morning of July 5, 1922.

As the messenger and his police guard made their rounds on a streetcar, Ray Renard and Bill Engler trailed the pair in a touring car, while four red hots waited at the trolley stop near Arsenal and Virginia avenues. After boarding the streetcar, the boys jerked out their guns, and while Chippy Robinson and Steve Ryan kept the cop covered, Izzy Londe and Oliver Dougherty snatched the messenger's satchel, which contained $21,200 in cash and $71,600 in checks.

Two weeks later, Harry Londo, Izzy Londe, and Elmer Runge stole $15,000 worth of diamonds from a Franklin Avenue pawn dealer. Runge was grazed by a bullet during the getaway. With their coffers refilled, the Egan's Rats were once again sitting pretty.

The Maxwelton Club was accessible from St. Charles Rock Road by a dirt path. The three-quarter-mile racetrack was not visible from the road, but the old grandstand still stood 300 yards to the left of the roadhouse. Four houses were located several hundred yards to the east, their occupants frequently aroused by gangsters loudly zooming their cars down the path to the roadhouse at all hours of the day and night. The Egans plotted crimes there and eventually would turn the place into their personal violent playground. As Ray Renard would later say, "Target practice was the order of the day out there."

The Rats spent some $50 a day on ammunition and had stockpiled a large arsenal of pistols and shotguns at the inn. Shooting went on primarily during the day, but also at night as the boys blasted away at empty whiskey and beer bottles, oil cans, trees, and a large water tank that was a favorite target. The hoods would sit or stand in the grandstand and shoot at targets in the center of the track, and they often would race their cars around the track at high speed, firing at targets as they roared past. The shots could be heard as far as a mile away.

The gangsters were casual about their target practice, and the houses nearby often were pierced by stray bullets. As one of the neighbors related, the Egans often would saunter onto the porch of the roadhouse without warning and open fire at one target or another. Children weren't allowed to play in yards that faced the roadhouse, and one family's Thanksgiving dinner was ruined by errant rounds from a gang shooting session.

On one occasion, some of the boys accosted a local farmer, stole his car, and took it for a drive on the racetrack. In their drunkenness, they careened off the track and into a ditch. Dint Colbeck smoothed things over with the farmer by apologizing and presenting him with a hefty cash tithe.

All the Egans became proficient with firearms, but the fastest and most accurate shooter among the crew was twenty-five-year-old David "Chippy" Robinson, who by the summer of 1922 was the most feared gangster in all of St. Louis. He regarded murder as "an art and a pastime" and scared even his fellow gang mates. Ray Renard painted this portrait of Robinson a few years later:

> "Time and time I have seen him gloat over a dying victim. He got a big kick out of watching them pass out. To him, there was nothing in life of greater importance than a well-planned, well-executed murder.
>
> "When he led the gang's 'firing squad' on an expedition, he always demanded the first shot.
>
> "His idols were gunmen and killers. Target practice was his principal off-time diversion. I have seen him fire at a tree for hours. The tree to his mind was a human being. He would shoot from all ranges while standing, sitting and running. He would drive his motor car at terrific speed as he reached the tree, empty his gat at it, grab the wheel and drive on. I've seen him shoot at dogs and cats, as well as trees and human beings.
>
> "Time after time I've seen him draw a gat, point it at some member of the mob who would leap to safety behind the bar

or under a table, just as Dint would grab his arm and tell him to lay off. He liked Dint, but Dint was afraid of him. Everybody in the mob was, because you could never tell when he might shoot you.

"On many occasions when some young punk who was just a hanger-on would come out to the club, I've seen this killer draw his gat and make him dance while he emptied his gun at the feet of the hanger-on ... to him that was great sport."

Dint Colbeck's inner circle consisted of the psychotic Robinson, likeable Steve Ryan, tough Ol Dougherty, and the monosyllabic Red Smith, who acted as Colbeck's bodyguard. Indeed, the two were inseparable, with Red often referred to as Dint's "shadow."

These men, along with some thirty-five or forty associates now comprised what once had been a 300- or 400-man gang. The Egan's Rats had become a violent, impulsive group of armed robbers and killers. Older gangsters, those who had been with the outfit since the Tom Egan era, pleaded with Colbeck to focus on bootlegging, but robberies gradually became the mob's primary source of income.

Members of the rival Egan and Hogan gangs had largely adhered to the terms of the truce set down in June by Father Tim Dempsey. The Egans had virtually forgotten about the Hogans until they began hearing rumors that Jelly Roll Hogan had been importing members of the Waxey Gordon mob from New York and was hunting for them. Despite the respect all the gangsters had for Father Tim, the cease-fire was about to be broken.

Saturday, September 2, 1922, was the second-hottest day of the summer as the temperature topped out at 98 degrees and the humidity climbed to 85 percent. At 9 p.m., it was still a sticky 87 degrees as Dint Colbeck, Red Smith, Steve Ryan, and Oliver Dougherty loitered on the south side of Locust Avenue a couple of blocks west of Jefferson Avenue. The four Egans, dressed in summer suits and straw boaters, did double takes as a car containing two of their enemies—Hogan gunman Abe Goldfeder and Max Gordon, a recently arrived triggerman from New

York—drove right past them. Neither gangster noticed Colbeck and his three partners jump into a green Essex touring car and start after them.

In the last block west of Jefferson, the Egans killed their headlights and pulled abreast of Gordon's Ford, unleashing a volley of shots at the Hogan gunmen. Goldfeder was hit in the jaw, chest, and left arm, while Gordon was shot twice in the head, one of the bullets blowing his left eye clear out of his skull. Amazingly, both men survived their wounds.

The Egan crew fell into police custody later that night when they were arrested with two pals, Whitey Doering and Pascal Morina, in a raid at the Wellston gambling resort run by former Bottoms Gang boss Tony Foley. Goldfeder and Gordon didn't name the Egans as their assailants, but everyone knew they had been the shooters. Father Tim Dempsey refused to believe that the boys would break the truce, but that's exactly what they did.

Despite public outrage over the incident, Dint Colbeck was at the height of his power. The outgoing thirty-two-year-old gang boss had an ever-increasing network of friends, as local businessmen, policemen, and politicians frequently trouped out to the Maxwelton Club to meet with him. If there was a favor Colbeck could do for them, he could count on receiving favors in return. If a friend got traffic ticket or wound up in a legal jam, one call to Dint would resolve the matter. Likewise, if Colbeck or any of the boys got in trouble, a friend would always help *them* out. It didn't hurt that Colbeck always sent his more respectable visitors off with plenty of beer and whiskey.

Ray Renard would later describe how Colbeck scored points with local big shots by helping them recover their stolen vehicles. Dint would have Renard steal a solid citizen's car, then call the person, commiserate about the loss, and offer to help find the vehicle. Miraculously, the missing vehicle would be discovered and returned to the owner, who in turn would be extremely grateful to the gang boss for getting his auto back undamaged. Many law-abiding St. Louisans enjoyed the allure of associating with a powerful gangster and were proud to say they were friends with Dint Colbeck.

But being a gangster wasn't always easy. Ray Renard later told of a time when he, Izzy Londe, and Oliver Dougherty were driving on Washington Avenue, plotting a payroll robbery, when they were spotted by police who pulled a quick U-turn to follow them. The three gangsters turned north on Tenth Street, and not wanting to face a concealed-weapons rap, they wiped down their pistols and tossed them out the car windows as they sped past the Tenth District police station.

A few days later, Renard was being tailed by Detective Sergeant Fred Egenreither, the same cop who had killed both Walter Costello and John Doyle in the line of duty. When Renard stopped at a lowered railroad crossing gate at Newstead and Duncan, Egenreither pulled up behind him, got out of his car, casually walked up to Renard's open driver's-side window, and punched him in the jaw.

Although the gang's national liquor-smuggling network was not as active as it once had been, the Rats had a large illicit beer operation in both the city of St. Louis and St. Louis County. Truckloads of suds would be delivered to the Maxwelton Club and then distributed to speakeasies and other niteries throughout the area. Saloonkeepers either bought Colbeck's beer or, after being issued threats and warnings, were violently put out of business.

Taking advantage of the turmoil of the Italian underworld, Dint also put the squeeze on Italian moonshiners, or "alky-cookers," in the city and county by sending the Licavolis around to their to exact tributes ranging from $100 to $500 a month.

Criminals often benefited from Colbeck's generosity, as he would sign bonds for their release when they got into trouble. It was a lucrative sideline, since there was little danger the crooks would forfeit the bonds and risk incurring the wrath of the Egan's Rats. The boys also operated floating dice and card games, as well as taking tribute payments from brothels throughout the city and county. All gang members got a cut from a heist, whether they had a hand in it or not. The book *The Three Musketeers* was a favorite among the men, and like the heroes of the Dumas classic, their motto was, "All for one and one for all." Ray

Renard described the fictional characters as the "original gang-sters," using swords instead of guns.

Colbeck insisted that gang members not involved in an upcoming caper establish an alibi. Often the boys would go to a friendly doctor's office for a checkup or chat with a local beat cop at the time the crime was taking place.

Dint Colbeck served as sergeant-of-arms of the Democratic City Committee and also ran for constable but was defeated in the fall of 1922. The loss hardly ruffled the gang boss, nor did concealed-weapons charges that were brought against Colbeck, Red Smith, and Chippy Robinson, who all beat the rap.

Despite the changes in the gang, one thing that hadn't changed was its code of silence; snitches were still terminated with extreme prejudice. Theodore Lange was a twenty-five-year-old truck driver who was set to testify against a lower-level Rat named Frank "Cotton" Epplesheimer. On November 15, several minutes after leaving a South Fourth Street saloon, Lange's car was overtaken at Tenth and LaSalle by a Ford coupe and he was shot to death. Insiders credited Cotton Epplesheimer with eliminating the threat to his freedom.

As winter began, the boys were busy planning another heist and a murder as well.

Peter Berg was a twenty-seven-year-old barber who formerly had operated a shop in the same block of Franklin Avenue where Willie Egan's saloon was located. Berg got into a fight with two friends, and Colbeck took the side of the latter pair. In the blink of an eye, Berg was no longer in the gang's good graces, and two of the boys were assigned to kill him. The barber was taking a steam with two friends at a Jewish bathhouse at 1026 High Street on December 3, 1922, when one of his companions called the Egan's Rats. The gang sent killers who arrived on the scene in no time. Cornered in the steam room, a terrified Berg attempted to use one of his companions as a shield, but the gangsters shoved him out of the way before shooting Berg dead.

The idea for the heist began when gang hanger-on Joe Powderly brought a tip to the Rats at the Maxwelton Club. Joe had been hanging around a bonded warehouse at 3960 Duncan

Avenue run by the Jack Daniel's Company. He said the place was loaded with good pre-war whiskey, extraordinarily rare during Prohibition, and that the warehouse apparently had very little security. The whiskey was to be sold to druggists, who under the law could fill doctors' prescriptions for alcohol as a medical treatment. Dint Colbeck didn't go on the job, but some ten or twelve of the boys did.

Driving in two trucks, with handkerchiefs tied around their faces, the gangsters arrived at the warehouse at 10:10 p.m. on December 8. Ray Renard, Red Smith, and Chippy Robinson accosted three guards making their rounds and marched them inside the building, where they were met by Joe Powderly. Oliver Dougherty, and Eddie Linehan, who, with some other young hoods, had been dispatched to round up the guards at two coal companies next door to keep them from sounding an alarm. Steve Ryan and Lee Turner went inside to begin loading the whiskey.

The gang's trucks were parked at the east side of the building, where there was a large, sliding steel door and a loading dock. When Linehan, Dougherty, and the others returned, Powderly gave the all-clear signal, the doors were opened, and the boys went to work while Robinson kept the watchmen covered. After threatening to blow their brains out if they tried anything, Robinson got the guards' overcoats when they complained of being cold, and even let one smoke his pipe.

After breaking into the case storage room, the boys began carting the booze out to their waiting trucks. Others found barrels of whiskey on an upper level and rolled them onto an elevator and then right out the door and onto the trucks.

The Rats, barely able to contain their excitement, grinned, laughed, and joked as they worked. They opened one of the barrels and began swigging whiskey as they loaded, with Chippy cackling with joy as he drank. Reaching into the barrel, he rubbed a handful of Jack Daniel's into his hair, saying it made him, "smell good."

Right in the middle of the joyous work, a loud bell went off, and the boys jumped at the sound. Robinson screamed that it was a burglar alarm and aimed his pistol at the hostages. When it was determined that the sound was just an overly loud telephone, one of the guards was marched over to answer it and got rid of the caller.

Within an hour of arriving at the warehouse, the gangsters were done, having loaded up sixteen barrels and 120 cases of "Tennessee's finest sippin' whiskey." Robinson marched the hostages into the basement and told them to wait there quietly for ten minutes. Running back upstairs, Chippy kicked over the open barrel with a laugh, spilling booze all over the floor. Since it was Prohibition, when the Rats left, the hostages went upstairs and helped themselves to what was left of the whiskey before summoning help.

The booze was divided among the gang members, and most of it was consumed, sold, or diluted and sold for even bigger profits. Many of Dint Colbeck's powerful friends got a bottle of genuine Jack Daniel's whiskey for Christmas that year. Ray Renard later said he was given one barrel and seven cases, which he sold for a total profit of $2,000. All told, the Egan's Rats netted at least $50,000 on the heist.

Around Christmas the Egans lost one of their most durable members. Clarence "Little Red" Powers had amassed quite a fortune from his tire and used-car businesses and decided to go legit. The boys didn't fight it and wished Little Red good luck before bidding him farewell. Little did any of them realize that the coming year would be the most eventful in the thirty-year history of the Egan's Rats.

9

MAELSTROM

THE CRESCENDO OF criminality began at 11:20 on the morning of January 12, 1923, when three red hots robbed an Anderson Laundry Company messenger of a $3,600 payroll in front of 3950 Olive Street.

Just after midnight on February 11, Oklahoma Red Deaver was drinking at the Mount Olive Inn in St. Louis County with a friend, Tony Pittaluga. Deaver was the Rats' mascot, always laughing and joking with the boys. The Egans loved Deaver, and harmless old Okie Red hated violent crime and refused to even carry a gun. Unfortunately, before the night was over, Deaver would be dead.

Into the Mount Olive Inn stomped Gus Dietmeyer, a huge, mid-level Egan gangster. While not generally associated with the muscle end of the gang, Dietmeyer had taken someone's life before, during the gang war of 1916-17. On this evening, Dietmeyer was in a bad mood. When Okie Red Deaver attempted to cheer him up by offering to buy him drinks and telling jokes, Dietmeyer responded with curses and snarls, threatening to kill the old safecracker if he didn't leave him alone.

Deaver got angry, yelling, "Hell, you ain't no gunman!" and knocked Gus sprawling with his fists. Dietmeyer jumped up with a .45 automatic in his hand, shot Okie Red dead, and wounded Tony Pittaluga for good measure. As he stalked out, Dietmeyer nudged Deaver's body with his foot, growling, "You now see how much of a gunman I am."

Dint Colbeck and the boys were furious that their lovable old pal Oklahoma Red Deaver had been killed for such trivial reasons. But although they yelled and screamed at Dietmeyer, he was not punished, either by the gangsters or the police. The Egans paid for Deaver's funeral, and Dietmeyer himself sent a bouquet of flowers.

The red hots had little time to grieve over Okie Red because they were once again on the warpath. The Egan-Hogan feud had petered out into a stalemate. Although the Hogans remained fearful and ever vigilant, the Egans had become bored with the gang war. Edward "Jelly Roll" Hogan went about his duties as beverage inspector surrounded by armed guards, while his brother Jimmy remained holed up in the apartment above the Cass Avenue blacksmith shop.

The gang's lawyer and spokesman, Jacob Mackler, also was fearful. As he related to a *Post-Dispatch* reporter, he had taken out a second life insurance policy worth $10,000 to be paid as a reward for the apprehension of his killers. Although Mackler wasn't a gangster in the traditional sense of the word, his name was still on the hit list that Dint Colbeck had compiled.

At the beginning of the New Year, probably just for fun or out of boredom, the boys had decided to bump off Jacob Mackler. That Mackler had a wife and three small children was of no consequence to the Rats. They put Mackler's house at 1119 Clara Avenue and his law office in the Times Building under surveillance, but the lawyer was always surrounded by a bevy of Hogan gunmen. A hanger-on called the boys late in the afternoon of February 21 and reported that Mackler was going "over the river" without his usual contingent of bodyguards.

Six of the Egans sped away from the Maxwelton Club in a coupe and a touring car. The six triggermen were never publicly named by stool pigeon Ray Renard, but it became apparent from his subsequent statement to the authorities that Dint Colbeck accompanied the "firing squad," something he usually didn't do. The boys followed Mackler into Illinois, where he conferred on a bankruptcy case with Justice of the Peace Armin Weiss and fellow lawyer J. S. Gollub. After finishing their business, the three men left in Mackler's sedan at six o'clock that evening and were spotted again by the Egans at Nineteenth and G streets in Granite City. The boys decided to wait until they were back in St. Louis before attacking, and they discreetly tailed Mackler as he made his way through Madison and Venice and onto the McKinley Bridge.

The Egan gangsters pulled to a stop at the east end of the bridge and had a quick conference. Colbeck decided to have the coupe take the lead, with the three remaining men in the touring car to follow as backup. Dint told his men not to kill Weiss or Gollub if they could help it. The boys then hurried to catch up to their quarry.

At 6:45 p.m., as Jacob Mackler was unhurriedly driving his sedan south on Twelfth Street, the Egan coupe pulled alongside near the intersection with Howard Street. Two or three gunmen opened fire with automatic pistols, peppering the lawyer's car with at least fifteen shots. Four bullets struck Mackler, one of them tearing through his neck and severing his spinal cord. As Mackler slumped dead over the steering wheel, the car veered to the right and crashed into a building. The coupe sped off into the night. Gollub staggered into the street, saw the touring car, and tried to flag it down without realizing it was filled with gangsters gawking at the carnage. The boys ignored Gollub's frantic signals.

The Hogan lawyer was buried in a respectful ceremony on February 24, and just a few hours later his killers hatched yet another murder plot. Two associates of the gang came to the Maxwelton Club late that night to discuss a problem with Dint Colbeck. One of the visitors had been having problems with former Egan gangster Little Red Powers. The man had called Powers and asked for a favor, but Little Red had snarled that he wasn't with the gang anymore. The unidentified Egan associate cursed, and the two men got into an altercation that ended with the associate threatening to kill Powers.

The mystery man and his partner knew Little Red was a dangerous man and still had powerful friends, so they had come to the Maxwelton that morning to get Colbeck's approval to slay Powers. After conferring, the Egans gave a thumbs-down verdict on Powers, telling the two visitors they could do what they wanted with the ex-gangster. Although Little Red was still friendly with the mob, the Egans had become extremely callous toward human life and didn't care if Powers was killed or not.

Powers had taken the two men's threats seriously enough to hole up at Belvedere Joe Gonella's Country Club in Olivette. That same night, when Powers retired to a one-room shack seventy-five feet west of the roadhouse, his friend Martin Wilson stood guard. The gang associate and his partner had driven straight from the Maxwelton Club to the Country Club, arriving in Olivette at six o'clock the next morning, February 25. Gonella had received a phone call from the Maxwelton telling him to make himself scarce. The two men marched up to the shack, flashing pistols at the bodyguard, who stepped aside.

When the two entered the shack they found Little Red Powers sprawled on the bed, fast asleep. They pumped eleven bullets into the gangster, who probably never knew what hit him. Wilson was mindful of Powers's friends and family and asked the killers to give him an "easy" wound, to make it look as if he'd put up a fight. Unfortunately for Wilson, the "easy" gunshot wound to his arm became infected, and he died within a month.

The police and press loudly speculated that Powers's murder was the work of Hogan gangsters in retaliation for the killing of Jacob Mackler. Hogan hoods were endlessly harassed and questioned, but the true story of Little Red's death wouldn't come out for another two years.

Father Timothy Dempsey offered to talk to the gangsters again, to try to get them to end the violence. But despite his good intentions, the red hots on both sides had been swept away by a tidal wave of hate, machismo, and violence, and no one could save them.

On March 10, 1923, Chippy Robinson, Ray Renard, a thug named Elmer Macklin, and a couple of others tried to rob a messenger for the long-suffering North St. Louis Trust Company. The messenger, William Pepper, fought like a bear, even after Chippy cracked him over the head with his pistol. In the end, the boys got only $360 for their trouble, and the bank awarded Pepper a medal he richly deserved.

Dint Colbeck had gotten word that several high-ranking police officials wanted to meet with him to discuss the gang war, and he decided to invite them to the Maxwelton for a conference. Before he did, however, one of the red hots, Elmer Runge, said he had a line on a fat bank in Wellston, right up the street from Tony Foley's casino. Dint decided to pull the bank heist before inviting the law into his lair.

Oliver Dougherty and Ray Renard reconnoitered the bank at 6200 Easton Avenue and decided it would be a cinch to hit. The job took place at ten o'clock on the morning of March 16. A seven-passenger Cadillac, with Ray Renard at the wheel, pulled up in front of the bank, and Oliver Dougherty, Izzy Londe, Elmer Runge, and Sticky Hennessey went inside. Dougherty and Hennessey worked crowd control while Londe and Runge scooped some $22,000 in cash from the teller cages. The gangsters piled back into their getaway car, which they abandoned on Natural Bridge Road before proceeding to the Maxwelton Club.

Later that night, as the boys drank and celebrated their score, Chippy Robinson decided to have a little fun with the rival Hogan mob. He called the county sheriff's department, saying he had a hot tip about the Wellston bank robbery, and then proceeded to name Harry Greenberg, Pat Scanlon, Humbert Costello, and Jelly Roll Hogan as the perpetrators. As a result of Robinson's anonymous tip, the four Hogan men, amid loud protestations of innocence, were arrested. Egan gangsters Runge, Londe, and Renard eventually would be charged with the crime, and their cases would drag on for quite some time.

The Hogans, angry that they once had again been humiliated by the rival Egan gang, began cruising the streets, looking for their enemies.

The Rats struck first, deciding to reprise their earlier feat by shooting up the Hogan house on Cass Avenue. Just after midnight on March 22, two carloads of Egan gangsters whizzed past the place, riddling it with bullets and buckshot from top to bottom. One projectile punched through a wall and door and then crashed into another wall just above the bed in which Jelly Roll Hogan's parents were sleeping.

Hogan may not have been a ruthless gangster, but he was outraged beyond belief by the second attack on his home. As a result, Jelly Roll, John "Kink" Connell, Humbert Costello, Harry Greenberg, Pat Scanlon, Charles Mercurio, and Frank Bova set out later that morning gunning for the Egan's Rats. Their enemies had disappeared, but whether the men checked the Maxwelton Club is unknown. The Egans were holed up there, and if the Hogans had shown, the resulting battle would have been an uneven bloodbath.

At two o'clock that afternoon, Hogan and his six helpers were arrested as they left his home after a lunch break. The boys boasted that they were "out after the Rats!" Police noted that Jelly Roll's sedan had recently been repainted from red to black. Hogan fondled a sawed-off, pump-action 12-gauge shotgun as he greeted the officers, claiming that he had been tipped off about an impending attack on his home. As he told police, "I received a telephone message Monday that something was coming off, and I had the gang planted in the house, all set for business. We had plenty of ammunition, and we sat up all Monday night and Tuesday night. They caught us napping tonight. or there would have been a different story to tell."

When the beverage inspector was asked if he wanted protection, Jelly Roll patted his shotgun and said, "Nah, the Hogans'll take care of themselves."

Two days later, the rival gangs collided again. At 7:10 p.m. on March 24, Jelly Roll Hogan and Humbert Costello were driving north on North Grand Boulevard, armed and dangerous. A few blocks south of St. Louis Avenue, a speeding coupe overtook them. A furious fight ensured, with hoods in both cars exchanging pistol volleys and shotgun blasts. As they approached St. Louis, Hogan's repainted Dorris swerved to the west side of the street and crashed into a tree. The Egans' coupe plowed into a thirteen-year-old schoolboy named Leonard Bickel, Jr., who suffered permanent injuries. The coupe made a squealing left turn onto St. Louis Avenue and vanished into the gathering dusk. Hogan and Costello hoofed it back to the boss's home, reloading their weapons as they ran.

Jelly Roll Hogan admitted his part in the shooting and fingered Elmer Runge and Izzy Londe as his assailants. The two red hots were soon arrested and brought before the beverage inspector at police headquarters. When Hogan was asked by police if he could identify Londe and Runge as his attackers, he snarled, "I'll identify them with a shotgun!"

Schooboy Leonard Bickel's injuries brought public outrage over the gang war to a fever pitch. Perhaps to blunt the outcry, both Dint Colbeck and Jelly Roll Hogan would provide money for the youngster's medical care. Six Hogan gangsters arrested a couple of days earlier were immediately hit with concealed weapons charges. Shortly thereafter, at two o'clock on the morning of March 27, two curtained sedans raced east on Lindell Boulevard, their occupants trading bullets with one another. The gun battle continued as the cars sped past North Grand, into the cutoff, and onto Locust, and the vehicles were last seen fishtailing north on Jefferson.

It was assumed that the cars contained members of the Egan and Hogan gangs who were trying to kill each other. Ray Renard would claim a few years later that the incident didn't involve either gang and was unrelated to the underworld war. But the public thought the gun battle was fought between the two rival gangs, and that's all that mattered.

The plate-glass showroom windows of the Hudson-Frampton auto dealership at 3301 Locust Avenue had been hit by gunfire from the two mystery sedans. The owner of the dealership painted on his bullet-pocked windows in large letters:

WHAT GANGSTERS ARE DOING IN ST. LOUIS. THEY WILL BE SHOOTING UP OUR HOMES NEXT! HOW LONG WILL ST. LOUISANS TOLERATE THESE JESSE JAMES TACTICS?

Later that morning, Jelly Roll Hogan was brought before President Phillip Brockman of the Board of Police Commissioners and Police Chief O'Brien for "questioning" about the gang war. The closed-door conference lasted two and a half hours, with all involved refusing to comment. Chief O'Brien gave strict orders to police to arrest all known gangsters, ex-convicts, and police characters on sight. A conference was also

Isadore "Izzy" Londe, left, and Elmer Runge were two of the more excitable members of the Rats and front-line participants in the bloody war with the Hogan Gang.

held with Justice of the Peace Jimmy Miles, who had been a conduit for the Egan gang for nearly thirty years. Father Timothy Dempsey intimated that he was trying to bring about a peace deal himself.

On Thursday morning, March 29, Jelly Roll Hogan ushered a *St. Louis Post-Dispatch* reporter into his home at 3035 Cass Avenue.

"Come on in, and see for yourself. I just want you to take a look," said Hogan, who was in an irritable mood, pointing out numerous bullet holes in the walls and furniture. "And listen, the police want me to get out of town. They've got the nerve to tell me that if I leave the city, the gang war will end. What about the dirty skunks who did that?

"My mother and father were asleep in that other room when those shots were fired into this house. The bullets passed over their heads. And the police tell me to leave town. They say if I get out of town, the gang war ends," Hogan said with a sarcastic laugh, ending his diatribe.

Edward Hogan Sr. told the reporter, "Eddie hasn't got a thing to do with this war. He's been dragged into it through no fault of his own. He is only acting in self-defense. He's kept busy inspecting soda-water factories. He's trying to earn a living with his state job. We're in a hell of a fix here. We're not safe in our own home."

Jelly Roll continued his lament to the reporter:

"I was inspecting a soda-water factory last Thursday when six of my friends were arrested on concealed weapons charges. I don't care what the police say. It's not me that's stretching this thing out. I never went gunning for anybody. I was arrested for having a gun in my automobile. I was carrying it in self-defense, and a jury acquitted me.

"This feud, as they call it, began when somebody spread the rumor that my brother, Jimmy, was one of three men hired by Max Greenberg to kill Bill Egan. That was a damned lie, and I'd like to know who started it. Why, one of the three men named as the murderers of Egan, John Doyle, later killed by detectives, was in jail in Ohio when Egan was killed.

"The other crowd seems to think that Jimmy is in the house here. Well, they're mistaken. He's not here, nor anywhere near. I'd like to know where I got the nickname of 'Jelly Roll.' That is something else that has been wished on me. None of my friends call me that. I haven't any idea how or where it originated."

Father Dempsey was quoted in the same article:

"I have had a talk with Hogan, and I am satisfied that he will call this war off. If I could just get him and Colbeck together I'd make them shake hands.

"You know, it's not Hogan and Colbeck so much as it is the irresponsible youths who delight in calling themselves Hogan gunmen or Egan gunmen. Now, if Hogan and Colbeck would only shake hands and pass out the word they are no longer enemies, I believe they other boys would put up their guns and quit shooting each other.

"Gossip is at the bottom of this whole thing. Somebody starts a rumor that Max Greenberg is in town or that Jimmy Hogan is to be killed within 48 hours, and the boys believe it all and go gunning for each other. They are fascinated by the glamour. They like to hear their exploits discussed. I am heartbroken. None of the boys belong to my parish. They represent various nationalities and creeds, but my heart goes out to them just the same, and I'd give anything I possess if I could only stop them."

Pictures and biographies of all the gangsters were featured in newspapers, and the police urged the courts to set bail for the gangsters at unusually high amounts, in order to keep them locked up longer.

One police official spoke disparagingly about his quarry to the *Post-Dispatch*:

"The average gangster is the most cowardly individual on the face of the earth. You could not get a fair fist fight out of any of them. They travel in groups and usually shoot from behind. Get him alone and the gangster will cringe with fear if you double your fists. He is a sneak of the lowest sort, and in spite off gang ethics, he will double-cross his best friend. He never works but wears good clothes and has plenty of money. He couldn't pay his bondsmen and lawyers if he didn't have the cash. If some of the paymasters who are held up would identify the robbers and then stick to the identification, there would be no more gangsters in St. Louis. Most of them would be in the penitentiary, and the rest of them would look for honest employment. A gangster would take a piece of candy from a baby's mouth."

The *Post-Dispatch* then offered this Darwinian assessment of the red hots:

The most impressive features in the physical makeup of most gangsters include a diabetic complexion, not exactly sallow, but a cross between lemon and chalk; a blank expression; round shoulders; small eyes, the dullness of which suggest death; and a drooping mouth. A crooked nose is considered a big asset because it suggests that the owner may have at one time been in an honest-to-goodness fight.

The gangster never talks, hence he gets the reputation that he carries secrets, but that is not the chief reason. It is merely because the average gangster could not hold a conversation with himself, much less anyone else. Always his eyes must be shifting to make it appear he is dodging enemies.

The eyes of Dint Colbeck and the rest of the Egan's Rats were probably rolling—at the police, the public, and the Hogans for making the gang war out to be much more important than it really was. On the night of March 30, an editor and reporter with the *St. Louis Star* came to the Maxwelton Club to try and broker a truce with Egans. Colbeck agreed to discuss peace.

Within the next twenty-four hours, the reporter returned with President Brockman and Chief of Detectives Hoagland. The three men met with Colbeck and several of the boys in one of the private rooms on the second floor of the roadhouse. Brockman warned the gangsters, "If you don't quit fighting, and the police can't stop you, we'll call out the militia." Colbeck stated flatly, "We'll quit if the Hogan mob quits. But if one of them follows one of my boys ten feet, the war will be on again."

Dint and all the members of his inner circle at the conference gave their personal word that they were done fighting. Everyone went downstairs, where Colbeck undoubtedly served drinks to the three guests.

The reporter had with him a signed note from Jelly Roll Hogan, written on official stationary, stating that he was done with the gang war. The scribe wanted Colbeck to write a similar note to the people of St. Louis, saying that he would publish both letters in the paper. Dint walked alone to a table and quickly scribbled out:

March 31/23,

To the people of St. Louis, I want to state that in so far as we are concerned the gang war in St. Louis is ended.

William P. Colbeck.

He then strolled over and tossed the note on the bar. The boys read it aloud and had a big laugh.

Sure enough, both notes appeared in the *Star*. But by early April 1923, Dint Colbeck probably could have cared less about finishing off the Hogan Gang. Something much bigger was occupying his attention, something that made the gang war seem insignificant by comparison.

Dint Colbeck had reached out to the burgeoning Cuckoo Gang, a group of crooks just as wild as the Egan's Rats. The Cuckoos controlled almost all of the South Side except for The Hill, and were primarily armed robbers, liquor hijackers, extortionists, and kidnappers, often victimizing fellow criminals as well as civilians. Ethnically, the Cuckoos were about evenly split between American-born whites and Arab-Americans, the latter being of Syrian extraction. The Cuckoos were bossed on the street by the three Tipton brothers, Ray, Roy, and Herman.

An associate of Roy Tipton, Max Simonson, had a tip for a huge score. During meetings at the both the Maxwelton and Sharpshooters clubs that spanned weeks, Colbeck and the Tipton brothers decided to act on the tip and rob a mail truck in downtown St. Louis. They spent days observing the truck until they knew its routine better than the messengers did, and by the first business day of the new month, the boys were ready. The night before at the Maxwelton Club, Dint Colbeck had told his men to prepare their alibis immediately, hinting that something big was in the works.

It was six o'clock on the morning of Monday, April 2, 1923, the day after Easter. The sky was overcast, the temperature mild, and the streets were still largely deserted. The working stiffs were still waking up and the late-night desperados had retreated to their lairs. It was a perfect time for a heist.

The mail truck set out from the post office at Eighteenth and Clark right on time to make its daily deliveries to branches throughout the city. As the truck headed east on Locust Avenue, a Ford sedan cut in front of it at Fourth Street and rapidly began to slow. As the mail truck driver braked to avoid the zigzagging Ford, a black Cadillac touring car glided alongside and two masked men jumped out. Brandishing a pistol and shotgun, the robbers hopped onto the running board of the slow-moving truck and, sliding into the cab, forced the driver to continue east on Locust. A third man muscled his way into the back, subduing the armed guard.

When the truck reached the north-south alley halfway between Second and First streets, the driver was ordered to turn right and stop after traveling about forty feet. The driver and guard were dragged out of the truck and held at gunpoint as men emerging from the Ford and the Cadillac rummaged through the vehicle, taking nine mail pouches. Within two minutes, the bandits were gone and the postal messengers were left in the alley with their ransacked truck.

Once again, newspapers ran extra editions whose headlines trumpeted the robbery, but the true value of the loot the gangsters got away with was not revealed to the public. Although payment was stopped on most of the payroll checks that were stolen, the gangsters reaped a huge bounty in unsigned, negotiable industrial bonds worth more than $2,400,000 dollars. *That's two point four million in 1923 dollars!* The size of this caper far exceeded anything the Egan's Rats had ever dreamed of.

However, the bonds still had to be fenced, and this presented a problem since the bonds could be rendered negotiable only by forging signatures onto them. But the bandits also had grabbed nearly $260,000 in cash, and this was promptly divided among the boys.

Ray Renard claimed he first heard of the robbery the next day at the Maxwelton Club while schmoozing with James "Sticky" Hennessey, who told him about the caper and how well it had gone. Colbeck assigned the pair to get rid of the Cadillac used in the robbery, and they departed to do so later that night.

With Hennessey behind the wheel of the Cadillac and Renard driving his own Hudson touring car, the pair made their way to a bar in Wellston, where they met Cuckoo chief Roy Tipton, Rudolph "Featheredge" Schmidt, William "Lucky Bill" Crowe, Clarence "Dizzy" Daniels, and Egan red hot Harry Londo. Tipton asked Renard to drive him and twenty-two-year-old Dizzy Daniels to a friend's house in Fenton before dumping the Caddy, and the three men drank some whiskey there before heading back into the city.

Apparently, the Cadillac began to have brake trouble, so the boys got a large rope and tied it to the back of Renard's Hudson to tow the disabled vehicle. They then continued up Gravois Road toward St. Louis. What happened next would be debated for years.

At 9:45 on the night on April 3, barely thirty-nine hours after the mail truck robbery, the two-car caravan was plodding up Gravois through Affton when motorcycle Deputy Constable

Edward P. Neu ordered the odd cavalcade to stop. The cars ground to a halt in front of St. George's Catholic Church at 8240 Gravois Road, where parishioners were just emerging from a meeting.

Just as the cars stopped, the tow rope between the Hudson and the Cadillac broke. Deputy Neu got off his motorcycle and knelt beside the disabled Caddy to examine the tow rope. The Hudson began to back up slowly, and a man, described as "twenty-eight years old, five feet nine, dressed in a light cap and tan raincoat," jumped from the touring car and snatched Neu's .38 service revolver from its holster. He fired two shots into the deputy's shoulder and chest. Neu slumped to one knee and moaned, "For God's sake, don't shoot me anymore!" The gunman leaned forward and fired another bullet into the lawman's mouth.

Two men, armed with a pistol and a shotgun, leaped out of the Hudson, quickly grabbed the shooter, and tossed him into the Hudson, which screeched off up Gravois, leaving the shocked churchgoers trying to sort what they had just seen. Two policemen pursued the fleeing auto and fired a slew of shots at it, but the Hudson disappeared at the intersection of Gravois and Morgan Ford roads.

It was never made clear who actually killed Deputy Constable Edward Neu. The slaying would come up briefly during the November 1924 trial of several prominent Rats in which Ray Renard was the star witness. Renard would declare in 1931 that he had been with Clarence "Dizzy" Daniels and Cuckoo boss Roy Tipton that night, and that Daniels had killed Neu. Daniels, who at the time was deep into a life sentence at Jeff City for another cop killing, would tell the *Post-Dispatch* in 1933 that it was actually Renard who killed the deputy constable, adding that he would detail the murder under oath. Interesting, particularly since Renard's deal with the government allegedly hinged on his assurance that he had never personally killed anyone.

In his eyewitness account to police immediately after the shooting, St. George parishioner Harold Briggs stated that a young, well-dressed man had jumped from the Cadillac and shot Edward Neu. Renard would later testify that the twenty-two-year-old Daniels inexplicably had gone berserk and cut down the lawman. This was certainly possible, as evidenced by the fact that the hot-headed Daniels would help kill a St. Louis city policeman and a hostage during a botched robbery a few months later. Briggs initially stated that five men jumped from the Hudson and dragged the shooter back inside the car; he later amended that number to two.

It's hard to believe that the smallish Roy Tipton and Ray Renard could muscle huge, adrenaline-crazed Daniels into the car by themselves. It is also unlikely that, in the wake of a high-risk job like the downtown mail robbery, the Cuckoo Gang boss would get into a car with a hood he had just met instead of riding with his trusted henchman Dizzy Daniels.

Although Daniels certainly wasn't an upstanding citizen, he basically said in his latter-day interview that Renard had panicked when Deputy Neu pulled them over and opened fire before he and Tipton could react. It is also important to note that there was noticeable bad blood between the Egan's Rats and the Cuckoo Gang after the night Neu was killed. It's also possible that Daniels' allegations were the work of a bitter "lifer" looking to stick it to a notorious snitch who had pinned another murder on him.

Interestingly, when Daniels came out with his allegations in 1933, Renard issued a terse no-comment statement from his California home, instead of the scathing denial one might expect. This could be taken as a sign of guilt, or simply that he was tired of discussing the subject.

Today, more than eighty years later, it's still impossible to determine who actually killed Deputy Constable Neu or why.

At four o'clock on the afternoon following Neu's killing, Ray Renard returned to the Wellston speakeasy where he had run into Sticky Hennessey and Featheredge Schmidt the night before. The two men followed Renard to the Maxwelton Club, wehre they walked around swinging a basket filled with more than $1 million in bonds, the Egan gang's share of the haul.

By this time, Dint Colbeck undoubtedly had heard of the previous night's events, but what he may have said or done to his dapper acolyte is unknown. It's probable that Dint, still flush from the robbery, could have cared less who Renard may have killed as long as he hadn't get caught. Colbeck and several shotgun-toting men drove off with their share of the bonds, stashing most of them at the Richmond Heights bungalow of Whitey Doering for safe-keeping until they could fence them. Little did the Egans know that an investigation of the gang was already in the works.

Just a couple of days after the murder of Deputy Neu, the two gang leaders who had been gunning for each other nearly came face to face. Dint Colbeck went downtown to the Municipal Courts Building to post bond for Ray Renard on a concealed-weapons charge. (Renard eventually would receive a nine-month sentence, which he would appeal.) As Colbeck and Renard stood in the courtroom, Jelly Roll Hogan and six of his men walked in; their trial on concealed-weapons charges was on the docket immediately after Renard's. Dint and Jelly Roll came within just a few feet of each other, but neither spoke nor looked in the other's direction, and they concluded their respective business in court uneventfully.

One man who moved easily between the Cuckoo Gang and the Egan's Rats was William "Big Bill" Rush. While not a tough guy, he enjoyed the company of the red hots, and when he opened a saloon and dance hall along the boundary between Granite City and Madison, Illinois, he invited all his friends to attend the grand opening on the night of April 5, 1923. Representing the Egans were Sticky Hennessey, Izzy Londe, and Lee Turner, and as the night wore on, Big Bill became nervous that the hoods would rob him.

The red hots became drunker and rowdier as the evening progressed. After midnight, Rush had an employee gather up all his cash and leave the premises. Upon seeing the man depart with the money, Hennessey angrily confronted a petrified Rush. Before Big Bill had a chance to explain his concerns, the three gangsters dragged him into a back room and shot him to death. Police found his body crumpled in a corner with four bullets in his chest.

Just two days after his sentencing on a concealed-weapons charge, Ray Renard was involved in another murder. William Crowe, known as "Lucky Bill" because of his knack for beating convictions, was fatally shot in his dingy Chouteau Avenue flat at midnight on April 12. Despite the fact that Crowe recently had been running with the Cuckoos, the police had reason to believe that the two men present when he was killed were Egan red hots Elmer Runge and Ray Renard. Police also suspected, but of course couldn't prove, that Runge had pulled the trigger on not-so-Lucky Bill Crowe.

Three of the Rats spent the next week on trial. On April 17, Renard was acquitted of pulling a February bank robbery in East Alton, Illinois, and a few days later Dint Colbeck and Chippy Robinson were finally acquitted on charges stemming from the robbery of the safe at John Ireland's home in July 1920. With the boys in the clear for the moment, they were free resume their lawless ways.

The original idea was to fence the stolen bonds gradually. They exchanged $50,000 worth in Chicago, and bondmaster Whitey Doering began reaching out to a man in Williamson County, Illinois, to help move more of the notes. Doering had become the Egans' unofficial liaison to the Charlie Birger gang, which was resurrecting schemes of robbing Illinois mail trucks and grabbing mining company payrolls. Then on April 19, the law made its first move.

Two weeks earlier, police had been alerted when a friend of Whitey Doering tried to pass some bonds to a St. Louis broker, who became suspicious and called the law. After days of surveillance, the cops raided Doering's Richmond Heights bungalow in force, recovering the Rats' entire share of the loot and shining a bright light on the Egan gang as the perpetrators of the downtown mail robbery. Doering, his wife, and a helper, David Weisman, were arrested, and they were soon joined by Ray Renard, Red Smith, Oliver Dougherty, Steve Ryan, Eddie Linehan, and William Meyer. All made bail but were plagued by thoughts of the million-dollar score they had lost.

A few days later, in the early morning hours of April 25, Fred Burke pulled a caper that netted some much needed cash for the gang's coffers. The job was a little-noticed harbinger of the crime methodology the intelligent Burke would employ to good advantage. The federal warehouse at 4116 North Union Boulevard was a storehouse for pre-war whiskey earmarked for medicinal use, and its tight security meant something special would be required to get inside. Burke decided to disguise himself as a police officer to fool the guards.

At 12:30 a.m., Burke, dressed in a policeman's uniform, knocked on the warehouse's door and asked the night watchman who answered if he would identify a burglary suspect. The watchman, seeing the blue uniform and the strapping Burke, immediately opened up, only to find himself staring at two pistols aimed at him. Four or five men appeared and a virtual replay of the Jack Daniel's heist occurred. It's not known who accompanied Burke that night, but the most likely culprits were his closest partners, Gus Winkler, Bob Carey, Ray Nugent, and possibly Izzy Londe and Milford Jones. The heist probably didn't involve Dint Colbeck's inner circle, since informant Ray Renard had nothing to say about it. The boys made off with a total of fifty barrels of whiskey with a retail value of $80,000.

The gangsters also had another mail robbery lined up, one they had been considering since mid-March. The tip had come from Thomas Saatkamp and Frank Hackethal, who owned a resort on Long Lake, near Staunton, Illinois. The Consolidated Coal Company's payroll was delivered every month by a train that stopped at Staunton. After an abortive robbery attempt the day after Whitey Doering's bust, the Rats exhaustively rehearsed for the job. They memorized their duties and devised a precise timetable for the heist. In light of the disastrous aftermath of the robbery in downtown St. Louis, Dint Colbeck was determined that this caper should succeed.

Once again, a nasty internal dispute arose before the caper. It came of the form of thirty-two-year-old hanger-on Joe Powderly, who had provided the tip on the Jack Daniel's heist in December. Ostensibly a stock trader, "Old Joe" had become quite cocky over the winter and spring, frequently bragging of his association with the Rats. Fascinated with gangsters, Powderly loved to tie on a good one and, with a rod in his jacket, boast of his exploits. Anyone could see that Powderly wasn't a gangster at heart. He had a wife and two children, a home at 4545 North Broadway, and had served as an artilleryman during World War I. But since he had become a wanna-be gangster, he had been spending precious little time with his family.

On the evening of May 3, Powderly got drunk in a bar up the street from his house. When someone tried to upbraid him, Joe shot the man through the shoulder, then beat a hasty retreat, probably reveling in the adrenaline rush. Such incidents drew a lot of heat, and when Chippy Robinson, who happened to be in the bar that night, saw how careless Powderly was, he made up his mind then and there to kill him.

Powderly was drinking at the Maxwelton Club on the night of May 24 and having a grand time among his idols. Sticky Hennessey and Chippy Robinson were buying Joe drinks and asked him if he'd like to go club-hopping, which precipitated a grand tour of St. Louis speakeasies and nightclubs. After the boys picked up a few girls, they made their way to Frank Hackethal's lake resort, which was a planning base for the upcoming mail robbery. The three men were boozing it up and laughing; everyone else in the place knew who they were and gave them a wide berth. The hoods also freely discussed how a couple of the red hots had robbed a St. Louis Dairy Company messenger of $3,500 a few days earlier.

Robinson asked Powderly if he had his gat with him. Joe quickly drew his pistol and poked it into Chippy's ribs with a laugh, which pissed off Robinson, who nodded and said, "Let Sticky see your gat." Powderly eagerly obliged, and after another round of drinks was ordered, Hennessey discreetly slipped the gun into his pocket.

Robinson glared at Powderly. "You know why I've brought you here?" he asked.

"What for?" Joe put a drunken half-smile on his face.

"To bump you off."

"Why— wha— listen—"

"I'm going to kill you."

His evening rapidly turning into a nightmare, Powderly probably was sorry he'd ever pretended to be physically tough. Feeling immense pressure in his bladder, he pleaded, "For God's sake … my wife," then instinctively tried to bolt from his chair. Chippy plugged him with four neatly grouped shots before Old Joe could move a step.

Robinson barked, "Leave the women. Let's get this bird away from here; they don't want any murders here." He and Hennessey dragged the still-breathing Powderly out the door and down the front steps, the gangster wannabe's head smacking the wooden planks as they descended. A carload of partygoers pulled up, and Sticky got the drop on them and took their car keys. The boys shoved the now-dead Powderly into the vehicle's passenger seat, while Chippy got behind the wheel and Sticky climbed in the back.

During the long drive back to St. Louis, Robinson decided he wanted to have a little fun and told Hennessey to prop up Powderly so he would appear to be alive to passing motorists. Robinson then stopped the car, lit a fat cigar, and placed it in the corpse's mouth, which was frozen open in final agony. Hennessey held the body up as Chippy drove and made conversation with the dead man:

"How's that smoke, Joe?"

"Like that cigar, kid?"

"How's it feel to be dead?"

"Are you enjoying the ride, kid?

"Why don't you talk, Joe?"

During the ghastly ride, Robinson kept cracking jokes and talking to the lifeless body of Powderly, who formerly had idolized the very same gangsters who killed him. Finally, the men reached the McKinley Bridge, and making sure no other cars would soon be crossing, Hennessey and Robinson hauled Powderly out of the car and slipped a few heavy rocks into his pockets. Chippy continued to talk: "Joe, you need a bath. Joe's all bloody, ain't ya, Joe?"

Grabbing Powderly by the back of his belt, the pair pitched him over the side and into the Mississippi River. The bloated body of the stock trader would wash ashore two weeks later, causing the police to scratch their heads about why he had been killed.

DEPRAVED

INDIFFERENCE

T HE STAUNTON MAIL robbery went down at 5:30 in the afternoon on Saturday, May 26, 1923, thirty-six hours after Joe
Powderly had been deep-sixed in the river. All the prepara-
tion and rehearsals were about to pay off. The money train left
St. Louis's Union Station at 3:40 p.m., heading east, and when the
train stopped at the station on the eastern edge of Staunton, the
guards began transferring the mail sacks to the postmaster, who
waited in a Ford sedan.

Earlier that day, Ray Renard, Sticky Hennessey, Izzy Londe,
and Frank "Cotton" Epplesheimer had left the Maxwelton Inn for
Frank Hackethal's resort on Long Lake. They later hooked up
with another participant, labor racketeer Charles "Red" Lanham,
who followed them to Staunton, where they met Red Smith and
Dint Colbeck at 4:30 in the afternoon, an hour before the money
train was due.

The boys then left for the village of Hamel, where a stolen
Cadillac Phaeton had been stashed. As Hackethal drove on
alone, the hoods piled into the Caddy and drove to Staunton,
arriving just as the train pulled into the station. Renard noticed a

Studebaker sedan parked by the curb outside the depot. Inside were Oliver Dougherty, Chippy Robinson, and Steve Ryan, all of whom were armed with sawed-off shotguns. Their job was to cover the first group of gangsters while they made the snatch.

As Postmaster Harry Kuehnen wrestled his bag out of the train and spoke with his guard, G. A. Roberts, Renard coolly cruised around the block and parked the Cadillac in a driveway along the street the messenger usually took to the post office. When the messengers took a different route, Renard zoomed after them, and when he caught up, Izzy Londe swung out onto the running board of the Phaeton, aiming a .45 at the messengers and yelling for them to stop.

Oblivious to the danger just to their right, the messengers continued to drive on slowly. Londe began cursing and pumped a few shots into their vehicle's windows and tires. Sticky Hennessey added another shot for good measure. The messengers stopped, and Red Lanham slid out of the Caddy and grabbed the mailbag from Roberts, ordering both messengers into the car and forcing them to kneel on the floorboard.

Ray Renard sped off toward St. Louis with his partners and hostages along dirt roads that were well oiled and relatively free of traffic. The three backups in the Studebaker, who never had to fire a shot, drove off leisurely. As Renard drew closer to the city, Dint Colbeck and Red Smith, who had been at the lake resort when the job was being pulled, began tailing the men. Not far from Edwardsville, Hennessey and Lanham transferred themselves and the loot to Smith's coupe, and Kuehnen and Roberts were released near the town. The Cadillac Phaeton was abandoned near Long Lake, and Renard, Londe, and Epplesheimer headed for the city in Renard's Chalmers.

By now, the authorities had been alerted to the robbery, and all bridges and roads into St. Louis were being watched by police. Foreseeing this possibility, Steve Ryan had proposed during the planning sessions that the boys use a boat to cross the river and enter Missouri at a spot of their choosing. It was ultimately decided that the men would split up and try to get into the city on their own. Stopping at a predetermined rendezvous in Venice, Londe and Epplesheimer boarded a streetcar and slipped into the city, while Red Lanham joined Renard in the Chalmers.

Renard dropped Lanham at his car in East St. Louis. Renard never explained how he got across the river, but by now police were checking cars on the McKinley and Eads bridges, and Lanham decided to hop a freight train to get back into St. Louis. The take from the mail robbery turned amounted to $45,000.

The Egan's Rats had been committing crimes at a fever pitch, and they had a new one in the works for June 1923. After all, the boys lived large and spent money hand over fist on cars, clothes, women, and parties. Their primary income was derived from robberies, but as Ray Renard would later say:

"Money split by the gang did the members little good. We had places to live and drove motor cars, but that was all come easy, go easy. All mine went for gambling and attorney fees. I've dropped $1,000 and $2,000 a night shooting craps; I've seen others of the gang do the same thing. And the next day I had to hunt another chance to commit a robbery to get money to pay a lawyer to defend me in some case. Believe me, the lawyers got plenty.

"Dint was supposed to have put some of his dough into bonds and stashed them away for a rainy day. I've got exactly forty cents in my pocket, and my wife has to work for a living."

The new job was another mining company payroll heist, this time in Pocahontas, Illinois. The Egan's Rats could not have imagined that the robbery would contain the seeds of their demise.

James "Sticky" Hennessey strolled into the Maxwelton Club on June 6, saying he had word of a great score: The Pocahontas Mining Company would be shipping its payroll on June 15 through the Illinois town of the same name, and the messenger would be a frail, elderly man who would be easy to strong-arm. Sticky and Oliver Dougherty were designated to lead the heist, and they were accompanied by younger, fringe members of the Egan's Rats: Bill Engler, Edward "Cocky" Leonard, and Bartley Martin.

Perhaps the most unusual participant was thirty-three-year-old Lee Turner. Although he had been with the gang for more than ten years, and to prison twice for auto theft, Turner was an airplane pilot. Having always been fascinated with flight, he used his share of the Jack Daniel's warehouse loot to enroll in flight school and soon became a member of the prestigious St. Louis Flying Club.

Despite Turner's enthusiasm, he was almost dangerously rough around the edges. While buzzing a friend's house on Telegraph Road, Turner's plane almost collided with a church steeple. Another time, he decided to show off for the boys at the Maxwelton Club, and as the Egans spilled outside on a cloudless spring day, clutching bottles of beer and laughing and pointing, Turner's craft when into a nose dive and headed straight for the grandstand. He barely managed to avoid a potentially fatal crash, and after repairing his plane, he proudly painted his name on the wings.

Lee Turner came up with the novel idea of using Turner's airplane as a getaway vehicle in the upcoming mail robbery. Dint Colbeck agreed, and it was decided that Turner would fly the loot back to the Maxwelton Club, while the others drove back to St. Louis. That way, they wouldn't arouse suspicion if they were pulled over and questioned by police.

Just before the Pocahontas job, the Egan's Rats were again involved in a murder. And once again, it involved Chippy Robinson and Ray Renard, who later would claim to have seen the whole thing. On the night on June 12, 1923, Renard and his pal Eddie Linehan were in the Suburban Inn in Wellston. The placed was packed with guys and dolls and gangsters and their molls, everyone drinking and dancing, and a popular local black jazz band cranking out tunes on the stage. After midnight, the two saw Chippy Robinson walk in with a young, voluptuous girl on his arm and take a table near them. The three nodded at one another, but things were visibly frosty. Renard was afraid of Robinson, who thought he was a spineless pretty-boy, and Linehan and Robinson had often feuded with each other.

Eddie Linehan was known as the second-most dangerous man in the Egan's Rats behind Chippy Robinson. While not in love with murder like Robinson, he was known to use his gun at the slightest provocation, drunk or sober. The twenty-two-year-old Linehan also nursed a deep hatred of police, the result of being blasted with a shotgun by an Illinois cop back in 1921. Linehan said what he wanted when he pleased, often getting verbal with Dint Colbeck himself. Often when he was drunk at the Maxwelton Club, Eddie would whip out his gat, curse all the Rats in the barroom, and dare any of them to shoot it out with him. No one took the challenge. Renard figured the only reason Eddie and Chippy hadn't had it out yet was because they hadn't both been drunk at the same time.

Renard and Linehan were at the Suburban Inn the night of June 12 when a popular black singer named Isaac Young walked into the clubroom. People stopped and greeted him as he made his way through the crowd. Chippy Robinson watched him work the room, then loudly called him over. According to Renard, the following transpired:

"Hello, Young." Robinson said.

The singer grinned, "Hello, Mistah Egan."

"My name ain't Egan."

"I know it ain't, but you're one of them Egans," replied Young, who probably never realized that his harmless banter was signing his death warrant.

Renard later guessed that Robinson was showing off for his girl when, quick as a flash, Chippy pulled out his gun and began waving it in Young's face.

"Put that away," Young said, a half-smile still clinging to his face.

Robinson flashed his psycho smirk, saying, "Listen, I want you to do a dance for my girl here."

Now scared, Young stammered, "I-I-I can't dance."

Robinson roared at the top of his lungs, "Do you know who I am? I don't care for anybody but me, see? I'm running this dump tonight, and what I say goes. Now you dance for us!"

Everyone in the joint had stopped whatever they were doing and were watching tensely.

Young pleaded, "I can't dance; that ain't my line!"

"Then sing us a song," Chippy growled, brushing the barrel of his pistol against Young's midsection.

"I don't work here. Get one of the other boys," the entertainer said.

Robinson's face twisted in rage as he yelled, "You're gonna sing, you black sonofabitch," and fired a shot at Young's feet without looking.

That was the final straw for Young, who, with a groan, made a dash for the exit. Robinson stood up and dropped the fleeing singer with a single shot to the back just as he reached the front door. Sitting back down and holstering his gun, Chippy knocked back his whiskey and screamed to the crowd, "If any of you motherfuckers open your mouths, I'll ..." Robinson didn't finish his threat; instead, he grabbed his date, stepped over the dying Isaac Young, and left.

Renard and Linehan watched silently as Robinson exited. Linehan cursed Chippy and reached into his jacket for his own pistol, but Renard stopped him. The two quickly melted into the fleeing crowd, none of whom had dared to move an inch while Robinson was still in the room.

The next day, Robinson was at the Maxwelton Club gloating over newspaper accounts of the murder. "Good shot, wasn't it?" he asked bartender "Baldy" Noonan. Then, smiling fiercely, he added, "A lot of guts he had, the dirty nigger, refusing to dance for *me!*"

Late in the afternoon on June 14, the day before the mail robbery was the take place, the six men taking part in the heist left for Pocahontas, Illinois. Lee Turner's airplane developed engine trouble, and he was forced to land in a farmer's field. The boys found him that evening after he had walked into town.

The next morning at 8:30, having been up all night, Sticky Hennessey and his crew struck, grabbing Postmaster John Green and the mail sack containing the mining company's payroll. The police were quickly alerted, but they never located the perpetrators. The gang members immediately left Pocahontas in their Cadillac and headed toward St. Louis, but this time the getaway didn't go as smoothly as in past Egan capers.

Tired and drooling for the payoff, the boys immediately tore through the mail bag but discovered it contained a mere $4,000.

The frustrated and enraged crew hastily divvied up the cash, then hit the road again for St. Louis. Whoever was driving took a wrong turn onto a rough, muddy road that jostled the boys to no end. The Cadillac touring car became stuck in a huge quagmire, and after a good deal of cursing and snarling, the boys were able to muscle the car out of its soggy trap.

Not more than two bone-rattling miles later, the Cadillac became bogged down in the mud again. The boys pushed and heaved, and nearly all of them at some point ended up falling into the knee-deep mud. An Amish man in a horse-drawn buggy passed by the huffing and puffing gangsters and asked if they needed any help, but they waved him away, although some of the nervier thugs fingered their pistols. After the Samaritan left, an argument ensued about how the crew would get back to St. Louis. It seemed that each man wanted to go a different way, while the driver repeatedly protested that *he* knew the best route.

Finally getting off the horrible country lane, the gangsters headed southwest. Seven miles from Collinsville, they stopped to put skid chains on their tires, to prevent a repeat of the earlier mud bath. When they finished, they pulled their hostage, fifty-year-old John Green, from the Cadillac and tossed him into a roadside puddle. As they approached Venice, the six robbers knew full well they couldn't drive across the McKinley or Merchants bridges because the police would be watching both structures. Ditching the Caddy, Dougherty led the crew down to the river's edge, where they gave fisherman Lloyd Lewis $2 to row them across the Mississippi in his open boat. Sometime after noon, nearly five hours after the robbery, the boys finally made it back to St. Louis. Stepping ashore at the foot of Bremen Avenue, the Egans walked to a nearby grain elevator to call the Maxwelton Club.

Sticky Hennessey dialed the roadhouse, and only Ray Renard and Cotton Epplesheimer were there. The latter was dispatched to North Broadway and Bremen to pick up the men. Renard would later say that he had been setting up his alibi all day, which was fortunate, since he was identified by several eyewitnesses as having participated in the robbery. Renard greeted the heist crew when they staggered into the club at about 1:45

p.m., exhausted, haggard, and covered with mud. Hennessey cursed a blue streak and said at one point, "We should have never gone." The boys then settled in for some much-needed liquid refreshment.

Lee Turner got in his car, picked up a mechanic he knew, and drove back to Pocahontas to repair and retrieve his plane. He took off at about 5:30 that afternoon and headed back to the St. Louis Flying Club near Bridgeton, Missouri.

The Rats were naïve to think that the police on both sides of the river would remain dumb forever. At 4:30 the next morning, the cops raided the Maxwelton Club and collared Bartley Martin and Cotton Epplesheimer. The former was passed out drunk, his head resting on his suit jacket, possessing a revolver and $462 dollars cash, his share from the job. A couple of hours later, Ray Renard was dragged out of bed after witnesses had identified his mug shot. Police heard the story about the mysterious airplane and promptly grabbed Lee Turner. Eddie Linehan was soon busted, even though he had not taken part in the robbery. Sticky Hennessey was next to fall into police custody, and soon all of the robbery participants except Oliver Dougherty had been rounded up.

Renard related how he and Eddie Linehan had traveled to Springfield, Illinois, to retain lawyers to handle their case, and both men protested to Dint Colbeck about having to stand trial and possibly serve time for a crime they didn't commit. Renard was currently out on appeal from two convictions, one for interstate theft and the other for concealed weapons, and it seemed as if his number finally might be up. Colbeck sought to assure his men that he would pay all their legal fees, and the matter was dropped as the summer began.

Yet another heist was in the works, this one a payroll robbery of United Railways, the city's streetcar provider, which was headquartered at Park and Thirty-ninth avenues. Fred Burke had come to Colbeck with the job, and he led Oliver Dougherty, Lee Turner, and four other red hots on the heist. Turner had been forced to make an emergency landing on June 23, 1923, at Bridgeton and demolished his plane when he crashed through a fence and into a barn. Turner had told Colbeck that he desperately wanted to be included in the new job, and Dint added him to the crew.

Ray Renard provided transportation for the gangsters in the form of a stolen Cadillac sedan, and the boys hit the UR at four o'clock on the afternoon of July 3. Five men barged into the building brandishing weapons. All wore masks except Burke, who was nattily dressed in a gray summer suit and straw boater. The huge gangster was described by witnesses as the leader of the holdup crew. Three men kept forty employees at bay while Burke and Dougherty rifled the treasurer's office, scooping $38,306 in cash into a white canvas sack. As they made their getaway, two UR employees shakily produced revolvers and opened fire on the fleeing bandits. Burke and his crew shot back, but no one was hurt.

The original plan was to divide the loot at Burke's Meramec River hideout. The boys cut south on Tower Grove Avenue and down through the park of the same name. The Cadillac turned right on Arsenal and then swung south on Morgan Ford Road, but in the vicinity of Gravois Avenue, the left-front tire popped completely off the wheel, much to the shock of the robbers. After driving noisily on the rim, the men pulled over and promptly carjacked a baker who happened to be passing by. Three of the Egans stayed with the disabled vehicle, while four others took the loot and sped off for Burke's cabin. The boys were furious with Renard for stealing such a lemon, which worsened his already decaying reputation with the Egan's Rats.

The month of July was blessedly quiet for the gang, after the frantic criminal pace of the year thus far. The only excitement was on July 14 when Lee Turner gave the boys at the Maxwelton Club a show with the new plane he had purchased with his share of the United Railways job. Turner botched the landing and rolled his craft. Once again, luck was with him and he was not seriously injured.

In the aftermath of the police raid in June, Dint Colbeck had begun casting friendly eyes on the former mansion of a municipal judge on Olive Road in Olivette. By the end of the month,

Colbeck had sold the Rock Road roadhouse (much to the unspoken relief of the long-suffering neighbors) and moved the Maxwelton Club to the Olive Road mansion. Even the large sign and gate leading to the roadhouse was taken to the new location.

The gang boss soon got word that the local branch of the Ku Klux Klan had brought the old roadhouse. Colbeck and the boys despised the Klan because it was both anti-Catholic and anti-bootlegging. A furious Dint decided that he would never let the "pointy heads" have what he still saw as his place.

On the night of August 4, 1923, the Klan held a huge initiation ceremony at the old racetrack. Some 6,000 spectators saw 1,000 men and 700 women sworn into the organization underneath two huge flaming crosses, while Klan-friendly lawmen stood guard at the head of the path to the roadhouse. The grandstand was filled to capacity, and 600 automobiles were parked on the premises, their license plates indicating they had come from all over Missouri and Illinois. Streetcars worked late into the night, as did hot dog vendors on the grounds.

Late that evening, after the meeting broke up and the crowd drifted away, three cars tried to enter the roadhouse drive. A sheriff's deputy attempted to turn away the visitors, which included Colbeck, Chippy Robinson, Steve Ryan, and Oliver Dougherty in the lead car. They were backed up by Ray Renard, Sticky Hennessey, Bill Engler, Barney Castle, and several others.

"Get the hell away from here!" the deputy told the men.

"Get the fuck outta the way, or I'll blow you up," Dint growled.

Recognition flashed on the cop's face, "Is that you, Mr. Colbeck?"

Sufficiently humbled, the deputy stepped back and the three carloads of gangsters roared onto the property. As they pulled up in front of the roadhouse, the boys grabbed four bundles of dynamite and walked inside the empty building. They placed the bombs in the basement against all four corners of the foundation. Lighting the fuses, four men dashed out and hopped into the cars, which were already heading for the exit. Four large explosions erupted.

The roadhouse was left standing, having sustained only moderate damage. The foundation was thicker than the boys had thought, and they hadn't used nearly enough dynamite for the job. If the Egans had stacked all the dynamite in one corner, they conceivably might have toppled the structure. Still, they accomplished their goal, as the Klan soon sold the property to the Laurel Hill Cemetery Association.

Nicknamed "Buster," Leo Vincent Brothers initially was one of several faceless "punks" who passed through the Maxwelton Club, grateful for anything Dint Colbeck happened to throw his way, such as stealing a car or beating up someone who had failed to pay a debt to a loan shark. Although he was well built and tough, he had been mercilessly bullied by Andrew "Big Boy" Kane. But by the summer of 1923, Brothers had gained standing within the Rats and was now a ruthless gangster who was quite proficient with a pistol. Kane was still a nobody.

Brothers hadn't forgotten the abuse he'd suffered at the hands of the oaf, and at eight o'clock on the night of August 5, he sought revenge on the "King of the Punks." Backed up by an unknown partner, Brothers waylaid Big Boy in front of 1709 Cass Avenue and administered a beating. Kane wound up being shot to death, and when police checked his corpse, they found little more than twenty cents and two lottery tickets in his pockets, a sign that Big Boy remained down on his luck to the last.

Lee Turner's lack of piloting skill finally caught up with him, with fatal consequences. Around suppertime on August 7, Turner was taking a friend named Walter Moore, a railroad fireman, up for a ride. A few days earlier, the St. Louis Flying Club had forbidden Turner to fly his plane because it had failed a safety inspection, but he simply waited until everyone had gone for the evening and climbed aboard with his pal.

As the pair soared through the humid summer sky, a portion of the material covering the wings ripped away and the plane went into a violent tailspin, plunging 300 feet to the ground. The aircraft crashed into a tree, and Moore was instantly crushed while Turner once again cheated death, sustaining only a broken leg, black eye, and cuts and bruises. In the hospital, Lee was still chipper, asking doctors if he would be healed by the time the International Air Races were held in early October.

During the seemingly lazy summer of 1923, another monster deal fell into the lap of the Egan's Rats. The caper was too big for a single gang, and a deal had been struck between several powerful politicians and gangsters in St. Louis, Indianapolis, and Cincinnati to "milk" all the whiskey out of the Jack Daniel's warehouse on Duncan Avenue. The operation would dwarf the heist the Egans had pulled off in December.

Among the top men in the deal were state Senator Mike Kinney and his lesser-known brother Willie, who was now the "gauger" at the warehouse. Others included Democratic City Committeeman Mike Whalen, former Bottoms Gang boss-turned-gambler Tony Foley, IRS collector for the Eastern District of Missouri Arnold Hellmich, former St. Louis Circuit Court Clerk Nat Goldstein, Cincinnati booze kingpin George Remus, and Tennessee distiller Lem Motlow.

Nearly $1.8 million worth of uncut Jack Daniel's whiskey was stored in the warehouse, and the plan was to gradually "siphon" it out in barrels that would be replaced by identical barrels filled with water. Dint Colbeck attended many planning sessions that summer in a downtown St. Louis office building with the Kinneys, Motlow, and others. Colbeck and the Egan's Rats were charged with safely stashing the whiskey until it could be sold, an aspect of the job Colbeck would also handle.

Dint sold shares in the purloined whiskey to gangsters all over St. Louis, as well as policemen, politicians, and anyone else who was trustworthy and could come up with the dough. Colbeck promised a return of at least $2,000 on an investment of $1,000, and sales were brisk. According to Ray Renard, the operation was a big success.

By August, the "milking" was underway. A metric pump and hoses were used to siphon the liquor into barrels inside a building 150 feet from the warehouse. When a whiskey barrel ran dry, another crew would fill it with water and reseal it. Renard and the boys stole a total of ten trucks to transport the booze. In the dead of night, the boys would drive up to the building where the stolen whiskey was kept, load the barrels onto the trucks, then drive the load to a barn on Olive Road not far from the Maxwelton Club where it was unloaded. Steve Ryan, Chippy Robinson, and Oliver Dougherty would take turns guarding the whiskey with a shotgun until the prospective buyers showed up to claim their share.

The operation went swimmingly throughout August and into September. Much of the booze was sent east to Cincinnati, where it was loaded onto waiting river barges for shipment north and south. Everyone made a killing on the caper. Colbeck would later say it took a million dollars to swing the whole deal, but in the end, profits topped $2 million.

In the months following the end of the Egan-Hogan gang war, Edward "Jelly Roll" Hogan and his men had been keeping an extremely low profile. They had to, as they spent most of the spring and summer of 1923 fighting to stay out of prison. James Hogan was dragged from hiding and sentenced to fifteen years for robbing bank messenger Erris Pillow two years earlier; however, his older brother called in some favors and was able to get the Missouri Supreme Court to set aside the verdict and grant a new trial. Ace Hogan triggerman Humbert Costello didn't fare as well when he was sentenced to twenty-five years for a 1920 jewelry store robbery.

Jimmy Hogan disappeared again, and rumors placed him as far afield as Texas. In truth, he had gone back to his apartment above the blacksmith shop at 2430 Cass Avenue. As time went on, the younger Hogan began to loosen up, since nothing had been heard from the Egan's Rats in months. Maybe the peace treaty really was on the square.

On the pleasant late-summer night of September 9, 1923, Jimmy made his first public appearance in more than two years. He walked with William McGee, the state representative who owned the blacksmith shop, to Michael Hogan's saloon at 2600 Cass Avenue, on the southwestern corner of the intersection with Jefferson Avenue. A large crowd was gathered inside and in front of the joint. Jimmy had a few drinks and relaxed, laughing and joking with old friends, including his first cousin Elmer

"Babe" Malone, Hogan hood Pat Scanlon, and many others. People remarked how good it was to see him and congratulated him on his recent marriage to a young girl, the ceremony having been held in secret.

The gang strife forgotten, Jimmy Hogan was having the time of his life. But unbeknownst to him, someone connected to the Egans had spotted him in the crowd, and the calm Jimmy was enjoying would soon be shattered.

Sticky Hennessey barged into the Maxwelton Club claiming that Jimmy Hogan had been sighted on Cass Avenue and asked Colbeck's permission to kill him. Dint showed how seriously he took the peace treaty when he told Hennessey: "Sure, but be sure you get the right guy." Hennessey and three other red hots grabbed their weapons and sped back toward the city.

At 9:30 p.m., Hogan was talking with Babe Malone and William McGee when a touring car approached from the south on Jefferson. As the vehicle turned onto Cass, three men sprayed the crowd with pistol fire. Babe Malone was shot through the forehead and killed instantly, while State Representative William McGee was mortally wounded in the stomach. Jimmy Hogan slid into a doorway at the sound of the first shot and was unscathed.

When Hennessey and his three partners returned to the Maxwelton, Colbeck asked them, "What luck?"

"We got him!"

"Are you sure?"

"Absolutely."

Sticky and the boys laughed and traded backslaps with the others present. A few hours later, Dint Colbeck got a telephone call. After returning the receiver to its cradle, he stalked back to where Hennessey and the others were drinking and playing cards. "You damn fools, you didn't get Hogan." he said.

One of the hoods asked, "Who did we get?"

"Babe Malone and Representative McGee."

Dint looked down at his men, "Well, it's just a miss; let it go at that." Everyone rolled with laughter.

The newspapers bemoaned the double murder and the possible revival of the Egan-Hogan feud. Colbeck, called in for questioning, denied that the war was on again. "You can take my word for it," he said. "When I told Chief Hoagland last April that the

Egan-Hogan scrap was at an end, I meant what I said. I'm sorry for what happened Sunday night."

When asked about the killings, Colbeck shrugged, saying, "I do know that three of the boys were full of moonshine Sunday and were riding about in a big touring car. They might have seen Hogan in the crowd at Jefferson and Cass and maybe took a few shots at him for fun. But it was the moonshine that was to blame and not the old gang stuff. That has been forgotten."

James "Sticky" Hennessey was publicly named as the leader of the moonshine-fortified shooters, and he was arrested in Clayton with Chippy Robinson and ex-Hogan- turned-Egan John "Kink" Connell, who were both released. Ultimately, prosecutors didn't have enough evidence to file murder charges, so they charged Hennessey with carrying a concealed weapon. One of the other shooters named was Thomas Skinner, but he skated as well.

Soon after the haphazard attempt to kill Jimmy Hogan, the wheels came off the Jack Daniel's "milking" operation. Willie Kinney was transferred by the government to a new location, and his replacement discovered during an annual check that the whiskey was gone. The scam hit the papers on September 21, 1923, and it was reported that there were 894 full barrels in the warehouse—but only one, the barrel nearest the door, was actually filled with whiskey. Although the disappearance of the booze was not technically a theft, both the Internal Revenue Service and Justice Department promised a long and thorough investigation. It didn't appear that fallout from the whiskey heist would touch the Egan mob, and besides, the gang had made a nice piece of change from it.

Wilbert R. Grant was known throughout the Midwest as an expert safecracker and bank robber. Nicknamed "Des Moines Billy," the forty-eight-year-old Grant pulled jobs all over the country and was respected by criminals everywhere. Grant was known for disdaining violence, breaking into banks in the dead of night and cutting into vaults, instead of storming the place in broad daylight and waving guns around. He lived with his attractive thirty-five-year-old wife, Rosie, in a posh suite at the luxurious Preston Hotel in

Chicago and sent his son to an exclusive parochial school. He and his wife dressed in the finest clothes and were bedecked in diamond jewelry.

In September, Grant, Rosie, and Grant's protégé Wilfred Stainaker traveled to St. Louis to fence some stolen bonds and to scout potential jobs. The trio set up headquarters at the Woodbine Hotel and made the rounds of the city, reaching out to the local criminals and checking prospects.

In late September, Des Moines Billy and his party visited the Maxwelton Club, and Dint Colbeck introduced Grant to the boys. A friendly, easy-going fellow by nature, Billy made fast friends among the Egan's Rats, buying them meals and drinks, hanging out with them, and trading good conversation. Rarely had the boys been exposed to a master criminal like Billy Grant, and they were star-struck by his sociability and good manners. Most of the people they dealt with were pretty rough and uncouth, but Grant almost seemed to be from another planet. Soon the safecracker, his wife, and partner were regulars at the Maxwelton.

Around ten o'clock on the evening of October 22, Grant, Rosie, and Stainaker showed up at the roadhouse, dressed to the nines as usual and in the mood for some club-hopping. Grant invited Chippy Robinson to join them, and the latter quickly jumped up from his table with a smile, and together they headed out.

After midnight, the four walked into the Plantation Inn, a roadhouse at 2905 Suburban Street in Wellston. Formerly the Suburban, the club had been sold and re-named in the wake of Robinson's murder of Isaac Young. The place was jumping with dancing couples and a jazz band, but Grant and company spotted Ray Renard and his date through the blue haze of tobacco smoke and waved. Renard visibly stiffened when he saw Robinson, but he pasted on a smile and joined the group for a few drinks. Everyone was laughing and having a good time, but Renard soon returned to his table, where he kept a wary eye on the volatile Egan triggerman.

By 2 a.m., the quartet had been partying for almost two hours and was having a swell time. Robinson had loosened up and was enjoying himself, drinking much faster than the other three. A clearly intoxicated Robinson began regaling the Grants with tales of his criminal exploits, telling them about robberies and killings in which he had participated.

Then Chippy asked Billy Grant: "You brought a lot of stuff to St. Louis with you, didn't you?"

"Some stuff."

"Getting rid of it?"

"Some of it."

"Watch your step; this is a hot town!"

They all laughed and ordered another round of drinks. The next time Renard looked over at their table, he saw that Robinson had whipped out his .45 automatic and was "pulling his old stuff." With a maniacal gleam in his eye, Chippy went on to brag about how good a shot he was, offering to shoot out the lights or make a waiter dance if the Grants wanted. Billy Grant, obviously afraid of attracting too much attention, told Robinson to put his rod away and be quiet.

"What are you afraid of, a pinch?" Chippy asked, becoming annoyed.

"I couldn't afford one, not tonight, anyway," Grant admitted.

"Carrying your stuff with you?"

Grant nodded wordlessly.

Robinson pressed, "Let's see it."

Grant probably wasn't scared at this point, but he almost certainly wanted to calm Chippy Robinson down. Seeking to placate the inebriated gunman, Grant discreetly drew a small automatic pistol and showed it to Robinson under the table.

For a few minutes, Chippy sat quietly while the other three nervously sipped their drinks and made a couple of awkward attempts at conversation. Renard watched these developments closely but fearfully, the way one might watch a killer crocodile as it stalks an unsuspecting wildebeest.

Then Robinson popped up from his chair and pointed his .45 at Grant. "Think I'll stick you up!" he crowed. Grant and his companions snickered and told Chippy to sit back down. Rosie Grant gently tugged at Robinson's sleeve to try to get him to sit down, but Chippy turned his venom on her, "Don't do that," he growled. Then he zeroed in on Billy again: "I gotta stick you up!"

Probably hoping to silence the loony gunman, Grant, Rosie, and Stainaker raised their hands. With a huge grin, Chippy frisked all three, taking their cash and diamond jewelry. The Grants clung to half-smiles, possibly thinking that when Robinson sobered up he'd give their swag back. But Ray Renard saw something that made him freeze in his seat: Robinson's face was beginning to change. As Renard described it, "His temples swelled, his jaws set, and his eyes narrowed. He looked like a mad dog."

Robinson gritted through his teeth, "Listen, I think you people are the kind of birds that would squeal on a guy."

Billy Grant was petrified for the first time, and Wilfred Stainaker started to stand on nerveless legs.

"I think I'll kill you," Chippy yelled as he pumped a shot into Grant. Rosie shrieked, and Stainaker jumped up, reaching for his hip, and was promptly plugged by Robinson, who then turned his gun on Rosie Grant, shooting her down as well. The club became as silent as a tomb, and Renard clutched his glass, praying he wouldn't be noticed.

The drunken Robinson swayed on his feet and began laughing as he yanked out his back-up pistol, a .38 revolver. Still cackling uproariously, he emptied both weapons into the three bodies. After his guns clicked empty, Chippy turned to the unmoving crowd, spat at them, and walked toward the door while tucking his pistols in his pockets.

Police were puzzled why the three safecrackers had been killed, postulating from the number of gunshot wounds that two or three men must have done the killing. The cops never figured out who the shooter was and surmised that Billy Grant probably had screwed someone on a criminal scheme. While the cops blindly groped for answers, the man who did the shooting sat at the Maxwelton Club and read about the investigation in the papers.

Chippy Robinson went on a two-week drunk after the triple homicide. Everyone in the gang gave him an extremely wide berth, including Dint Colbeck himself. Chippy would talk of the killings for months afterward, and perhaps for the first time in his career, he showed remorse. He would later claim that Rosie Grant haunted his dreams. To anyone who would listen, Robinson would moan, "Jesus, I'm sorry I killed that woman. Her eyes … big, blue eyes. I see them all the time."

Times were tense around the Maxwelton Club as the leaves fell and autumn began. Many of the Rats were facing criminal charges, most notably for the disappointing Pocahontas mail robbery. Cash was running short, so the boys quickly knocked off the Park Savings Trust Company in Hi-Pointe on November 6. The only confirmed participants were Ray Renard and Bill Engler. They made off with $2,380 but the job nearly turned tragic when Engler's pistol discharged accidentally, nearly hitting a little girl.

A week later a murder contract fell into the Egans' lap when an anonymous gangster came to the Maxwelton Club to recruit men to kill Italian bootlegger Leonard Catanzaro, whom he alleged had been a member of the group that had killed Ben Milner and Ben Funke at the Rigoletto Inn in 1920. He initially asked Ray Renard, who later claimed to have turned down an offer of $5,000. Two other Egans (never named by Renard) accepted the contract and contacted the victim under the pretense of buying a case of whiskey. On the evening of November 13, Catanzaro drove the two red hots to a suitably deserted neighborhood to do the deal, and they shot him to death after he pulled to a stop at the corner of Prairie and Evans avenues.

Thirty-six hours later, the boys would again steal the payroll of the Consolidated Coal Company. After a night of drinking and card playing, Ray Renard, Chippy Robinson, Oliver Dougherty, Steve Ryan, and Izzy Londe headed to Collinsville, Illinois. When company messengers went to withdraw the payroll money, the gangsters followed them back to their office. As they unlocked the door, Robinson surprised them with a shotgun and his partners relieved them of the payroll, which amounted to $14,300 in cash and $164 in silver coins. As the boys screeched away from the office building, one of them tossed the coins out the car window with a laugh.

Looking to get a line on a second payroll job, Dint Colbeck dispatched Whitey Doering to Williamson County, Illinois, to talk with bootlegging boss Charlie Birger to see if he would be interested in pulling a job with the Rats.

Doering and his gofer David Weisman had recently been convicted of participating in the April downtown mail robbery, and he was currently free on a $90,000 bond pending appeal. Knowing that a twenty-five-year sentence in Leavenworth Federal Penitentiary in Kansas awaited him, and that he probably wouldn't be able to enjoy the spoils from whatever caper he managed to set up, Whitey was in a foul mood as he set off on the trip to Illinois.

At 9:30 p.m. on November 18, Doering arrived at the hamlet of Halfway, Illinois, for his meeting with Birger. The main feature of the village was a large roadhouse, into which the Egan gangster walked. Whitey had no way of knowing that the backwoods crime boss had gotten into a scrap at roadhouse just two nights earlier and killed the bartender, so his temper was short as well. Doering inquired about robbery possibilities, and Birger basically told him to get lost. Both men yanked out pistols and blazed away at each other. Birger survived his wounds, but Doering did not.

Just after Whitey Doering's funeral, two Egan red hots got into a lethal dispute. Twenty-two-year-old Harry Londo and twenty-one-year-old Elmer Runge were great friends, and both had been with the Rats for quite a while. The latter was noted as the flashiest dresser in the gang and was married to the niece of the deceased Willie Egan. Londo dressed like a bum but was just as volatile as his pal. Why they had a falling out is still a mystery. According to Ray Renard, "I don't know exactly what happened. Maybe Harry used some wrong dice on Elmer; maybe Elmer took a bottle of Harry's booze or borrowed something without asking him. Anyway, it was something that didn't amount to much, but they swore to kill each other."

Elmer Runge knew that Harry Londo's main running buddy was a man known only as "Tony." Runge got Tony to lure Londo to a meeting at the corner of Eighth and O'Fallon at 9:30 on the night of November 30. As Londo walked north on the west side of Eighth Street to keep the appointment, Tony pulled up in a car as the former passed a vacant lot at 1289 Eighth. Londo noticed the car, but since he couldn't see who was inside, he kept walking. As soon as Tony slowed, Runge sprang from the vehicle, clad in a spiffy Chesterfield overcoat, and quickly pumped a bullet into the back of Londo's head.

Later, at the Maxwelton Club, Runge freely boasted of killing Londo. Several of the boys told him he was wrong to have killed his longtime friend. Barney Castle let the youthful gangster have it, saying it was a "dirty job." Elmer rubbed his gat under Castle's chin and breathed, "Listen, you asshole, if you don't like it, you can have some of the same!"

Elmer Runge had been on less than good terms with Dint Colbeck and the boys for quite a while, and his killing of Harry Londo left him totally estranged. After Runge threatened Barney Castle, the Egans decided the time had come to kill him. Runge fully expected the Rats to come after him, so he decided to remove himself from the scene for a while. Since he was facing trial on burglary and larceny charges, Runge decided to go before the judge and offer to plead guilty in exchange for a two-year term at the Boonville Reformatory.

At 2:50 p.m. on December 5, less than a week after killing Londo, Elmer Runge parked his sedan on Fourteenth Street north of Pine and began walking south toward the Municipal Courts Building to give himself up. As he swaggered across Pine Street toward Chestnut, about two blocks from his destination, an old, muddy Ford sedan filled with his old pals approached. Runge saw them coming and dashed across the street into an alley halfway down the block that ran between Fourteenth and Thirteenth streets. The Ford quickly followed, and three men quickly leaped out and collared the unarmed Runge.

The largest of the trio, probably either Red Smith or Steve Ryan, grabbed the neatly dressed killer and smacked him over the head a couple of times with his pistol while asking him, "Who was with you when you killed Londo?" The bleeding Runge spat, "Fuck you!" The large man viciously pistol-whipped Elmer, breaking his nose, splitting open his scalp, and crushing bones in his face. Runge finally gasped out the name of his accomplice and sank to his knees, at which point the big man shot him in the base of his skull. The three thugs jumped back into the Ford, drove to the end of the alley, and turned north on Thirteenth before most passersby even realized there was a dead man laying in a puddle of cold, mucky water in a back alley.

James "Sticky" Hennessey had been drinking heavily over the last couple of months, ever since he'd been busted for the ho-hum Pocahontas mail robbery. He had indeed been "full of moonshine" during his sloppy attempt to kill Jimmy Hogan. Whispering began in Egan circles, saying that Hennessey would be the next to join the growing list of murdered gangsters. Still, Sticky continued to loaf around the Maxwelton, brooding and drinking until he couldn't see straight.

This was exactly what he was doing at midnight on December 13, when his brother-in-law Izzy Londe sat in with him. The latter wasn't doing so hot either, having already blown his stake from the Collinsville job. Londe mentioned that Fred Burke and his pals had headed up to Detroit and that he was thinking of joining them. Sticky figured he could leave town, since he'd just be another federal fugitive. The twenty-three-year-old Hennessey's future wasn't looking very bright—but there was always whiskey.

An hour later, Hennessey and Londe staggered out of the club into the cold and pouring rain. Climbing into Hennessey's high-powered sport sedan, the two roared off down Olive Road.

Later, Izzy Londe told the *Post-Dispatch* what happened next:

> "He had her wide open. I don't know how fast we were going, but it was fast enough. I knew something was going to happen, but I didn't want to ask 'Sticky' to slow her down.
>
> "The road was straight and just a smooth as a skating rink. All of a sudden we skidded, and 'Sticky' lost control. We hit a telephone pole and knocked it loose. The car kept going. I tried to crawl from the front seat to the back of the car when, zowie, we hit another pole.
>
> "That was the end of it. The pole fell over on the car and 'Sticky' was caught below the load. I felt a pain in the head and was kind of dizzy. I got out of the wreckage, but 'Sticky' never moved. I spoke to him, but he did not answer."

A neighbor who heard the crash rushed to the Maxwelton Club to notify the Egans. Oliver Dougherty and Baldy Noonan set off in the rain to find Sticky and Izzy. They soon arrived at the horrific scene where Hennessey lay dead and Londe lay on the ground, having sustained relatively minor injuries.

If there was in fact a plot against Hennessey, he cheated it by dying in an alcohol-related car wreck. As soon as he got out of the hospital, Izzy Londe headed on up to Detroit to join Fred Burke.

DOWNFALL

A S 1924 BEGAN, Dint Colbeck was distributing his usual holiday gifts to local politicians, businessmen, and police officials. Despite the recent murders, Colbeck was at the
height of his power, swimming in money and dealing ruthlessly
with anyone who crossed him. He surrounded himself within his
core group of gunmen: Chippy Robinson, Oliver Dougherty, Red
Smith, and Steve Ryan. By now, Dint was relying exclusively on
this quartet for advice about gang matters. The four were muscle
artists who possessed virtually no business sense, which may
explain some of Colbeck's more senseless decisions. The resulting gaffes were apparent to other Rats, though none dared to
complain verbally.

Some expressed their displeasure with their feet, among
them Fred Burke and Izzy Londe, who had left for Detroit. The
Egan's Rats were never tightly knit to begin with, and some members began casting their lots with other gangs, notably the
Cuckoo Gang. The Licavoli brothers and cousins had joined the
Russo Gang, the crew of American-born Sicilian gangsters that
was now attached to the Giannola Gang, which was alternately
known as the Green Gang or the Green Ones.

Six of the boys started off the New Year by robbing the West St. Louis Trust Company at 4101 Easton Avenue of $26,850 dollars on January 15. Ray Renard, desperate for cash to pay his mounting legal fees, then concocted a plan to swipe a load of tobacco and resell it. He and Bill Engler made their move on January 25, trailing a truck filled with the cash crop from the American Tobacco Company. They hijacked the vehicle at Laclede and Spring avenues, while it was en route to the Terminal Railroad depot.

The hoods kicked the driver loose and drove to a friend's barn on The Hill, where they transferred the tobacco to another truck before setting off for Affton, Missouri, to sell the load to an associate. The truck broke down in front of 3934 Shaw Avenue. Beating a quick retreat, Renard returned with a mechanic a few hours later, only to find police officers milling around the disabled truck and its load of stolen tobacco. Renard cursed in frustration and slid down in his seat as they drove past the scene.

Eddie Linehan and Ray Renard were due to stand trial in Springfield, Illinois, in mid-February for the Pocahontas mail robbery. The others taken into custody, Cotton Epplesheimer and Bartley Martin, had been released when witnesses failed to identify them. The only members of the Egan's Rats being tried were Linehan and Renard, who ironically had *not* participated in the robbery. Both men knew this, and by late January were growing increasingly angry and worried. It appeared to them that they were being thrown to the wolves.

The pair had never been the most popular guys in the gang, and both agreed that Dint Colbeck was offering them up as a sacrifice to the government, as well as getting rid of two potential rivals, especially the dangerous Linehan. A disgruntled Renard drove to Pocahontas to personally question all of the government's witnesses and ask if they had evidence indicating he had taken part in the heist. When Colbeck heard of Renard's grandstand play, he was furious, as was Oliver Dougherty, who hadn't yet been fingered for the robbery.

Downfall

Renard and Linehan were called on the carpet at the Maxwelton Club by Dint Colbeck, who told them, "Listen, I can fix it up so you and Eddie can get only eighteen months on that job if you want to take a plea."

Renard shot back, "I'm innocent, and I'm not going to take any prison term on it. I won't take eighteen minutes. I'm going to trial. If Linehan wants to take a plea, he can, but not me."

Colbeck had been speaking primarily to Renard, so Linehan fixed his boss with a hard glare and snarled, "*I'm* going to trial, too!"

"Well, I just *asked* you," Dint breathed, meeting Linehan's gaze with an equally icy stare.

Both hoods left the meeting more convinced than ever that Colbeck was planning on getting rid of them.

Soon after, Renard went to Springfield to meet with his lawyers. The attorneys went over the case and then told Ray they needed $5,000 more to cover their fees, with $3,500 due as a down payment before they went to trial. Renard and Linehan had another sit-down with Colbeck, who was joined by Dougherty, Engler, and Lee Turner. Renard asked Colbeck to "take care" of his legal fees, as he had originally promised. The gang boss shrugged and said he didn't have the cash on him, and suggested that the dapper getaway driver borrow the money from friends. Dint reiterated that he would "take care" of Renard.

This was too much for Linehan, who exploded with profanity, targeting Colbeck, Dougherty, and anyone else in the vicinity. Aiming a finger at Dint, Eddie growled that he would see them all in hell before he did any "wrong time" for them. Colbeck put up his hands in a placating gesture and said, "Don't worry, Eddie, we'll take care of you." Linehan seemed not to notice the boss's chilling grin as he said this.

By early February, Renard was visibly a nervous wreck. Weight was falling off his already slender frame and dark circles had developed under his eyes. Borrowing what money he could from his friends, he weighed which was worse, federal prison or possibly a bullet in the head from his partners. Linehan wasn't losing sleep over what was happening, but his drinking increased and he spent little time with his wife and two young children.

Early on the morning of February 10, Eddie Linehan sped into St. Louis on his way home after a night of power drinking at the Maxwelton. He decided to stop at a popular saloon on the southwestern corner of Vandeventer and Natural Bridge. The place was run by a popular old sneak thief named Edward "Putty Nose" Brady, and Jimmy Miles Jr, son of the deceased jurist, filled in behind the bar. At 5 a.m., the place was jumping, virtually vibrating with loud music, dancing, and conversation. No one in the place was even remotely sober. Neighbors had already complained, and earlier in the evening, Patrolman William Anderson had warned Miles to keep things quiet.

Shortly after the already sloshed Linehan showed up, Anderson returned to the bar and asked Miles when he was going to close. Anderson, without taking off his mittens, got the crowd's attention and announced that everyone had to go home. The Egan gunman sprang from his chair in defiance of the policeman, and Anderson, a respected officer who didn't like to use brutal force unless necessary, attempted to reason with the intoxicated thug. After a few moments, Anderson finally had taken enough guff and frisked Linehan, confiscating the gangster's holstered .45 automatic.

Telling Linehan that he was under arrest, Anderson grabbed him by the arm. Someone handed the Rat his hat and overcoat, and Miles grabbed his beer and followed the two men out the back door. Stepping out into the cold pre-dawn darkness, the men stopped on the sidewalk. Anderson was holding Linehan and the holstered pistol with both hands.

When the officer attempted to put on his cap, he momentarily released his grip on Linehan's arm. Moving remarkably fast for someone so drunk, Linehan snatched the beer bottle out of Miles's hand and broke it over Anderson's head, sending the policeman sprawling. Linehan barked, "Gimme my gat!" and Miles picked up the holster and handed it over. Eddie then jerked out the .45 pistol and pumped three rounds into William Anderson's head and neck, killing him.

Two days after killing Patrolman Anderson, on February 12, Eddie Linehan was pulled over by police while riding with Ray

Renard on Etzel Avenue. The men explained that their trial was to begin the next morning in Springfield and that they were trying to round up their witnesses.

That same night, Renard went to the Maxwelton Club, where a long conference involving Dint Colbeck and his men had just concluded. The primary topic of discussion was Eddie Linehan. The gang boss didn't care that Eddie had killed a cop, but Dint was worried that Linehan eventually would try to take over the mob. The others wanted Linehan dead because he was always threatening to kill them and because he had been careless enough to escape from the scene of the cop killing in an Egan-owned taxicab. It was decided at the meeting to do away with Eddie Linehan.

When Renard entered the club, Colbeck called him aside and said, "I want you to go out and get Linehan right away. If he asks you what I want, tell him I want to talk to him about that case that's coming up tomorrow."

Renard found Linehan at his girlfriend's house at Page and Hamilton and told the half-dressed and irritated gangster that Colbeck wanted to see him. Eddie pulled his clothes on and the pair headed toward the Maxwelton.

Arriving around midnight, they found Colbeck gone, and Linehan snarled, "That's a swell way to do, make a date with a guy!" As he turned to leave, another gang member persuaded Eddie to wait for the boss. The three men sat down and had a few drinks. The only people in the place were about a dozen members of the gang, who were drinking, playing cards, and talking in low voices, a normal night at the Maxwelton.

After a while, Eddie went into a smaller, adjoining room where he sat alone at a corner table with a cold glass of beer and read newspaper accounts of his murder of Patrolman Anderson. Three men playing poker on the other side of the room didn't even look up when he entered.

Colbeck appeared, stuck his head in the doorway, and said, "Hello, Eddie, old kid."

Linehan deciding to be civil, replied, "Hello, Dint. Wanted to see me?"

"Yeah, I'll be there in a minute."

Stepping back into the barroom, Colbeck motioned for

Chippy Robinson, Steve Ryan, Red Smith, and Oliver Dougherty to join him in the toilet for a quick whispered conference. When they emerged a few moments later, the four henchmen casually drifted into the side room one by one, crowding around the card table to watch the game. Linehan, absorbed in his newspapers, didn't notice them come in. Then he heard someone say, "Oh, Ed-die!"

Linehan looked up to see his boss aiming a .45 automatic at him. "You lousy bastard!" Dint yelled. Eddie leaped out of his chair and let out a groan of either fear or rage just before Colbeck shot him through his Adam's apple. Quick as lightning, Robinson, Ryan, Smith, and Dougherty spun around from the card table, shooting as fast as they could squeeze the triggers of their guns and marching toward the corner where Linehan's bloody body jerked with the impact of each bullet they fired into it. At least one of the gangsters rammed a fresh clip into his .45 and emptied it into the Linehan.

After what seemed like an eternity, the room fell silent, a heavy cloud of gun smoke drifting through it. Renard heard one of the "firing squad" mutter, "He'd have killed two or three around here if we hadn't got the louse." The boys wrapped Linehan's body in a blanket, carted it out to one of their cars (making a point of hauling the corpse past the terrified Renard), and drove into the city. Eddie Linehan was dumped on Goodfellow Avenue near Penrose Street, where he was found at 2:40 a.m., shot nineteen times in virtually every part of his body.

Ray Renard slithered out of the Maxwelton Club that night on jelly-like legs and disappeared. He didn't show up in Springfield the next morning for his court appearance. Police announced that the missing hood was the prime suspect in the murder of his co-defendant. Meanwhile, his lawyers had successfully argued for a continuance until March 18.

Police rounded up the usual suspects, including Dint Colbeck himself. Chief of Detectives Hoagland, who had seen Eddie Linehan's bullet-riddled body when it was discovered on Goodfellow, flew into a rage at the sight of Colbeck and unleashed his frustration over decades of crimes linked to the Egan's Rats.

Downfall

The detective got into a shouting match with the gang chieftain that was overheard by a cub reporter for the *Post-Dispatch*, which later printed an abbreviated, sanitized version of their dispute:

"What about Renard? What became of *him*?" Hoagland asked.

Dint replied, "I didn't see him. If he was out there I didn't see him. He might have dropped in during the night. You know I've got a big cabaret out there and a lot of people hanging around. I can't keep tabs on all of them."

Hoagland attacked, "Your gang of cutthroats and murderers is giving us a lot of trouble. I heard one of your taxicabs was at 'Putty Nose' Brady's saloon when Policeman Anderson was murdered Sunday morning."

"They're not my taxicabs. I'm just a stock-holder in the company. Your men have checked up on all the calls made Saturday night and Sunday morning. They ought to know whether one of them was at Brady's or not."

"Who was Linehan going to have for his alibi witnesses at Springfield?" Hoagland asked.

"I don't know. I'm not interested. I guess Renard could tell you that."

"Yes, if we found Renard, he'd be as dumb as you are. Funny, he had been missing since Tuesday noon, when he was seen with Linehan. Did he think he'd stand a better show going to trial without Linehan?"

Dint insisted, "I tell you, Chief. I don't know a thing about it!"

"Well, they're your gangsters, and you're a mighty poor leader, if you don't know anything about them!" Hoagland snapped.

At one point, Colbeck blurted that he had been shot during the gang war, revealing to outsiders for the first time the Hogan Gang's attempt on his life in the winter of 1922. The gang boss was soon released on bail, and police had no ideas about who killed Eddie Linehan, except a vague notion that Ray Renard may have done it.

In the weeks following the Linehan homicide, a new faction of Egan's Rats began hanging around the Maxwelton Club. The group was composed of several youths from West St. Louis and Wellston, most of whom were as hangers-on, but they earned Colbeck's respect when they hit the Bank of Maplewood on Manchester Avenue for $8,500 on the morning of February 26. The leaders were two World War I veterans-turned-crooks, twenty-four-year-old Lester Barth and twenty-seven-year-old Dewey Goebel.

Barth, short and squat, was a deadeyed triggerman and armed robber. Goebel, the brains of the group, was tall and sleek, with clear blue eyes. Despite their differing appearances, the dumpy, overall-clad Barth and the cool, Germanic-looking Goebel were best friends and added some deadly reinforcement to the gang.

When Ray Renard emerged after a brief spell in hiding, he found the Egan gang was giving him the cold shoulder. He was forced to sell his car to pay witness fees and then was faced with the logistical nightmare of getting his alibi witnesses to Springfield for the trial, which began on March 18. The jury, after receiving the case, remained out for quite a while, which Renard and his attorneys saw as a good sign. During the deliberations, Ray called Colbeck and updated him on the trial's progress.

"It looks all right for me!" he told the gang boss.

Dint deadpanned, "Is that so?"

Ray was flabbergasted. "What's the matter with you, are ya sick?" he asked.

Colbeck again replied in that flat voice, "Nothing's the matter with me."

Renard hung up the phone, convinced that it was only a matter of time before he would end up like Eddie Linehan and countless others.

Luck was with Renard as the trial ended in a hung jury and the government decided it didn't have enough evidence to mount a retrial. If Colbeck and the Rats had been counting on Renard drawing a lengthy prison sentence that would take him out of circulation, it now seemed they would have to get rid of him the easy way.

After beating the robbery rap, Renard returned to the Maxwelton Club, where everyone avoided him like the plague. He tried to talk to Oliver Dougherty, but Ol, who was still worried about being indicted himself, just barked at him to stop talking about the case. Dint Colbeck soon showed up, and he and Renard talked, the latter complaining about his remaining legal troubles, particularly that his bond on the interstate theft case was due to expire in early April.

Colbeck promised to help, and Renard, wanting to believe him in a last gasp of loyalty, reached to shake Dint's hand. Colbeck raised his hand and pointed his index finger at the dapper car thief. Renard understood this to be the sign of death, sort of the Egan's Rats version of the Mafia's "kiss of death."

Sitting down alone, Renard drew his pistol, placed it on the table, and ordered and sipped another drink as he considered his options. Out of the blue, Ray's wife showed up at the club and sat down with him. Fully aware of his troubles, she told him that she had decided to face the music with him. Eventually, Renard talked his wife into leaving, and he remained at the table, tense and very mindful of the recent fate of Eddie Linehan.

Colbeck walked back over to the table, and Renard instinctively reached for his gun. Dint asked, "What's wrong?"

"What do you mean by giving the finger?"

Dint laughed, "Can't you take a joke?"

"Not that kind."

"Well, I was just kidding. Listen, Ray, forget that stuff. Do you know the way out to Lake Hill?"

"Sure I do."

"Will you go out there with me tomorrow?"

"What for?"

"I want to look at some property. … I want to know what you think of it."

Since Ray had sold his car, Colbeck suggested they take his vehicle, or better yet, have Red Smith drive him. "Red knows the way out there," Dint told him. "Why don't you take him?"

Renard nodded and agreed to meet Colbeck the next afternoon at Lake Hill. He knew full well that something was amiss, as

Dint never involved Renard in his personal business. The worried gangster realized that if he ever got into a car with Red Smith, he'd never get out of it alive.

Returning home, Renard's troubled mind raced as he considered his options: He could either go to Lake Hill or run. Ray chose the latter, and he and his wife hastily packed their bags. At Union Station, they boarded a train for Chicago, changed trains there for Los Angeles, and upon arriving in California, took a bus to Tijuana, Mexico. Having forfeited his bond in the interstate theft case, Renard was automatically slapped with a seven-year sentence, to be served at Leavenworth.

Back in St. Louis, the government turned up the heat of the Egan's Rats on April 8, when it returned six indictments against gang members for the downtown mail robbery a year earlier. Steve Ryan, Red Smith, Chippy Robinson, and Gus Dietmeyer were arrested. Also named in the indictments were the absent Ray Renard and Cotton Epplesheimer, who tried to run but eventually was caught.

Since Renard had jumped his bond, the Egan gangsters had trouble making bail since no bondsmen wanted to post for them. This infuriated Dint Colbeck, who responded by offering a $3,000 bounty for Ray Renard, dead or alive. The gang boss sought Senator Mike Kinney's help in raising money for the hoods' bonds, and at first Kinney refused, which strained their relationship. Kinney finally acquiesced and posted bonds of $60,000 each for Robinson, Ryan, and Smith. Dietmeyer and Epplesheimer remained incarcerated.

In order to pay his crew's mounting legal costs, Colbeck led some of the lesser-known gang members on a raid of the Granite City National Bank on the morning of April 25. The Rats netted $63,000 in cash from the payroll of the Granite City Steel Works.

While all this was going on, Colbeck briefly was confronted with a challenge from the Italians. Vito Giannola had finally prevailed over Dominick Giambrone and was seeking to gain a foothold in the local bootlegging scene. Colbeck made it clear to Giannola that he would be the sorriest sonofabitch in the world if he tried to infringe on the Rats' territory in the city or in St. Louis County. The Green Ones opted to set up their stills across the river in Madison County, Illinois.

In his twenty-five years, Ray Renard had gone from petty thievery (to help his mother) to burglary, grand theft auto, and armed robbery, and he'd joined the toughest gang in St. Louis, which was now hunting him. To someone who had spent his whole life in the Midwest, Tijuana seemed like another planet to Renard; the weather, language, food, and atmosphere had a big effect on his emotions. He had no desire to leave and had obtained a low-risk job as a gambling house guard. Ray liked nothing more than to nosh on carnitas, take in a dog race, and watch the sun set over the Pacific with his wife.

At heart, however, he was still a gangster. So when word reached the border town in early May that Dint Colbeck had put a bounty on him, Renard became enraged and decided to return to Missouri to confront his former pals.

Just after arriving in St. Louis, Renard was at his sister-in-law's flat on North Thirteenth Street, attempting to sleep in the bedroom. Mindful of the fate of Little Red Powers, he had a pistol just inches from his hands. As he drifted in a state of semi-sleep, he heard a strange noise. Grabbing his gat and sitting up, he saw Oliver Dougherty creeping toward him in the darkened bedroom.

"Stick 'em up, Oliver!" he growled, "and keep 'em up. No monkey business, or I'll kill you!"

Ol shrugged. "Aw, Ray, you've got me wrong," he said, as if he hadn't been pushing Dint Colbeck to execute Renard for the last few months.

Some profane badgering ensued, and Dougherty finally said, "You've got us all wrong."

"No, I haven't!" Renard shot back.

"Yes, you have! You've got the mob thinking you've done a lot of talking."

Dougherty tried to calm Renard by pretending that he had no intention of harming him. Ray lowered his gun and declared that he was ready to surrender and accept a seven-year sentence for freight robbery. Ol asked him to call Colbeck and tell him that, then walked out of the room. Renard peered out of the bedroom window and saw carloads of gangsters pull up outside the flat. Dougherty went out and talked with them.

Walking back inside, Oliver said, "Dint wants you to call him. He's waiting."

Both men knew there was no telephone in the flat and that Renard would have to leave the building if he was to make the call. Ray barked for Oliver to go outside and wait, then slipped out the back door, climbed up to the neighbors' flat, and used their phone to call Colbeck.

"You did a bum trick by leaving!" Dint scolded when he took Ray's call.

"It would have been a bum trick to take me out riding and kill me, wouldn't it?" Renard replied.

"You've got me wrong."

"Well, why did you put in the paper that you would pay $3,000 for me?"

"We had that seven years fixed for you, so you wouldn't have to serve. And then you ran off," Colbeck chided.

"Yes, to keep you from killing me."

"Well, what are you going to do now?"

"I'm ready to turn myself in. Maybe you'd like to send some of your friends in the cops after me."

Afterward, Renard ran down to tell Dougherty of his conversation with the gang boss. Oliver told him not to worry, that he was going to stick up a messenger across the river the next day and he'd make sure his commissary had plenty of cash. The next morning, Ray Renard surrendered to federal authorities and was promptly sent to Leavenworth Federal Penitentiary.

Since succeeding his brother in the General Assembly more than a decade earlier, forty-nine year-old Mike Kinney was now one of Missouri's most powerful state senators, representing the Thirty-first District (St. Louis). A successful legislator, Kinney was by nature quiet and reserved, more like his brother-in-law Willie Egan than his own sibling Thomas. He was temperate in his personal habits; he never drank, smoked, cursed, and rarely even raised his voice. Kinney preferred to dabble in real estate rather than saloons and gangsterism.

With the Egan's Rats increasingly running amok, and with the Justice Department turning up the heat in its investigation of the

Jack Daniel's milking scheme, Kinney sought to put some distance between himself and the gang. Relations between the state senator and Dint Colbeck were frosty because of Kinney's reluctance to post bail for the mail robbers. And when he saw the feds were loaded for bear as they closed in on the Rats, he tried to avoid Colbeck altogether.

Because of his elected position, Kinney maintained a home in St. Louis, but he actually resided with his wife and daughter in Oakland, catching a commuter train into the city each morning. At eight o'clock on the unseasonably cool morning of June 3, 1924, Kinney was waiting at the Missouri Pacific station on Sappington Road. Witnesses said he seemed agitated and was continually pacing. As a brand-new Essex sedan passed by the station heading north, a young man dressed in overalls jumped out and dashed toward the senator, firing a pistol. Kinney was hit four times: in the jaw, in the chest and once in each arm. Collapsing to the ground, he passed out as the man jumped back into the Essex and was driven away.

The media thunderously reported the news of the attempted assassination. When Kinney's condition stabilized, he said he didn't know who had shot him. His main political rival, Edward "Jelly Roll" Hogan, quickly issued a statement proclaiming his innocence. Looking through a mug-shot book, Kinney fingered a twenty-six-year-old escaped mental patient named Hammie Shane as his assailant. A statewide alert was issued, and Shane was soon discovered in Hayti, Missouri, where he had been hiding since before the shooting. Rumors circulated that the attack was gang-related, but Kinney, who would fully recover from his wounds, steadfastly refused to comment on his brush with death.

It was never determined who was responsible for the attempt on Kinney's life. Many thought the shooter may have been a "lone nut," but there was at least one other person in the car, which would seem to indicate a conspiracy of some kind.

Ironically, no suspicion was ever seriously cast on Dint Colbeck or the Egans. Mike Kinney was no longer of any use to them after the bail dust-up, and notably, Kinney gave no further assistance to the Egan's Rats after the shooting, ending thirty-five years of collusion between the Kinney family and the gang that still bore the Egan name. Could Colbeck, furious over the senator's indifference to their plight, have requested a meeting with his former benefactor and then sent a pistol-packing killer in his place? Perhaps, but the truth likely will remain elusive forever.

Rotting in his Leavenworth prison cell, Ray Renard smoldered. Gone were his fat bankroll, fancy suits and cars, bottles of cologne, gorgeous showgirls—all the glitz of the gangster lifestyle had been replaced by a gray uniform and a number. The Egans had given him $100 and sent him off to prison, and Renard had received a couple of letters from Oliver Dougherty but nothing from any of the others.

As summer progressed, he continued to brood. Dreaming of his wife and the life they could have had in Mexico, Ray's brooding evolved into anger. After all the work he had put in with the Egan's Rats, all that he had endured, all the people he had seen murdered for trivial reasons, he had kept his mouth shut. And when he stayed with the gang after the Linehan slaying, they ended up tossing him away like a piece of garbage.

Sometime in July, Renard sent a detailed, multi-page letter to St. Louis-based federal prosecutor Horace L. Dyer. Shortly afterward, he was transferred to Atlanta Federal Penitentiary and placed in protective custody. Federal agents continued to debrief him, and as time passed, it looked as if Renard would have his vengeance, one way or the other.

The last indictments against the Egans Rats stemming from the downtown mail robbery came down on August 13, 1924. Dint Colbeck was taken into custody, just after his re-election to the Democratic City Committee. Also arrested was a blind attorney and bondsman named Walter A. Kelly, who was charged with helping to dispose of the stolen bonds. As a mere formality, two deceased Rats were also listed in the indictment, Harry Londo and James "Sticky" Hennessey.

For the first time, the extent of the government's sixteen-month investigation was revealed. A five-man task force of four postal inspectors and a notoriously tough city detective named

Downfall

John Carroll was responsible for collecting the incriminating evidence. The earlier convictions of William "Whitey" Doering and David Weisman were just the icing on the cake.

The Egans knew the feds had talked to Ray Renard, but they didn't think their former pal would have the guts to face them in court. The Rats were worse off than they could have imagined, for Renard had laid both the downtown mail robbery and the Staunton heist on the gang's doorstep (the authorities had been in the dark about the latter robbery until now). The Egan crew was set to stand trial first for the downtown heist and then for the Staunton job.

In the weeks preceding the first trial, the boys didn't bother to keep a low profile. Needing cash to pay their ever-mounting legal fees, the Rats robbed the Wellston Trust Company at 6212 Easton Avenue once again on September 19. The take was around $40,000 in cash.

The defendants in the downtown mail robbery caper were Dint Colbeck, Chippy Robinson, Steve Ryan, Oliver Dougherty, Red Smith, Leo Cronin, Rudolph "Featheredge" Schmidt, Max Simonson, Cuckoo Gang boss Roy Tipton, and attorney Walter Kelly. The trial began on Thursday morning, October 30. All the Rats were dressed impeccably, but Robinson got off on the wrong foot by showing up late for court. The government presented its case, calling witnesses who placed the gangsters on Locust Avenue on the morning of the heist and detailed how Simonson and Kelly had been the main fences for the bonds. The feds were saving their big bombshell for last.

Shortly after 9 a.m. on November 1, the courtroom in the Federal Building in St. Louis was cleared and steel shutters were closed over the windows to prevent any possible snipers from firing into the room. Armed guards roamed the hallways and surrounded twenty-five-year-old Raymond Renard as he walked briskly into the courtroom, setting off waves of murmuring among the large crowd inside the courtroom.

Now the rumors had been confirmed: Renard was indeed the government's star witness. Neatly dressed in a dark-blue suit, white shirt, and tan shoes, Renard sat down. Visibly nervous, he furiously chewed a wad of gum and squirmed in his seat as the defendants glared at him.

Renard began by telling the court how he happened to join the Egan's Rats, how he was assigned to dispose of the Cadillac used in the robbery, and how he had seen the defendants with the bonds the next day. The many weapons seized at the Maxwelton were displayed for the jury, just to remind them that they were dealing with violent gangsters. One of the armaments, the personal property of Dint Colbeck, was a mean-looking Army-issue Browning automatic rifle (BAR.) Ray eventually relaxed and was actually smiling as he wound up his testimony.

The defense team hammered away the best they could, painting Renard as untrustworthy, devious, and hinting that he, along with others, had pulled the job and was now trying to pin the blame on the innocent Egans. Renard declared, "I could tell this story five years from now, or twenty-five years from now, just as I have told it here."

Defense attorney Patrick Cullen snapped at the witness, "You have never worked a day in your life, have you?" Renard retorted, "That's wrong. I have worked! I'm no angel but intend to live an honest life after I do my seven years in Atlanta. I'm man enough to take my medicine."

The case went to the jury on November 3, and after three days of deliberation, they announced they were unable to reach a verdict. Judge Faris scheduled a retrial for January 13, and the gangsters were released on bond pending their trial for the Staunton heist.

That trial began the next week under heavy security in Quincy, Illinois. The defendants were Colbeck, Robinson, Ryan, Dougherty, Smith, Red Lanham, Cotton Epplesheimer, Gus Dietmeyer, and Frank Hackethal. Star witness Ray Renard and another witness, Thomas Saatkamp, were placed under elaborate guard at local hotels. Renard told what he knew about who had participated in the raid and how Colbeck was the gang's boss. Defense counsel's attempts to paint Renard as an incompetent witness because he was a convicted felon failed to hold water. Colbeck and Steve Ryan were the only defendants to take the stand; both claimed not to know anything about the robbery and to barely know Ray Renard at all.

Dint and the boys couldn't have held any illusions about how long the odds were or how things would turn out. Basically, it boiled down to which scumbag the jury believed.

At 10:30 a.m. on Saturday, November 15, the jury returned from twenty-three hours of deliberation and ripped out the heart of the gang that had terrorized St. Louis for more than thirty years. All nine members of the Egan's Rats were found guilty on all counts. For robbing the U.S. Mail, a mandatory sentence of twenty-five years was pronounced, and the judge decreed that the men were to be incarcerated immediately.

Judge Fitzhenry declared, "This crime is one of the most dastardly I've ever known of, except, of course, crimes involving human slaughter. Fortunately, there was none of that in this offense. These defendants are entitled to get all the law provides."

All the men stood and stated that they accepted the verdict. Only three-time loser Oliver Dougherty showed any emotion, his voice cracking slightly as he spoke. As the gangsters were shackled and led from the courtroom, they reasserted themselves, smiling and cracking wise for reporters as they left.

Colbeck, grinning, his derby pushed back on his head, was asked if he thought he had gotten a fair trial. He replied, "You heard what I just said in the courtroom when the judge asked me if I had anything to say. I told him, 'No, sir,' that we had a fair trial, and if the jury saw fit to convict, there's nothing we could do.

"Anyhow, I've been in tight places before. I went 'over the top' in France, and I didn't cry then and I won't cry now."

Steve Ryan and Cotton Epplesheimer waved and winked at reporters, but the others were stoic as they climbed into a police truck. At 12:53 the next morning, ten hours after the verdict was read, a Kansas-bound train pulled into Quincy, Illinois, and the nine convicted Rats were led to a car that had been specifically added for their transport. Their old lives were suddenly dead and buried as they were bundled off to spend the next quarter-century in Leavenworth. The end that had been approaching all year for the Egans was finally upon them.

In the face of all this, the gangsters remained in good spirits as they boarded the train. Dint Colbeck was relentlessly cocky

and cheerful, and the boys followed his example, faithful sub-
jects to the end. When Red Lanham began cursing about Judge
Fitzhenry, Dint admonished, "Quit beefing, Red. We've got it in
the neck, and we'd be poor sports to holler. We've got to take
things just as they come."

Lanham perked up, "Where's that bench-legged guy? Is he on
the train?" Oliver Dougherty had been referred to by a witness in
the trial as a "bench-legged man." Ol piped up with a sarcastic
squint, "Yes, the bench-legged guy's on the train. He'll be the
humpbacked guy before the next twenty-five years are up!"

The same witness had called Cotton Epplesheimer the
"peaked-faced man," and Cotton quipped to his fellow prisoners,
"Yes, and that peaked face will be filled too!" Colbeck and Lanham were handcuffed together and shared a seat; such was the
case for Robinson and Hackethal, Dougherty and Dietmeyer, and
Smith and Ryan. Epplesheimer sat alone. After the conductor
collected their tickets, he flashed his pass and said, "All the way!"
Chippy Robinson pulled out an address book with his free hand
and, showing a blank page, said with a smirk, "All the way!"

The train proceeded west into Missouri, rolling over rivers
and through forests, fields, and sleeping towns. In the dimly lit
car, the men chatted into the night, sipping coffee and munching
sandwiches before gradually drifting off to sleep. As the sun
brightened the bleak Kansas landscape, only Colbeck and Lanham were still awake. When the gray, looming structure of Leavenworth Federal Penitentiary appeared on the horizon, the men
became tense and grim. Lanham began quietly muttering about
how he had been framed. Cotton Epplesheimer wordlessly
stared out the window.

Entering the prison grounds, the train coasted to a stop, just
as the Sunday church service was letting out. Notes from the
church organ floated eerily in the morning chill, and towers containing guards armed with rifles loomed above the new arrivals,
creating a sense of claustrophobia among the Egan crew. The
inmates emerging from the church glanced furtively to see who
was arriving.

Dint Colbeck talked gravely to one of the reporters who had
ridden the train to cover the gang's incarceration, but he didn't
hesitate or display any nervousness. His shoulders were still

squared, his military bearing carrying over into his new life. Red Lanham wordlessly surveyed the surroundings, and Red Smith's face remained as blank and grim as ever. Chippy Robinson still sported his unsettling smirk.

Dint Colbeck, left, and eight other members of the Egan's Rats were sentenced to twenty-five year terms at Leavenworth Federal Penitentiary on the testimony of their former pal Ray Renard, right.

The men were lined up as one of the main trusties, Chicago labor leader "Big Tim" Murphy, passed by. They were then unshackled and led into the main cell house, stripped to the buff, examined both inside and out, and issued blue denim overalls and jumpers. A total of $2,400 cash was taken from the men and deposited in their commissaries. As Warden William Biddle lectured the new arrivals on the prison's rules, tears welled up in Steve Ryan's eyes, but he quickly brushed them away.

An hour later, as the train was preparing to depart, the Egans were sighted again, dressed in their blue uniforms and walking in the main yard. Colbeck was on point, striding briskly and erect, the leader to the end. Lanham trailed him, his head down. The others followed, and Robinson, bringing up the rear, grinned one last time at the reporters looking out the train windows.

The men were assigned cells in D Block, the most secure cellblock in the prison. Colbeck and Smith were in D116, Dietmeyer and Robinson in D134, and Dougherty and Ryan in D303. Colbeck was put to work in the tin shop, an assignment that came closest to utilizing the skills he had acquired in his plumbing career. Ryan went to the stone shop, where he spent much of his time breaking and shaping rocks with a hammer and chisel. Dietmeyer and Robinson were assigned to the kitchen, Lanham to the laundry, Dougherty to the tailor shop, Epplesheimer to the steel shop, and Smith and Hackethal to the boiler shop. The boys settled into their new lives and even claimed as their own a portion of the prison yard adjacent to the power house, nicknaming the spot "Grand and Olive" after a familiar St. Louis street corner.

The boys were returned to St. Louis in January 1925 for their retrial on the downtown mail robbery. All of them looked good and seemed unruffled by prison life, except for Red Lanham, who already possessed what cons and war veterans called "the thousand-yard stare."

All of them were found guilty and sentenced to seven years, to run concurrently with the time they were already serving. At 9:45 on the night of January 19, the nine Rats boarded a Leavenworth-bound train at Union Station, leaving St. Louis for the last time. As they boarded, Mabel Robinson, Chippy's wife, who once put a bullet in his leg when she caught him cheating on her, broke through the crowd of police and grabbed her husband, as if she could physically stop him from leaving. Tears rolled down Chippy's face as he hugged Mabel, and then he motioned for police to take her away.

Their convictions for the Staunton heist finished the Egan's Rats as a major organized crime power in St. Louis. A handful of the gang's members still remained, but they had scattered like cockroaches exposed to bright light. Many were still wanted for the Pocahontas mail robbery. Eddie Leonard and Bartley Martin soon surrendered for their part in the job and ended up with their pals at Leavenworth.

The Egan crew from Wellston went right back to work, however. Two nights after the final verdict was handed down, they attempted to rob the Eagle Park roadhouse between East St. Louis and Venice, Illinois. Watchman Melvin Norvell and his girlfriend Pearl Ridge opened fire on the thugs. Norvell and robber Hollis Byram were killed, and three others were wounded. It was later discovered that the proprietors, John and Catherine Gray, were protected by the Cuckoo Gang, which got word to the upstart Egans to stay out the East Side.

Just three weeks after the Staunton convictions, "Cocky" Walsh and Louis Mulconry robbed a Mazda Lamp Works messenger of an $11,000 payroll. The police were all too familiar with this type of heist, and less than two hours later, the cops found Walsh and Mulconry at the Maxwelton Club chuckling over their score.

Lee Turner, Barney Castle, and Bill Engler were federal fugitives. Castle had run all the way to Los Angeles and formed a small crew of his own. Their first job was a disaster, with Barney being shot to death while trying to rob a postmaster of a $150,000 payroll in El Segundo on April 3, 1925. Engler and Turner eventually would join the rest of the group at Leavenworth.

By the summer of 1925, the Egan's Rats were mostly a distant memory, but the Wellston crew was still wreaking havoc, pulling stickups and assaulting people with furious abandon. With the Maxwelton Club closed, they retreated to their haunts around Bartmer Avenue in St. Louis, a rough stretch of bars and pool halls known as "Hell's Half-Acre." With Lester Barth in prison for robbery, Dewey Goebel attempted to assert himself over the wild young hoods, who seemed more concerned with drinking, senseless robberies, and basking in the fame of the former Egan mob. One of them, Don Hoffman, reportedly boasted that the Wellston gang would take over the town and make everyone forget about the Egan's Rats.

Their final job took place in the early morning hours of October 5, 1925. Two carloads of gangsters showed up at a roadhouse on Upper Creve Coeur Lake owned by James Quin. A rugged ex-Navy man, Quin was not someone to be intimidated, and he yanked out a .38 revolver and a .45 automatic and shot it out with the robbers and chased them out to their cars. Vincent Goedde and Don Hoffman were riddled with bullets and fell dead as they reached their Ford coupe. Quickly reloading his .45, Quin pumped the whole clip into the driver, eighteen-year-old James Tully. The other car sped off into the night.

Quin was not charged; indeed, police marveled at his marksmanship. Running in the darkness over uneven ground, Quin had managed to inflict seventeen wounds with just twenty-one shots.

Whatever was left of the Egan gang evaporated after this episode, and Dewey Goebel embarked on a new career as a freelance hit man and armed robber.

After the trials, Ray Renard returned to Atlanta to finish his seven-year sentence. In early 1925, Renard had begun a series of lengthy interviews with newsmen from the *St. Louis Star*, telling the complete story of his life as one of the Egan's Rats, laying bare his soul as well as the inner workings of the gang. The series ran daily for almost a month, as thousands of readers in St. Louis scooped up copies of the *Star* to read Renard's confession.

In March, after the series was finished, Dint Colbeck was interviewed at Leavenworth but refused to comment on Renard's stories. He asked the reporter to say hello to his friends in St. Louis, as did a noticeably spacey Chippy Robinson. Then the men went back to work, Chippy peeling the potatoes, Dint fixing leaky pipes, Steve breaking rocks, Red shoveling coal, Ol mending pants ... and so things went.

The Egan's Rats, a gang that had existed in some form or another since the early 1890s, had finally passed out of existence, the victim of changing times, greed, violence, and carelessness. The Rats might well have passed from the nation's consciousness forever—and been totally ignored by modern-day crime historians—except for one man ... the man who got away.

THE MAN WHO
GOT AWAY

THE INDUSTRIOUS FRED Burke had traveled to Detroit in late 1923, joining with former Egan's Rat Johnny Reid, who ran a speakeasy there at Third and Peterboro. This bar became Burke's headquarters while he was in town. Joining him were Gus Winkler, Izzy Londe, Milford Jones, Bob Carey, and Ray Nugent. Through Reid, Burke and the boys met members of the local mob, a group of Jewish hoodlums from the North End known as the Purple Gang.

Reid was one of the Purples' top liquor distributors, keeping speakeasies around the city stocked with the gang's booze. Despite their friendship with Reid, the Burke crew had little interest in bootlegging, maintaining the Egan gang penchant for the fast, easy buck. A popular rendezvous for the boys was a gambling joint owned by former Egan rival John J. "Baldy" Ryan at 21 East Elizabeth Street. Ryan's place served as a sort of way station for any ex-St. Louis crook who happened to be in Detroit.

Their first notable caper took place March 10, 1924, when four of the hoods stalked into the Book Building in downtown Detroit and held up John Kay's jewelry store. Brandishing .45

automatics, they demanded that Kay open the safe. Kay coolly stalled, and the frustrated gunman finally bound and gagged the old man and left, making off with a mere $7,000 worth of jewels from the showcase. The wily jeweler's bluff had worked—the safe contained nearly fourteen times that amount of loot.

The crew might have gotten away clean, but two nights later a drunken Fred Burke caused a scene in a restaurant at Joseph Campau and Sherwood streets. Police responding to the disturbance pulled up in time to see Burke stagger to his car and attempt to drive away. They quickly overtook the blitzed gunman and locked him in the Chene Street Station drunk tank. The cops found almost all of the jewels in the automobile's **side** pockets. Burke was immediately sent back to prison for a parole violation.

A short time later, Izzy Londe, Bob Carey, and a hanger-on named James Callahan were also in custody. Burke and Londe went to trial, but the latter was only robber the jeweler could identify, which resulted in a ten- to twenty-year sentence for Izzy in Marquette Prison, a forlorn bastion in Michigan's Upper Peninsula. Humbled by Londe's fate, Carey made a point to bombard John Kay with threatening phone calls whenever he was in Detroit, just to make sure the old jeweler wasn't thinking about eventually fingering him.

On October 22, Burke walked out of Jackson Prison right into the arms of St. Louis detectives, who were lying in wait to bust him for the United Railways robbery of July 1923, which informant Ray Renard had laid at his door. Soon after making bail, Burke returned to Michigan and went back to work.

Fred Burke and his men didn't limit themselves to Detroit. Indeed, they were just as comfortable in St. Louis, Chicago, Toledo, St. Paul, Kansas City, or Cincinnati. Burke became known for his cleverness in planning crimes; his use of police uniforms to fool victims was a prime example. Also known for his diverse weaponry, Fred pioneered the use of bulletproof vests by criminals and soon was packing a Thompson submachine gun, a weapon with which he would become noted as an expert marksman.

Their main line of work in Detroit was known as the "snatch racket," kidnapping wealthy businessmen and gamblers, collecting a large ransom, then driving the victims across the state line, usually to Toledo, Ohio, and cutting them loose. Burke had made a science of the racket, perfecting it to the extent that gamblers throughout Detroit lived in fear of what was known as the "St. Louis Gang." Some of the crew's more notorious victims were noted gamblers Lefty Clark, Danny Sullivan, Ruby Mathias, Lincoln Fitzgerald, Dutch Weinbrenner, and Charles "Doc" Brady.

Also joining Burke in Detroit was Charles "Tennessee Slim" Hurley, a St. Louis crook and associate of Johnny Reid. John "Pudgy" Dunn, the hulking former Egan gunman who had sworn to avenge his brother Cherries, joined the crew as well. Of course, only Burke, Carey, and Reid even vaguely remembered Dunn, and the intervening years had made him much more brutal and ruthless—and just as trigger-happy as his brother had been.

Pudgy Dunn proved as much one night in January 1924 when he offed William Riley, his safecracking partner, whom he accused of ratting him out as the killer of Robert Koch back in 1914. While out on bail a year later, after a mistrial in the Riley case, he would go out drinking with the boys and nearly kill Tennessee Slim Hurley in a fight. Dunn ultimately would be convicted of manslaughter in death of Riley and would draw a ten-year sentence.

On January 10, 1925, just a couple of days after Tennessee Slim was shot, the Purple Gang and the former Rats pulled one of their first recorded jobs together when they attempted to rob a gambling den at 2439 Milwaukee Avenue. The joint was run by thirty-year-old Raymond Bishop, a former stick man for Lefty Clark who had recently opened up his own operation. Joe Bernstein, leader of the Purple Gang, had recommended the place for the heist and was on the premises at 3 a.m.

The gambling den had closed for the night when three men entered through a second-story skylight and hid in the bathroom until the owner retired to his office to count the night's take. Bernstein had told them not to expect any resistance, so the hoods were surprised when Bishop opened fire with a .45. A close-quarters gun battle ensued, and when the smoke cleared, Ray Bishop and one of the robbers, Arthur Wilson, lay dying. The other crooks fled the scene, one of them jumping out of the second-story window in his panic. Bernstein and a handful of other gamblers remained behind to explain to police what had happened.

Fred Burke was picked up in a sweep after the Hurley shooting and charged with jumping his bail in the United Railways case. Identified by multiple witnesses as the unmasked robber, Burke, in true Egan style, plotted a caper to help pay his legal fees. He and three others made off with nearly $30,000 from the Farmers National Bank in Louisville, Kentucky, on April 2, but not before shooting a teller who tried to play tough. All four men— Burke, Pascal and Paul Morina, and Larry Dougherty, younger brother of the imprisoned Oliver—eventually were identified by witnesses. The latter three were convicted and promptly sent to Leavenworth, where they reunited with other members of the Egan's Rats.

Due to stand trial for the UR caper, Burke got into more trouble when he, Gus Winkler, and Milford Jones were chased through downtown St. Louis as suspicious characters on June 5, 1925. The men tossed their pistols out of the window of their car, while police fired about a dozen bullets at them before they crashed into a telephone pole at Main and Clark streets. A bullet had passed through the left shoulder pad of Burke's suit. The cops found three different jackets and straw hats inside the car, as well as a leather pouch that contained what was described as a "submachine gun" (actually a 7.63mm Mauser C96 broomhandle automatic pistol).

Police believed the men were waiting either to rob or kill someone, and the three were hit with concealed-weapons charges. Winkler was sent back to serve nine months in the city workhouse for felonious operation of a motor vehicle, stemming from a previous heist when he hit and seriously injured a little girl during the hectic getaway.

Seven hundred miles away, at Marquette Prison in Michigan's Upper Peninsula, Izzy Londe had no intention of serving out his full sentence and concocted and escape plan. Somehow, the ex-Rat had arranged for four pistols to be smuggled inside, and on June 29, 1925, he made his bid for freedom. Using a guard as a shield, Londe and three other convicts scaled the wall. After trading shots with other guards, the four men escaped into the surrounding forest, leaving their hostage behind. But as lawmen and volunteers began combing the forests and roads looking for the escapees, it became apparent that Izzy hadn't quite thought things through.

On foot in an unfamiliar, tangled wilderness, the cons headed on a roughly southwestern course for the Wisconsin border. After stealing a small car, they were confronted by a roadblock near the village of Sagola just after midnight on July 4. After failing to punch through the line of squad cars, a furious gun battle erupted. Izzy Londe's lungs were punctured by a shotgun blast, and Eddie Weisman and Joe DeFlorio also were seriously wounded. Vance Hardy was the only escapee to elude the searchers, staggering into the pitch-black woods and disappearing for the next few months. Eventually, all four would end up right back at Marquette. What role, if any, that Fred Burke and his pals may have played in the escape attempt is unknown.

Despite considerable evidence pointing to his guilt, on November 12, Burke was acquitted of all charges in the UR robbery. The presiding circuit judge was beside himself, saying it was an "insult to intelligence" that the jury had not found Burke guilty. The exasperated jurist described the jury as "incompetent," and as for Burke himself: "I have no more respect for this defendant than I do a human rat."

When Gus Winkler got out of the workhouse, he promptly rejoined his friends, and together they robbed the North St. Louis Trust Company at 3500 North Grand Boulevard on the morning of May 18, 1926, getting $30,000 in cash for their efforts. One of the crew kept the customers at bay with a sawed-off shotgun while his partners emptied the teller cages, yelling and cursing at the frighten employees until they obeyed every command. The suspects, in addition to Winkler, were Burke, Bob Carey, Ray Nugent, Milford Jones, and former Egan gangster Louis Mulconry.

The men remained in and around St. Louis until the beginning of August, when they were summoned to Detroit by bar owner Johnny Reid, who had been targeted for extortion by Sicilian mobster Mike Dipisa.

A hijacker and confessed killer, Dipisa had a bad reputation in Detroit's underworld, stemming mainly from an embarrassing incident in which he had tried to stick up a Purple Gang-connected bookmaker and was targeted for retaliation by the Purples (Dipisa returned the bookmaker's jewels). Seeking to bolster his rep, Dipisa moved against Johnny Reid only because Burke and company had dropped out of sight.

Trouble started in early August 1926, when Clarence "Bud" Gilboe and his friend Paul Clark entered Reid's saloon and demanded a cut of his profits, using Mike Dipisa's name. The former Egan gangster responded by jerking a hidden revolver and opening fire on the two extortionists. Tennessee Slim Hurley (who actually hailed from Virginia) also was in the bar and shot at the startled hoods as they dashed outside. One of the bullets grazed an innocent barfly who had his beak in a mug of beer when the fireworks began.

The incident wasn't reported to the police, but Reid knew who was responsible, being quite familiar with the Purple Gang incident. After getting his place cleaned up, he immediately got on the phone—and within a day, Fred Burke and his partners were on their way back to Detroit.

Mike Dipisa was out in front of a "blind pig" (speakeasy), on Hunt Street late in the evening of August 10. A few hours earlier, two men had shown up at a pig Dipisa ran at 72 Winder Street, talking mean and asking for him. As he stood talking to a group of people in front of the Hunt Street joint, a car containing three men cruised by and opened fire. The shots went wide, and Dipisa quickly rounded up two of his henchmen, Phillip Cusmano and Joseph Marino. "Come on!" he told them. "Someone just took a shot at me, and I think I know where to find them!"

Driving directly to Third and Peterboro, the three found Johnny Reid's place dark and empty. Puzzled, they cruised the city streets for hours, looking for any sign of Reid or his sidekick, Tennessee Slim. Dipisa was driving, while Cusmano and Marino sat armed and ready.

At 2:40 a.m., the three found themselves downtown. Turning north on Broadway, they were startled to see a large sedan appear out of nowhere and pull alongside. The car was bristling with the ex-Egan's Rats, and Johnny Reid himself was behind the wheel. They opened fire on Dipisa's car with pistols. Dipisa ducked down, as did Cusmano and Marino, who barely managed to return fire since neither dared expose any part of himself to the hail of bullets. The cars raced up Broadway toward Grand Circus Park, trading shots not more than ten feet apart. Amazingly, no one was injured.

Making a screeching turn east on Madison, Dipisa eventually outdistanced his assailants, although his car looked like a sieve. Two foot patrolmen had seen the gun battle, and they commandeered a passing taxicab to search for the combatants. They spotted Dipisa's bullet-ridden roadster and chased him to Woodward and Elizabeth, where they took him and his two goons into custody. The boys smartly had ditched their pistols before being arrested, and by noon, Dipisa was free on a writ of *habeas corpus.*

Johnny Reid was frustrated that he and the other ex-Rats had missed their opportunity to kill Mike Dipisa. Reid and his pals decided to raid the restaurant of Papa Leo Giorlando at 2968 Brush Street, one of their quarry's favorite roosts. Reid, Tennessee Slim Hurley, Fred Burke, Milford Jones, and Bob Carey all downed glasses of whiskey in Johnny's saloon, loaded their pistols and headed for Giorlando's place.

The restaurant was located in the basement, and at 1 a.m. on August 12, just twenty-two hours after the Broadway shootout, the five hoods approached the entrance. Several people were eating and drinking as Reid and Burke stepped through the doorway, followed by Hurley, Carey, and Jones.

Pulling their pistols and opening fire, Reid and his buddies made Papa Leo's seem like a saloon in a Hollywood western. A blizzard of .38- and .45-caliber bullets swept the dining room, shattering glasses and plates on tables, bottles of booze behind the bar, and peppering the door leading to the kitchen. Joseph Guastella, part-owner of the café, and chef Cesare Genovese were cut down by the fusillade, and waitress Marion LeBeis was wounded in the leg and fell under a table. A half-dozen bullets struck a grifter named Louis Ross, who would survive. Car thief Mariano Milito was wounded in the left thigh. Papa Leo Giorlando managed to bob and weave his way through the hail of bullets, crashed through the rear door, and lumbered off into the night. The five shooters dashed back to their car and roared off into the night.

Police raided underworld haunts in force in the wake of the two very public shootings. Dipisa himself was very rattled and laid low in his East Side hideout. On the afternoon of August 13, two carloads of gangsters traded shots on Brush Street, less than a block from Papa Leo's. Two associates of Burke were arrested, giving their names as John Shearer and Joe Puffer.

Mike Dipisa had had enough. At a meeting with plucky saloonkeeper Johnny Reid, he explained that the two extortionists, Bud Gilboe and Paul Clark, had used his name without his knowledge and that he did not send them. Reid, enjoying watching the popcorn gangster squirm, agreed to peace, but only if the two extortionists were turned over to him. Dipisa readily acquiesced. Gilboe and Clark soon were lured to a meeting with Reid, abducted, driven into what is now Lathrup Village, Michigan, and pumped full of holes.

Having neutralized Mike Dipisa within two weeks, Gus Winkler and Milford Jones returned to St. Louis, where their old pals in the Cuckoo Gang were facing problems with Sicilian mobsters similar to those Johnny Reid had encountered in Detroit. The Cuckoos decided to go on the offensive against the Vito Giannola-led Green Ones.

On the night of September 23, the Cuckoos rushed the entrance of the Submarine Bar at Fourteenth and Locust and attacked a group of gangsters who had just finished listening to the Jack Dempsey-Gene Tunney heavyweight title fight on radio. Three men were killed and at least three others wounded. The similarities between this attack and the one at Papa Leo's in Detroit a month earlier have led many historians to conclude that the lead triggermen and planners were none other than Gus Winkler and Milford Jones.

Back in Detroit, Bob Carey, Ray Nugent, and the recently arrived Tony Ortell invaded the home of real estate broker Edward Loveley on Halloween night 1926. After the three trussed him up, they made off with $40,000 worth of diamonds, furs, and some expensive antiques. Carey and Nugent, identified from mug shots as the perpetrators, dumped the loot and fled west, winding up in Los Angeles, where they were hauled in on suspicion of robbing a jeweler. Both were extradited to Detroit to stand trial for the Loveley caper. Police took extra precautions after getting word that Fred Burke was planning a commando-style attack on the train to rescue his partners, but the trip east proved uneventful.

Johnny Reid's relationship with the Purple Gang was beginning to fray, in part because a drunken Tennessee Slim Hurley had killed a young lounge singer named Melba Rhodes in a Cass Avenue speakeasy at 6 a.m. on September 20. The singer's sister just happened to date Purple triggerman Eddie Fletcher, and she was still so distraught a month later that she tried to kill herself. Thinking that Fletcher might have shot her, police arrested him and his partner, Abe Axler. Reid kicked Hurley out of his inner circle, but the Purples were still irked.

Then, with Burke out of sight and Jones and Winkler in St. Louis and Carey and Nugent in Los Angeles, Mike Dipisa surfaced again.

When his brother was killed in a holdup attempt in November 1926, Dipisa blamed Johnny Reid, and the attack on his family spurred the humiliated gangster to retaliate.

On Christmas night, Reid was celebrating at the Log Cabin Inn on East Adams Avenue in downtown Detroit. He was soon joined by Abe Axler and Eddie Fletcher, and the men talked and drank for several hours. At about four o'clock, Reid struggled to his feet and walked slowly out into the cold, dark morning. He *had* to walk slowly, as he was seeing triple by now.

Climbing into his sedan, Reid aimed the vehicle north on Woodward Avenue, heading toward his apartment at 3025 East Grand Boulevard. He pulled into the alley in back of the building and cut the engine. Reid hadn't realized that someone had been watching him all night, or that his departure from the Log Cabin Inn had been observed. Or that a hit man was now crouching in the alley with a sawed-off shotgun. Despite his inebriated state, Reid sensed movement behind him—and then everything exploded in a red haze.

The Wayne County Medical Examiner listed the cause of death as "traumatic cerebral hemorrhage" on Reid's death certificate, a polite way of saying his head had been blown apart by a shotgun blast. Johnny Reid was nine days shy of his thirty-sixth birthday. Nearly 400 people attended his funeral three days later, including Fred Burke, Gus Winkler, and Milford Jones. The mourners spoke proudly of the charity work Reid had done around Christmastime.

Trying to get a line on who killed their friend, Fred Burke concluded that the shooter was a recently arrived jewel thief from Chicago named Frankie Wright, who had been hired personally by Mike Dipisa. Burke and Winkler were unable to trap Wright, but as the New Year of 1927 wore on, they would get a helping hand from their friendly neighborhood gangsters.

The Purple Gang also wanted Wright very badly, suspecting him of killing one of their top narcotics purveyors, Jake Weinberg, on February 3, 1927. To make matters worse, along with two New York burglars, Joseph Bloom and George Cohen, Wright was trying to muscle in on Burke's snatch racket. Since arriving in Detroit, the jewel thief had been living it up, staying in an expensive suite at the Book-Cadillac Hotel and spending freely in the city's cabarets.

While the hunt for Johnny Reid's killer continued, the Burke crew encountered trouble. Once he returned from California, Bob Carey promptly jumped his $15,000 bond in the Loveley case and went back to work. He befriended two Missouri ex-cons, James Ellis and Leroy "Doggy" Snyder, both of whom had relocated to Detroit and sought to join up with Fred Burke. Carey sized up the two on the night of March 16, 1927.

Bringing along Tony Ortell for company, the four men went on a toot and played poker at the Lewis Cass Apartments at 129 Charlotte Street. The men drank heavily, littering the room with empty whiskey and beer bottles. At some point, as Ellis displayed a winning hand, Carey and Ortell drew their gats and shot to death both Ellis and Snyder, whose bodies were found the next day by a maid. A queen of spades was found concealed up Ellis's sleeve, so police guessed the thug had been caught cheating. Carey and Ortell had left their fingerprints all over the room, so along with the forfeited bond Carey now had a double-murder rap hanging over his head.

When his carelessly brutal buddy Bob Carey left town again, Fred Burke decided to lure the crafty Wright into the open. Gus Winkler called Wright and told him his good friend, gambler Meyer "Fish" Bloomfield, had been kidnapped, and that if he paid a ransom, he could retrieve his friend unharmed. The Purple Gang was apprised of the plan and formally hired Burke to avenge the deaths of both Johnny Reid and Jake Weinberg. Purple boss Abe Bernstein sent his two best triggermen to accompany Burke: the diminutive Abe Axler and Eddie Fletcher, known as the "Siamese Twins."

Wright coughed up the ransom, and Winkler told him he could find his pal inside Apartment 308 at the Milaflores Apartments, located at 106 East Alexandrine Avenue.

At 4:30 on the morning of March 28, Frankie Wright pulled up in front of the Milaflores Apartments along with Joseph Bloom and George Cohen. Apartment 308 was located at the far end of the narrow hallway on the third floor. At the opposite end of the passageway was a stairwell that doubled as a fire exit. Inside this doorway stood Abe Axler, Eddie Fletcher, and Fred Burke, the Siamese Twins armed with a .38 revolver and a pair of .45s, while Burke, who towered over the pint-sized killers, sported a Thompson submachine gun with a 50-round ammunition drum. They waited in silence, Axler occasionally tugging at the tip of his cap, a nervous habit he had. Finally, they saw their prey approach.

Wright, accompanied by Bloom and Cohen, strode purposefully down the hallway to Apartment 308, their hands in their pockets, fingering their pistols. As Wright rapped roughly on the apartment portal, the fire door at the other end of the hall burst open, and Burke and the Twins unleashed a storm of lead at the three hapless thugs. The withering machine-gun and pistol fire ripped into the three gangsters, who didn't even have time to scream as they tumbled to the floor, hot rounds continuing to slam into their bodies.

When the shooting finally subsided, one of the victims let out a final, strangled groan. Someone, probably Fletcher, screamed, "Get him! Get him again!" and Burke let go with another long burst from the Thompson, again spraying the bodies as they lay crumpled in front of the apartment's door. Their weapons now empty, the killers vaulted down the stairs, out the back door, and into a waiting car driven by Gus Winkler, who sped them away from the carnage.

Back upstairs, Frank Wright was still clinging to life despite fourteen gunshot wounds. The bodies of Joseph Bloom and George Cohen were so riddled with bullets that the coroner would be unable to determine just how many times they had been shot. At the hospital, Wright tried to explain why he and his pals had gone to the apartment, but he was incoherent most of the time. When asked if he remembered the faces of the killers, Wright replied, "The machine gun worked. That's all I can remember." He described the shooting as "awful," and at seven o'clock the next morning, Frank Wright died of his wounds.

This was the first time the infamous "Tommygun" had been documented as being used in Detroit's gangland warfare, and police correctly suspected that Wright had been murdered in revenge for Johnny Reid. Burke and Axler were pulled over and arrested the next evening while driving on Woodward Avenue. Police couldn't pin the "Milaflores Massacre" on Burke, but no one connected with the case doubted he was the triggerman. When Burke's prints were run, it was discovered that he was wanted for the Farmers National Bank holdup in Louisville two years earlier, and before long, Fred Burke was in Kentucky facing a host of legal problems.

While Burke was in Louisville, an event transpired that would shake the foundation of the Egan-Purple alliance.

Twenty-nine-year-old Ted Werner had been a lower-level member of the Egan's Rats when Burke and the rest of the boys were in St. Louis. After being acquitted on an armed robbery charge in 1923, Werner had left town and knocked around the Midwest. After the Rats went to Detroit, Ted joined them for a brief time, hitting it off Purple Gang leader Joe Bernstein so well that the two soon opened a gambling joint outside New Orleans named the Victory Inn. But soon after the Milaflores Massacre, a dispute arose between the two, and Werner was shot and killed at an apartment he shared with Bernstein in the Crescent City on April 16, 1927.

Later that spring, Gus Winkler, Bob Carey, and Ray Nugent abducted popular Detroit gambler Mert Wertheimer, expecting to reap a potential six-figure ransom. They drove him to Chicago and held him captive at a North Side flat on Grace Street. It turned out that Mert was not only protected by the Purple Gang but also a good friend of Chicago crime boss Al Capone. Winkler and his wife, Georgette, had moved into the Leland Hotel when Gus was contacted by an emissary of Capone, who wanted to arrange a meeting.

Knowing that Wertheimer was stashed only a couple of blocks away, Winkler was nervous as he informed Carey and Nugent that Capone wanted a sit-down. The latter two had no desire to accept an invitation to their own murder and wanted nothing more than to get out of Chicago as soon as possible. Gus persuaded them to accompany him to the meet and, hoping to make the best possible impression, cleaned up his partners and gave them a crash course in manners and etiquette.

About the third week of May 1927, the three ex-Egan's Rats walked into Al Capone's spacious office at the Hawthorne Hotel in Cicero, Illinois. The meeting was enlightening, as the Chicago boss was quite personable while he explained to his guests how the kidnapping racket was going south and told them that such talented men as themselves should get into a real business. Winkler enjoyed the evening chatting with Capone, but to his dismay, his partners drank freely from Al's brandy decanter and before long, their nerves guzzled calm, Carey and Nugent had their feet up on Capone's desk and were talking loudly and joking like the crude, violent hoods they were. Big Al just laughed good naturedly at their antics, and then took the three men out to a sumptuous dinner.

Capone generously offered each man some cash. Winkler thanked the crime boss, telling him he didn't need the money, but right on cue, his cohorts grinned and snatched up the cash. Winkler was pleased with the way the meeting had gone, but he was angry with his pals for their boorish behavior.

Mert Wertheimer was released immediately, and Carey and Winkler soon settled in Chicago. Nugent went back to the home he recently had purchased Toledo, Ohio, in the 2300 block of Upton Avenue, where his wife, Julia, lived with their two children. Gus and Bob began hanging around the bar of the Hawthorne Hotel, ingratiating themselves to Capone's men. Gus and wife Georgette moved into a nearby apartment.

Fred Burke was still in Detroit snatching gamblers for ransom. Unfortunately, his racket was so successful that hoods all across the city were trying to imitate it, most notably a gang led by Charles "Legs" Laman. Burke found himself getting blamed for jobs he hadn't pulled, and the Purple Gang was growing increasingly frustrated with him. Fred wasn't too thrilled either with the group of racketeers whose reputation far exceeded their competence.

To make matters worse, Burke had finally figured out that the Purples had killed his good friend Ted Werner in New Orleans. When questioned by the Egans, the Bernsteins brushed them off, probably thinking they were drunken hicks that could be used and discarded at will. The ex-Rats began planning retaliation against the Purple Gang, and Burke snatched up his Tommygun, intending to cruise the North End and shoot the first Purples he saw.

On the night of July 21, 1927, Louis Fleisher was at the Exchange Café drinking with his good friends. The Exchange, located at 9136 Oakland Avenue, served as a hangout for the Purples, and exactly a year earlier, Fleisher had killed New York gangster "Two-Gun Willie" Glanzerock right outside. With Fleisher this night were his best friend, Henry Kaplan, and two youngsters, Edward Fecter and Sam Drapkin. At 10:30 p.m. the four left the café and walked a few doors south to their car. They stood next to the vehicle, talking for a few moments, giddy from the booze, the camaraderie of friends, and the warm summer evening.

At that moment, a sedan cruised by and raked the group with submachine gun fire. Kaplan was hit five times and died later at Henry Ford Hospital. Fleisher took a round through his left side. Four slugs hit Fecter, one amazingly glancing off his forehead, and Drapkin was struck five times in his right arm and shoulder. All were treated at the hospital and released.

Police incorrectly assumed that the attack on the Purples was retribution for Louis Fleisher's killing of Willie Glanzerock, since the attack had happened near the anniversary of Glanzerock's death. For his part, Fleisher, when questioned about that murder, said Two-Gun Willie had tried to hijack a load of booze from him, but he "beat him to the draw." Police charged him with Willie's murder, but a judge ruled that Fleisher had acted in self-defense.

Ten days after the Oakland Avenue attack, Fred Burke pulled his last major job in Detroit, with Abe Axler and Eddie Fletcher helping him snatch a North End merchant named Abraham Fein. The Siamese Twins at the time were unaware of Burke's strike against their gang. The trio was assisted by Bob Carey's brother-in-law Joseph O'Riordan. After the shootings and Fein's kidnapping, Detroit had become a dangerous place for the former Rats, and a confrontation between the two groups was imminent.

Purple Gang boss Abe Bernstein invited Gus Winkler and Fred Burke to a peace meeting where they could settle their differences. The pair was instructed to report to David Banks's suite in the Carlton-Plaza Hotel at 2931 John R Street, where the Bernstein brothers would be waiting for them. Burke and Winkler were naturally suspicious, as the Milaflores Massacre had been set up in precisely the same manner. They sent Raymond Shocker, a bootlegger pal from St. Louis, in their place. Shocker was to check things out and then, if everything was kosher, telephone Burke and Winkler. If things weren't as they should be, Raymond was to get the hell out of there as fast as he could.

Shocker arrived at the Carlton-Plaza on the evening of September 6, and after being greeted in the lobby by David Banks, the bootlegger made his way up to the third floor suite. There, one of the most dangerous Purples, Irving Shapiro, stood waiting. A submachine gun was stashed in the closet, and Shapiro had been instructed to use the Thompson on Burke, Winkler, and whoever else was with them. Shocker stepped into the room and, seeing no one but Shapiro, immediately rushed him.

During the vicious scuffle, Shapiro broke Shocker's nose and cheekbone and knocked out two of his teeth. When the St. Louis bootlegger staggered back, instinctively raising a hand in self-defense, Shapiro put a bullet through it. He fired again, hitting

Shocker in the shoulder, and pulled the trigger a third time, but the gun jammed. Shocker, despite his wounds, grappled with Shapiro and Banks, the latter of whom got him in a full nelson while the former used the jammed pistol to beat Shocker within an inch of his life, fracturing his skull. Shapiro and Banks retrieved the submachine gun, locked the door behind them, and ran downstairs and out into the street.

After the Purple Gang's botched attempt on his life, Burke left Detroit forever, promptly reported to Chicago, and was introduced to Al Capone. In light of subsequent events, the first meeting between Burke and Capone perhaps could best be described as "love at first sight."

13

"NOBODY SHOT ME"

BY THE FALL of 1927, Fred Burke and all the main members of his crew were regulars at the Hawthorne Hotel in Cicero. The only man missing was Milford Jones, whose steadfast refusal to work with Italians left him the odd man out; the only gang he would work for was the Cuckoos in St. Louis. Jones had always marched to his own beat.

The former Egan's Rats met many members of Al Capone's gang, reuniting with Claude Maddox, formerly from St. Louis, who owned a dive on the North Side called the Circus Café, as well as his partner, Tony Capezio. Capone's number-one hit man was Jack McGurn, a handsome former boxer and avid golfer who, although Sicilian, went by his Irish ring name. Also around was Louis Campagna, a short, wiry tough guy known as "Little New York"; Rocco DeGrazia; Frank Rio, Capone's bodyguard; youthful gangster Tony Accardo, who one day would become boss of the Chicago mob; and Willie Heeney, a former Rat and current Capone fixer. Since Heeney had left St. Louis in the late 1910s, Burke and the rest weren't especially close to him.

Their most important new friend was more like them than the rest of Capone's goons. Fred Goetz was thirty years old, and it was never known exactly how he had ended up working Capone. Born into a respectable Chicago family, he earned an engineering degree from the University of Illinois. Joining the new Army Air Corps, Goetz was commissioned as a second lieutenant at the beginning of World War I. Well-spoken, unfailingly polite and courteous, he was of above-average height and well built, with handsome features, neatly parted blond hair, and clear blue eyes. Goetz looked like a lifeguard, which he had been, working at a Lake Michigan beach until 1925.

However, there was something else behind the pleasant face and blue eyes, something darker. Goetz had been arrested for trying to rape a seven-year-old girl during his time as a lifeguard, but he beat the rap and began committing armed robberies and ran a bootlegging still with a couple of friends in Springfield, Illinois. Soon after, he appeared in the Capone mob for the first time.

Goetz would later use the alias Ziegler, but Burke and the boys knew him as George Goetz. His true talent lay in contract murder and armed robbery. Goetz often would head to a small midwestern town and rob a bank, and within a week, he could be found shooting someone down on a Chicago street corner. Utilizing his considerable intelligence, Goetz developed novel ways of taking out his targets, including using a sawed-off, 12-gauge pump shotgun that he hid in a golf bag with his clubs, in case a quick assignment arose. He jokingly referred to the weapon as his "twelve iron" and picked up the nickname "Shotgun George" from this weapon of choice.

He also was credited with inventing a time bomb with leather straps that he would tie around a kidnapping victim in order to force a ransom payment. Rarely raising his voice, Goetz was, according to one FBI agent, capable of "generous kindness and consciousness cruelty." The bank robber/hit man's best friend and valet was Byron Bolton, a former Navy machine-gunner-turned-armed robber, whom some of the boys may have known in St. Louis, where he was originally from.

In the fall and winter of 1927–28, the Capone mob was dog-fighting with a group of gangsters led by Joe Aiello, who was frustrated that Big Al was blocking his takeover of the Chicago chapter of the Unione Siciliana, ostensibly a benevolent society that took care of the Sicilian community but increasingly served as a criminal organization. Aiello had repeatedly tried to kill Capone and then reportedly offered a $50,000 bounty for anyone who could remove the crime boss. Aiello would prove no match for his rival.

Chicago's local election in April 1928 was a brutal affair known as the "Pineapple Primary." Rival gangs attacked reform candidates and their supporters, tossing bombs, or "pineapples," into speakeasies, offices, and homes. The Burke crew, which Capone referred to as the "American boys," used Claude Maddox's Circus Café at 1759 North Avenue in Chicago as its headquarters and in all probability worked for Capone in both the Aiello war and the Pineapple Primary.

Not all of Burke's time was spent working, however. Despite his murderous reputation, at heart he loved nothing more than to hunt and fish, play practical jokes, and guzzle beers with his buddies. A caddy at a Chicago-area golf course later recalled occasions when Capone, Burke, McGurn, Campagna, Goetz, and others arrived to play a round. The gangsters were loud and boisterous, betting on swings, horsing around, and drinking freely from flasks.

By the later holes, the men would be quite intoxicated and often would begin a game of "Blind Robin," in which one thug would lie on the ground with a golf ball balanced on his chin while one of his pals teed off. When Capone was on the ground, none of the boys dared use anything larger than a putter. The muscular Burke was the most feared player in the bunch and could wield a driver with terrific force.

Virtually all of the hoods cheated relentlessly (they were criminals, after all), and on one occasion Jack McGurn went after Burke for nudging his ball. During the ensuing brawl, Burke bloodied his opponent with powerful haymaker blows, but he tired fast and ex-boxer McGurn then jabbed his way to victory over the winded Burke.

Amid this violent yet happy atmosphere, the former Kansas farmboy once known as Thomas Camp was now at the pinnacle of his criminal career—and the caper that would gain him the greatest notoriety was yet to come.

That spring Ray Nugent cooked up a caper in his hometown of Toledo, Ohio. He suggested to the boys that they could hit an American Securities truck, blow open its portable safe, and get away with more than $200,000. The job was set for April 16, and Gus Winkler, Bob Carey, George Goetz, Nugent, and a cantankerous ex-con named Charlie Fitzgerald took part. The men succeeded in snatching the truck, but then they discovered that the idiotic Nugent had forgotten to bring the explosives. They decided on the spot to cart the safe back to Nugent's garage and cut into it with a blowtorch.

After gingerly loading the safe into the back of their car, the boys had just pulled off when two police officers, George Zientara and John Biskupski, happened upon the scene and gave chase. The robbers drove at a furious pace, taking corners sharply and zigzagging through neighborhoods. The driver in all probability was Gus Winkler, one of the best getaway drivers ever to come out of St. Louis.

After losing the cops, the thugs headed for Nugent's garage, where they frantically cut into the safe. Just as they extracted the loot, Patrolmen Zientara and Biskupski located the men. One of the robbers peeked around the corner of the garage, saw where the cops were hiding, and opened up on the pair with a submachine gun, mortally wounding Zientara.

Capone scolded his American boys for pulling such a harebrained scheme that almost landed them all in prison. Then Big Al smiled and told the crew he had a new job for them, something very important, and that there was no one he trusted more to handle it.

Al Capone was originally from Brooklyn, New York. His mentor and first boss was Frankie Yale, owner of a Coney Island dance hall called the Harvard Inn, where Capone worked as a waiter and bouncer. It was there, during a fight over a girl, that Al received the scars on his left cheek that would mark him forever and spawn the nickname "Scarface." Yale was the powerful head of Italian organized crime in Brooklyn, and during Prohibition he arranged for whiskey shipments to his friend Capone, who had gone to Chicago in 1919 or early 1920 to avoid a murder rap in

New York and was working for Johnny Torrio, a lieutenant of vice lord "Big Jim" Colosimo.

Yale was linked to at least two sensational murders in Chicago. The first occurred in 1920, when it is believed he took out Colosimo, who had been neglecting his illicit businesses to pursue a beautiful young singer. Torrio was made manager of Colosimo's vice empire and, with Capone's help, expanded the operation into bootlegging, racketeering, and other lucrative enterprises. The crime cartel would become known as the Chicago Syndicate. In November 1924, Yale again came west and is believed to have perpetrated the "handshake murder" that took out North Side Gang leader Dean O'Banion in his flower shop.

By 1928, however, the relationship had soured between Yale and Capone, who was now the undisputed leader of the Syndicate since being handed the reins by Torrio in 1925. Among reasons were Yale's refusal to back Capone's choice for president of Chicago's Unione Siciliana, and also because Yale allegedly was allowing many of Al's booze shipments to be hijacked before they left New York.

That spring, Capone began pondering retaliation against Frankie Yale. He chose three of the American boys for the job: Fred Burke, Gus Winkler, and George Goetz. Louis Campagna was designated to accompany the men because of his familiarity with New York City.

On July 1, the four men were searching New York City for Yale and cruised by his Manhattan apartment and his regular haunts in Brooklyn, particularly his speakeasy, the Sunrise Café. According to most accounts, the killers lured Yale out of the Sunrise about 4 p.m. with a cryptic phone call telling him that something was wrong with his wife, Lucy. Yale jumped in his bullet-proofed, coffee-colored Lincoln coupe and turned north onto New Utrecht Avenue.

When he noticed four hard-eyed men in a Buick sedan staring at him at a stoplight, Frankie floored the accelerator, and soon both cars were weaving in and out of traffic on the busy thoroughfare. Yale suddenly veered left onto Forty-fourth Street, the American boys close on his tail. Unfortunately for the mob boss, the dealer had neglected to bulletproof his car's windows.

One of the gunmen opened fire at the Lincoln's back window with a Thompson submachine gun before they had closed the distance. The weapon's 100-round drum magazine misfed after just nine rounds, and as the triggerman snatched up another Tommygun, the Buick pulled alongside the Lincoln. Yale was riddled with buckshot and submachine gun bullets, and his coupe veered onto the sidewalk, crashing into the front stoop of a house where a Jewish woman was giving a Bar Mitzvah for her son. As the Buick screeched to a stop, one of the gunmen jumped out, ran over to the totaled Lincoln, and emptied a .45 automatic into Frankie Yale's head.

Leaving their car a few blocks away, the killers headed for the Staten Island Ferry dock and then New Jersey. Although they left their weapons behind in the car, one of the men discreetly brought the functional Thompson with him as they made their escape.

The crew had been instructed not to communicate with anyone in Chicago, but police traced phone calls made by Louis Campagna and George Goetz to their women back home, which confirmed their theory that Capone was behind the murder. Investigators found that the Buick sedan had been purchased at a Nash dealership in Knoxville, Tennessee, a few days before the murder. They also traced some of the pistols left behind in the car to Miami, and linked the jammed Thompson to Chicago sporting goods dealer Peter von Frantzius, who was known to have sold submachine guns to members of the Capone mob. But despite these and other leads, the killers were never arrested.

Frankie Yale's slaying marked the first time a Thompson submachine gun had been used in a hit in New York City. Thus, New York became the second major American city whose underworld had been introduced to the formidable Thompson by former members of the Egan's Rats.

Despite the heat from the Yale hit, Capone was pleased with Burke and Winkler; after all, they had accomplished their mission. Another job of extermination was on the horizon as fall began. Tony Lombardo, Capone's good friend and president of the Chicago Unione, had been gunned down on September 7 in broad daylight in front of hundreds of people in the Loop, presumably in revenge for Frankie Yale.

Joe Aiello still hadn't given up his ideas of getting rid of Capone, and he had formed an alliance with Big Al's archenemies, the North Side Gang. Composed primarily of Irish and German hoods, the North Siders had warred on and off with Capone over the last four years. Their popular leader, Dean O'Banion, had been murdered in November 1924 by the now deceased Yale and two others, and his friends had sworn vengeance. The new boss, Hymie Weiss, made several spectacular but ultimately unsuccessful attempts to kill Capone, and on one occasion, in September 1926, he led a cavalcade of cars past the Hawthorne Hotel and shredded the place with hundreds of submachine-gun bullets.

Soon thereafter, Weiss was taken out in a Tommygun ambush on State Street, right outside the North Siders' headquarters. His successor, Vincent "Schemer" Drucci, was killed in a scuffle with a detective, and that left George "Bugs" Moran in charge of the North Side Gang. Despite his depleted crew, Bugs Moran became a major thorn in Capone's side, muscling in on his Near North Side speakeasies and gambling territories. Because of its location, the Circus Café, headquarters of Fred Burke and the other American boys, was right in the line of fire.

In the fall of 1928, Capone and some close friends gathered at a resort that George Goetz owned near Couderay, Wisconsin. It was at this meeting, attended by Frank Nitti, Fred Burke, Gus Winkler, George Goetz, Byron Bolton, Rocco DeGrazia, and others, that a plan arose to kill Moran.

The final straw came on January 8, 1929, when the new president of the Unione Siciliana, Capone's pal Pasqualino Lolordo, was gunned down in his home, reportedly by Joe Aiello and the North Side Gang's best triggermen, Frank and Pete Gusenberg. Capone was furious and immediately made plans to remove Bugs Moran from the land of the living, once and for all.

Capone was sick with pneumonia through most of January, so Burke and Goetz took over planning the hit. Just as Dint Colbeck had done with the Egan's Rats, Burke put out the word that the boys at the Circus Café should "find an alibi." Capone hit man Jack McGurn parked himself in a hotel suite with his blonde girlfriend, Louise Rolfe, and didn't emerge for days.

The main meeting place of the North Side Gang was a dingy garage at 2122 North Clark Street known as the S.M.C. Cartage Company. The gang's trucks were repaired there, and truckloads of illicit booze were also delivered to the address. It was decided to lure Moran to the garage and kill him there. As for gaining entry, Burke would use the ruse he had developed in St. Louis, posing as a police officer.

The primary hoodlums involved in the hit would be Burke, Goetz, Gus Winkler, Bob Carey, and Ray Nugent, with Byron Bolton, Claude Maddox, Tony Capezio, Raymond Shocker, and Tony Accardo acting as lookouts and backup. Little could Fred Burke and all the rest of the former Rats have imagined that they were about to cross the line separating hit men from mass murderers.

At 10:25 on the morning of February 14, 1929, forty-year-old Pete Gusenberg, his brother Frank and five others were waiting in the rear of the S.M.C. Cartage Company. It was dim inside the garage, which was lit only by a single 200-watt bulb, and also cold, as the inside temperature hovered near the outside mark of eighteen degrees. At least ten trucks and cars were crammed inside the building, forming a small passage to the front office, which the gangsters seldom used. The men were in a small open area in the back against the north wall. Pete watched his breath plume in front of him, wishing Moran would hurry the hell up.

Why Bugs had called this meeting, no one seemed to know. All Moran had told Gusenberg was to be at the garage in the morning, and Pete had gotten there early, after waking his wife, Myrtle, for another go-around. He could still taste her musk on his lips. Grinning to himself, he glanced around the room at his pals. Frank Gusenberg, Al Weinshank, James Clark, and Adam Heyer crowded around the coffeepot, talking in low tones. Reinhart Schwimmer, the optometrist hanger-on, was standing off to the side trying and failing to join the conversation. Mechanic John May, who was under one of the trucks twisting wrenches, had brought along his Alsatian dog, which Pete petted briefly. Pete had always liked dogs, but one thing he didn't like was what he steadfastly referred to as "the wops," Capone and his mostly Italian mob.

The Syndicate had inflicted many losses on the North Siders over the last few years. Moran and his boys had gotten their licks in, but the scales were never even. Pete Gusenberg had gotten out of Leavenworth in 1926 and later that year had taken part in the drive-by attack on Capone at the Hawthorne Hotel. Add his own exclamation point to the hit, Pete had his driver stop while he grabbed his Tommygun, got out of the car, walked up to the front door of the restaurant where Capone was cowering, and fired an entire 100-round drum of ammo into the dining room.

Pete had liked Hymie Weiss, who he thought was perhaps the one guy who could have beaten Capone, but Hymie was long gone, as were many others. The North Siders always seemed to come up snake eyes against the wops. Pete and brother Frank had tried twice to kill Jack McGurn. On one of those occasions, the Gusenbergs caught him in a phone booth and pumped enough lead into him to sink a ship—but the big-nosed hit man had survived.

As he headed toward a table in the S.M.C. garage, Pete thought he heard a car in the alley behind the building. Suddenly, the wooden double doors facing the alley were yanked open, bathing the rear area in dull-gray light. Two uniformed cops strode inside and started yelling about a raid, aiming their .38 revolvers at the North Side crew. Gusenberg was annoyed but felt they had nothing to worry about, since there was no booze on the premises.

Pete quickly sized up the cops. The apparent leader was big and mean looking, and had a gravelly voice with a slight twang, meaning he was probably some yokel from Nebraska or Iowa. His partner was a bit shorter, with blond hair and cheeks that were red from the cold. He had cold blue eyes, and his lips were curled into a weird half-smile. Pete had seen that look before, on the faces of killers on the street and queers in stir. It was the smirk of a psychopath, but before this could completely register, the cops began pushing Pete and the others up against the brick wall. The seven North Siders lined up with their hands on the wall, and one of the cops began to frisk them. Pete felt his gat being yanked out of his pocket.

Gusenberg was standing second from the left, with a couple of chairs crammed between him and the wall. Frank was on his left and Al Weinshank on his right. Pete heard John May and Reinhart Schwimmer complaining that they weren't *really* gangsters. Knowing that the gang was well connected with the local police, he decided to pipe up: "What a pain in the ass! We'll be out in just a couple of hours!" A beat later, he heard someone behind him murmur, "Shhh." The voice was so soft and melodic it had to be the psycho, and Gusenberg thought this surely must be the strangest bust he'd ever been in. Usually, the bulls yelled and cursed and smacked you over the head, but this time not a word was uttered after the hoods were lined up facing the wall.

Seconds ticked by, and Pete still heard nothing from the cops; the only sounds were Gusenberg and his pals breathing. Then, from behind, he thought he heard whispering.

At that point, the world exploded in an ear-splitting chatter. Pete felt a cord of pain rip across his lower back, exploding up and down his body, snatching his breath away. Underneath the deafening roar, he thought he heard Frank scream, and then another bolt of pain shot along his shoulders and neck, rendering his whole body numb. In a moment of stark clarity, Pete saw his blood splatter on the bricks of the wall. Feeling himself falling, his brain was still unable to comprehend what was happening, and before it could, Pete's thoughts were scrambled by another stream of .45-caliber bullets.

A few moments earlier, while Pete Gusenberg and the others were waiting inside the S.M.C. garage for their boss to arrive, a delivery van lumbered up North Clark Street. A block north of the garage, as its driver, a newspaper delivery man named Elmer Lewis, entered the intersection with Webster Avenue, a Cadillac sedan swerved left into Clark, trying to beat a red light. Lewis smacked into the Caddy's left fender.

Pulling over, the truck driver panicked when he saw that he'd hit a police car, a detective-model Cadillac with decals and all the other police trappings. As Lewis rushed over, a man hopped out of the car, laughed, and waved him off. Lewis would later describe him as five feet ten, 175 pounds, with a light complexion, "American" rather than "Italian," dressed in a blue suit, with a matching fedora and a chinchilla overcoat.

Lewis climbed back into his truck and drove off, noticing that the Cadillac had stopped a little farther down Clark. Meanwhile, a 1926 Peerless sedan had eased into the alley that ran behind the S.M.C. Cartage Company, stopping by the wooden double doors. One witness reported that two men in police uniforms got out of the vehicle and walked through the double doors into the garage. Once inside, they lined up the seven men they found there, from left to right:

- Frank and Pete Gusenberg, North Side gunmen
- Albert Weinshank, labor racketeer
- Adam Heyer, business manager for the North Side Gang
- James Clark, extortionist and triggerman
- John May, ex-safecracker and mechanic
- Reinhart Schwimmer, optometrist and gang hanger-on

Once the North Siders were up against the wall, one of the cops walked into the narrow passageway and opened the front door of the garage, letting in two men dressed in civilian clothes from the Cadillac. With the four men standing about ten feet behind the North Siders, they whipped out their weapons, which included two Thompsons, one fitted with a fifty-round ammo drum and the other with a twenty-round box clip, plus two sawed-off, pump-action 12-gauge shotguns.

Two of the killers opened fire without warning, raking the seven gangsters with neat streams of submachine-gun fire at waist and head level. One of the victims, mechanic John May, apparently looked over his left shoulder at the sound of the first volley, because one of the shotgun killers blew away the left side of his head with a load of buckshot. The other shooter blasted Reinhart Schwimmer in the torso for good measure. The North Siders, literally torn to pieces by the withering crossfire, crumpled to the floor. One of the machine-gunners then knelt down and sprayed the line of corpses one final time, after which they put the final part of their plan into effect, a little charade designed to fool any witnesses.

Mrs. Jeanette Landesman, who lived in a flat above a tailor shop next door to the garage, heard muffled clattering coming from next door as she was ironing clothes. Peeking out her window in curiosity, she saw two men in fedoras and overcoats march out of the garage with their hands in the air while two men in police uniforms herded them into a Cadillac detective sedan at the curb. Another witness remarked on the "long guns they were pointing at the backs of the men." The Cadillac lurched away from the garage, sounding its siren as it moved into traffic. Falling in behind a streetcar, the Cadillac's driver cut left into the oncoming lane, zoomed around the trolley, and pulled back to the right just in time.

Taking into account the muffled noises, the "prisoners," the "cops," and the careless way the Cadillac had driven off, Mrs. Landesman got one of her neighbors, Charles McAllister, to investigate. Entering the front door of the garage, threading his way between the parked cars and trucks, McAllister was struck by the smell of gunpowder and cordite—and what he saw next would haunt him for the rest of his life.

Seven bodies lay sprawled on the greasy garage floor. Blood and brain matter were everywhere, with the claret running in streams down the slightly sloped floor toward a drain. A large dog, chained to a truck, was moaning sorrowfully. The most startling sight was the blood-drenched man on the floor crawling toward him. When the mortally wounded Frank Gusenberg found his voice and asked, "Who is it?" McAllister's control broke and he ran to call the police.

Despite being hardened by Chicago's vicious gang wars, the cops were shocked by what they found inside the S.M.C. Cartage Company that morning. Al Weinshank, Adam Heyer, John May, and Reinhart Schwimmer lay on their backs, heads oozing blood and brains, eyes staring sightlessly into the void of death. James Clark was lying sideways by the wall, and Pete Gusenberg had slumped across the seat of a chair. Police noted how a large portion of May's skull was missing, and how some bullets had torn Gusenberg's pants right on the seat, creating an obscene sight.

Inspector Tom Loftis, first on the scene, briefly questioned the wounded Frank Gusenberg, who would only mutter, "I won't talk," or "Cops did it." The gangster was rushed to the hospital, and a huge crowd had formed outside, jostling for a better view as the bodies of the others were hefted into an ambulance.

At Alexian Brothers Hospital, Gusenberg clung to life, but he steadfastly refused to say anything about the shooting, mumbling only, "Nobody shot me." He died at 1:30 that afternoon, three hours after the murders. Gus Winkler's wife, Georgette, would later say that, at the very same time, her husband and Bob Carey sat by the windows in their apartment and discussed "mistakes" that had been made during the hit. She also would describe how on other occasions George Goetz would clown around by showing up in a police uniform and banging on the couple's door. Apparently, the rest of the men involved in the slayings had gone to Rocco DeGrazia's house immediately afterward.

Police searched for a motive and suspects in the unprecedented slaughter. It was thought at first that police really *had* done the killing, but 255 detectives on the force were soon cleared and pressure focused on the Circus Café. Fred Burke and his pals immediately decided to split up and go their separate ways. With the police clutching at straws, a disgusted and appalled public demanded results. For the first time, the American people saw bootleggers and gangsters not as romantic heroes, but as ruthless killers—and they would never again think of organized crime as a benign enterprise.

Al Capone, who just happened to be in Florida when the shootings went down, of course denied all responsibility, but now the public could see the wizard behind the curtain, and recognized Capone for what he was: Chicago's brutal overlord of crime. The St. Valentine's Day Massacre, as the slayings were soon called, perpetrated by former Egan's Rats from St. Louis, probably ensured that Capone's name would become synonymous with *gangster*.

The Chicago police were getting much closer to finding the perpetrators of the killings than it seemed. A few days after the massacre the charred remains of the Cadillac used in the hit were found in a garage near the Circus Café where it had exploded and burned while being cut apart with a blowtorch wielded by Tony Capezio, who was severely burned. The scorched Peerless sedan was found abandoned in Maywood, not far from a house owned by Claude Maddox. Inside was a pocketbook belonging to Albert Weinshank. The cops evidentially didn't make the connection, and for decades it was incorrectly assumed that the killers had used only the Cadillac.

Ten days into the investigation, two detectives following leads to St. Louis discovered that ex-Rats may have been involved. Soon, the cops announced they were seeking Fred Burke and "James Ray," as two of the killers. James Ray may have been an alias used by either Gus Winkler or Ray Nugent, but a mug shot of Ray published in the March 6, 1929, edition the *Chicago Tribune* shows a large, square-jawed man with hard eyes and thinning hair. Thus, Ray was neither Winkler, Nugent, nor anyone else known to be in the Burke crew. His identity remains a mystery today.

By April, the police secured two indictments in the massacre, against Capone hit men Jack McGurn and John Scalise. The latter would be murdered before standing trial, and the charge against McGurn would be dropped for lack of evidence. McGurn and girlfriend Louise Rolfe later would be convicted of conspiring to violate the Mann Act, which prohibited interstate transport of females for "immoral purposes," when visiting Capone in Florida. The two later married, and their convictions eventually were overturned by the U.S. Supreme Court.

So who really carried out the St. Valentine's Day Massacre? The killers' identities remained in doubt for years, but the police had a pretty good idea that Fred Burke and former members of the Egan's Rats performed the hit at Capone's behest. But for whatever reasons—corruption, indifference, lack of hard evidence—the crime was never officially solved.

It's impossible to know for certain who did what that morning. Based on the available evidence, it seems the uniformed policemen who entered the garage through the back door were

Fred Burke and George Goetz. Once the North Siders were lined up against the wall, one of the pair opened the front door and let in Bob Carey and Ray Nugent, who were masquerading as plain-clothes cops. Getaway driver supreme Gus Winkler probably drove the Cadillac, and the Peerless in the back alley may have been driven by Claude Maddox. Byron Bolton and Jimmy Morand were the lookouts posted across the street from the garage, and others, perhaps Tony Capezio and Tony Accardo, may have been on North Clark Street as additional lookouts and/or to possibly frustrate any attempt to pursue the killers.

But there was a problem with the slayings, a big one. Although they successfully wiped out some of the North Siders' top movers and shakers, Burke and company had missed their main target: gang boss George "Bugs" Moran. One popular account has it that Moran was walking toward the garage with bodyguards Willie Marks and Ted Newberry when they saw the Cadillac pull up out front, and not wanting to get involved with what they thought was a police shakedown, the trio quickly beat it.

Moments before, Byron Bolton, watching from a rented room across the street, had seen a man (probably Albert Weinshank) he thought was Moran enter the garage, and telephoned the Circus Café to alert the hit squad. When the killers entered the garage and surprisingly found themselves faced with seven men, they made a simple and brutal on-the-spot decision to kill everyone and get out fast.

Capone allegedly was infuriated that Bolton had mistaken someone else for Moran, and that his Syndicate was taking tremendous heat for the crime. George Goetz eventually succeeded in talking Capone out of killing Bolton.

An interesting side note to the massacre: Valentine's Day just happened to be Goetz's thirty-second birthday.

The killers had scattered to the four winds by April. Fred Burke stopped off in St. Louis before journeying to Kansas City. Gus Winkler and his wife joined Louis Campagna, Bob Carey, and George Goetz at a cabin near St. Joseph, Michigan, but cabin fever set in after a month and the Winklers got a place of their own in Gary, Indiana. Ray Nugent took off for Miami, looking to settle there permanently.

Winkler soon reunited with Burke at a bar in Calumet City, Illinois. Burke explained how he had renewed acquaintances with master midwestern bank robber Harvey Bailey, and that there would be some work for Winkler and him in the future. With the weather getting warmer, the men decided to take a vacation.

Gus and Georgette Winkler and Burke and his girlfriend Viola drove to a large cabin that Burke had near Grand Rapids, Minnesota. Bob Carey decided to tag along at the last minute. They spent a lazy summer in the backwoods of northern Minnesota, fishing, hunting, and playing endless holes of golf. The only bad part was that Burke and Carey were drinking so heavily that both usually were in the bag by mid-afternoon. While they vacationed, the massacre investigation began to stagnate. Burke was still wanted along with the mysterious "James Ray," but the police had no idea where they were.

As autumn approached, the Burke crew had to return to Chicago. With Capone in a Pennsylvania prison on a concealed-weapon charge, the Syndicate's temporary boss, Frank Nitti, who was not too fond of the American boys, had been quite cavalier in paying them, and money was getting tight. Burke and Viola settled down in a cottage on Lake Michigan near St. Joseph, while the Winklers returned to Gary. Burke and Winkler were later suspected of plucking $93,000 from a ripe bank in Peru, Indiana, on October 18, 1929.

One night in December, Winkler joined Bob Carey for a drink at a roadhouse in Calumet City, where he was introduced to Harvey Bailey and his gang of bank robbers. The Bailey Gang had just stolen more than $300,000 in bonds from a Wisconsin bank and was looking to stash them for a while. Carey talked Winkler into driving the bonds to Burke's lakeside house, but just after Gus reluctantly made the trip to Michigan, the roof fell in.

On December 14, Burke, who later was determined to have been drunk, had a minor fender bender in St. Joseph. When he tried to flee the scene, Patrolman Charles Skelly hopped onto the running board of the car Burke had hit and gave chase. Burke shot the patrolman three times, killing him. When the cops raided the lakeside home of one "Frederick Dane," they found

Viola, the stolen bonds, pistols, shotguns, two submachine guns, a bulletproof vest, and thousands of rounds of ammunition—but no Burke.

A nationwide alert was issued, prompting Chicago authorities to run ballistics tests on the two Thompsons found in Burke's hideout. The results showed that both weapons had been used in the massacre on North Clark Street, and that one of them had fired the bullets that had been extracted from Frankie Yale's body in Brooklyn in July 1928. Burke became the most-wanted man in America, his mug shots gracing the front pages of newspapers from coast to coast. He dropped out of sight and hid on a farm owned by relatives of Harvey Bailey near Green City, Missouri. The other shooters ran as well, with Winkler and his wife spending the winter in Texas.

After the murder of Patrolman Skelly, Fred "Killer" Burke remained in hiding in rural Missouri, leaving only to make brief jaunts to Chicago or Kansas City. Winkler returned to Chicago, where he parlayed his relationship with Al Capone into a powerful position in the Syndicate. Bob Carey dropped off the grid, and Ray Nugent remained in South Florida, where he had opened a saloon. George Goetz stayed in Chicago and continued his career as a bank robber and hit man. With the principals out of sight, the massacre investigation ground to a standstill.

In June 1930, Burke married a seventeen-year-old girl, and a month after the wedding, he was suspected of cornering Chicago hood Thomas Bonner at his cottage in Newaygo County, Michigan, and killing him for trying to give Burke up to the Chicago police. The victim's wife stated that Burke had been accompanied by an intoxicated blond man who held his gun in his left hand, but it was never determined if that man was George Goetz.

If the FBI's Ten Most Wanted Fugitives list had existed at this time, Burke certainly would have headed it. On September 13, he and Gus Winkler were identified as two of the three men who had robbed the Merchants Trust Company of South Paterson, New Jersey, of $18,000.

Fred Burke's downfall came six months later when a Green City handyman and gas-pumper who was an avid reader of detective magazines recognized wealthy Kansas City business-man Richard White as Burke. The cops showed up at his farm hideout on the morning of March 26, 1931, and he was soon extradited to Michigan to stand trial for killing Charles Skelly. Other jurisdictions were brushed off, including Chicago, whose prosecutor claimed he had enough evidence to convict Burke of the St. Valentine's Day Massacre. The ex-Egan's Rat pleaded guilty to killing Patrolman Skelly and was sentenced to life at Marquette Prison, where he would die of a heart attack on July 10, 1940.

By 1930, Gus Winkler had become one of the Capone Outfit's top men in the gambling trade and controlled rackets on the North Side. Other members of the mob, notably Frank Nitti and Paul Ricca, were jealous of Capone's relationship with Winkler. The lanky getaway driver was involved in a serious automobile acci-dent near St. Joseph, Michigan, on August 5, 1931, and suffered severe injuries, including the loss of his left eye.

While in the hospital, Winkler was incorrectly named as the perpetrator of a $2 million bank robbery the previous year in Lin-coln, Nebraska. Much to the chagrin of his fellow Italians, Capone put up Gus's $100,000 bond. Winkler then contacted the actual robbers, probably the Harvey Bailey Gang, and arranged for them to surrender the stolen bonds. As Winkler recovered from his injuries, one of his partners checked out permanently.

Ray Nugent continued to operate his bar in Miami, despite the fact that he drank as much booze as he sold. Often a guest at Al Capone's Palm Island estate in Biscayne Bay, Nugent was arrested for drunken driving in March 1930 along with Al's brother Ralph. When his prints were run, Miami police found that he was wanted for the Toledo armored-car heist and killing, and for a second-degree murder in Cincinnati. Nugent was arraigned in the latter case but jumped his $10,000 bond.

Rumors soon circulated that he was buying his beer and whiskey from non-Outfit sources, and he dropped out of sight. Sometime during the summer of 1931, Raymond "Crane-Neck"

Nugent disappeared without a trace and was never heard from again. Rumors again flew, including one that claimed he had been lured to Chicago and buried alive in the Indiana sand dunes southeast of the city. Two decades later, his long-suffering wife had him declared legally dead in order to collect his military pension.

Bob Carey was essentially ostracized from Chicago because Al Capone had become tired of his boozy unpredictability and wanted nothing more to do with him. He replaced his old buddy Fred Burke as America's most-wanted man, and by the winter of 1931, on his own for the first time in his criminal career, he was wanted in seven or eight states. He was still being sought for the Chicago massacre (although he was never publicly named as one of the killers), the double murder in Detroit, the killing of Patrolman George Zientara during the Toledo armored-car heist, and countless other capers. His reputation was such that authorities would suspect him of having a hand in the March 1932 kidnapping of aviator and hero Charles Lindbergh's baby boy.

Carey used a host of aliases during his career, making it quite difficult for law enforcement and future crime historians to pin down all his crimes. Among the aliases he employed were Conroy, Davis, Sanford, Sanborn, and Newberry (his middle name).

Appearing on the East Coast in early 1932, he and his common-law wife, Rose, worked out a blackmail racket in which Rose would bed Washington lawmakers while Bob discreetly took pictures that they would then use to squeeze the politicians. It was later found that two of the public officials who fell into the trap were U.S. Senators.

That spring, the couple moved to New York City, renting a second-floor railroad flat at 220 W. 104th Street. Carey moved in a large printing press and was soon producing high-quality counterfeit $5 bills to augment his income from the blackmail scheme. Despite his newfound success, Carey, a hopeless alcoholic for years, was still drinking heavily, which may explain what happened next.

According to a reconstruction by the New York Police Department, sometime after 11 p.m. on July 29, 1932, Rose followed Carey into the flat's bathroom, where he shot her three times. Then, kneeling over the rim of the bathtub, Carey blew his brains out with a .45 automatic.

Gus Winkler should have been at the top of his game in 1932. The St. Valentine's Day Massacre had faded from the public consciousness, he controlled most of the rackets on Chicago's North Side, and he'd gained almost complete autonomy in the Outfit. But with Al Capone in prison on tax-evasion charges, Burke locked up for murder, Carey dead, and Nugent dead or gone, Winkler was feeling increasingly isolated.

Gus was now surrounded by hoodlums he didn't trust, the foremost being Frank Nitti and fellow massacre gunman George Goetz. Winkler got into deeper trouble when an associate, former North Side Gang member Ted Newberry, got a couple of detectives to try and kill Nitti. But the wily Italian known as "The Enforcer" beat the odds and survived his gunshot wounds, and it was Newberry who was promptly rubbed out. Even though Winkler had nothing to do with the hit, Nitti harbored lingering suspicions about him.

In addition to running several gambling clubs, Gus landed a lucrative contract to distribute 3.2 beer (recently legalized by a change in the Prohibition law) for the 1933 Chicago World's Fair. Winkler also ran a protection service for bank robbers and was part owner of a garage where they could have special modifications made to their getaway cars, such as devices that produced smoke screens and oil slicks. Life was good, and he and Georgette lived in a lavish Lake Shore Drive apartment. Winkler had finally hit the big time.

But on June 17, 1933, Winkler's friend Verne Miller was accused of helping to gun down three policemen and a federal agent in an attempt to free longtime bank bandit Frank Nash, who was also killed in the parking lot of Kansas City's Union Station. The so-called Kansas City Massacre did for rural bank robbers what the St. Valentine's Day Massacre did for big-city bootleggers: showed the public that these men were not good-hearted latter-day Robin Hoods, but truly dangerous and often vicious individuals.

Winkler, who was perhaps trying to sever his ties with the

violent end of the business so that he could concentrate on his gambling and nightclub operations, was observed making discreet visits to the Bankers Building office of Melvin Purvis, top "G-man" in the FBI's Chicago field office, to give him tips on where to find Verne Miller. The fact that Winkler was getting cozy with the FBI was just too much for Frank Nitti to handle. And Gus, deeply distressed by the "suicide" of a good friend and business partner under suspicious circumstances, had every reason to be worried.

At 1:40 p.m. on October 9, 1933, as Winkler was approaching a Roscoe Street distributing company owned by Cook County Commissioner Charles Weber, a green delivery truck cruised by and its occupants opened up with shotguns. Seventy-two buckshot pellets ripped into the gangster, who died at a hospital thirty minutes later while gasping the Lord's Prayer. When notified of the thirty-three-year-old Winkler's murder, Weber growled, "I wish they had given him a hundred and seventy-five slugs instead of seventy-two. We ought to get rid of all those fellows."

Gus Winkler was the last notable ex-Egan's Rat operating in the Midwest at the time of his death. The lead triggerman in his murder eventually was determined to be George Goetz, who was accompanied by former Circus Café gangster Tony Capezio.

Goetz himself didn't have much time left. He'd been splitting his activities between the Outfit and the Barker-Karpis Gang, with whom he participated in several robberies and kidnappings. Standing outside a Cicero restaurant on the night of March 20, 1934, Goetz was struck by shotgun blasts that blew off most of his head. The only one of Capone's American boys now left in the Outfit was Claude Maddox, who was totally loyal to Frank Nitti.

Byron Bolton was arrested in Chicago along with a handful of the remaining members of the Barker-Karpis Gang after a brief shootout in January 1935. During his interrogation, Bolton told agents a detailed story about how he had participated in the St. Valentine's Day Massacre with the Fred Burke crew. Bolton's claims were corroborated by Georgette Winkler and a Chicago detective named William Drury, who had stayed on the case long after every else had given up. Bank robber Alvin Karpis, a close friend of George Goetz, would later tell the same general story to Capone biographer John Kobler.

However, FBI Director J. Edgar Hoover saw no need to investigate Bolton's claims because murder was a state offense. When the media broke the story a year later, many declared the St. Valentine's Day Massacre solved, but once again, there were no prosecutions. Claude Maddox and the other surviving members of the Circus Café gang were questioned but to no avail. And there the matter finally lay, with no one ever convicted in what remains one of the most notorious crimes in American history.

DENOUEMENT

WHILE FRED BURKE and his crew were shaking up the country, Dint Colbeck and the rest of the boys were pining away in their cells at Leavenworth. Spirits had not been good, and one of the boys, Bartley Martin, suffered a breakdown and was transferred to a mental hospital, where he ultimately committed suicide on July 2, 1926.

That same year, as the months slowly passed and their appeals inevitably failed, Colbeck came up with the idea that his imprisoned pals should write to government officials, confessing to the crimes and absolving Dint of any guilt, so *he* could be released from prison. Steve Ryan and Oliver Dougherty, who had gradually grown to resent Dint, were furious over the scheme, and their anger led to a huge brawl. Afterward, the warden decided to split up the Egan hierarchy. Colbeck, Chippy Robinson, Red Smith, Gus Dietmeyer, and Frank Hackethal were transferred to the Atlanta Federal Penitentiary, while the others remained at Leavenworth. In 1936, Cotton Epplesheimer would be sent to the new federal prison at Alcatraz, isolating him even further.

While at Atlanta, Dint studied theology and served as an assistant to the Catholic chaplain. One of his cellmates, from May 1932 to August 1934, was none other than Al Capone, who finally had been nailed by the feds and imprisoned for income tax evasion. Big Al assisted Dint in the chapel for a time. By the time Capone was transferred to Alcatraz in August 1934, Dint had taken over as boss of the prison radio department and was responsible for operating the telephone switchboard. Twice during his stretch at Leavenworth, Colbeck was granted compassionate leave and allowed to return to St. Louis—in 1935 to attend the funeral of his brother, and in 1938 to say goodbye to his mother. Colbeck wept freely at her burial.

The years crept by for the men in stir, while the world rushed on outside the gray walls. With so many of the Egan gangsters out of the picture, the mantle of organized crime in St. Louis fell on the Cuckoo Gang, led by Herman Tipton. The Cuckoos defeated various factions of the Italian underworld in a gang war that at one point had four discernable sides, and they banded with the Shelton brothers to battle the Birger Gang for control of bootlegging on the East Side.

When the Birger mob was eliminated in 1930, gang leader Carl Shelton ordered the Cuckoos out of the East Side, but because of the hefty profits he was reaping there, Tipton refused. This sparked a bloody internal war when Shelton convinced gunman Tommy Hayes to battle Tipton for leadership of the Cuckoo mob. Hayes prevailed, but he was gunned down in April 1932, probably on the orders of Shelton, who had come to believe that Hayes had turned against him. His death essentially marked the end of the Cuckoos as a major force in the St. Louis underworld.

While Dint and the rest of the boys were serving their terms, the ex-Egan's Rats who weren't in prison had either gone legit or were pulling capers with other gangs or on their own. After being exiled from the Detroit underworld in 1926, Charles "Tennessee Slim" Hurley, former partner of Johnny Reid and Fred Burke, went first to Kansas City and then ended up back in St. Louis. Slim took a job at the Wellston dog track and attempted to muscle his way back into the action. Hurley soon rubbed the wrong guys the wrong way, which he had a habit of doing, and on October 25, 1927, he was taken for a classic one-way ride. Shot once in the back of the head, his body was found floating in Elm Slough, an arm of Horseshoe Lake, about four and a half miles east of Granite City, Illinois.

In the wake of the destruction of the "Wellston faction," Lester Barth and Dewey Goebel became freelance killers and armed robbers. The two were suspected of participating in many heists and murders, including that of Missouri State Senator Joseph Mogler on December 2, 1929. The next year, they were hired by disgruntled Cuckoo gangster Tommy Hayes to help in his bid to take over the St. Louis rackets.

At dawn on October 2, 1930, Barth and Goebel crept toward an isolated shack near Valmeyer, Illinois, that was used by the Cuckoos as a whiskey plant. They riddled the building with submachine gun fire, killing two men and wounding three others, and were subsequently targeted for retribution. While driving to their hideout on The Hill on the morning of November 22, they were overtaken by the Cuckoo Gang's "gun car," a bulletproofed, maroon Hudson sedan, and were machine-gunned to death near the corner of Columbia and Macklind avenues.

Spurning an offer to join up with Fred Burke and his crew, lower-level Egan thug Louis Mulconry had stayed in St. Louis during Prohibition but remained close friends with Burke. After giving aid to Burke while the latter was on the run, Mulconry found himself embroiled in the Cuckoo Gang's internal war. The doughy gangster was slain in a dramatic gunfight on Weber Road in Carondelet on December 19 in revenge for the murders of fellow ex-Rats Barth and Goebel a month earlier.

Tony Ortell, the violent and rather inept Egan safecracker/recruiter, was busted in New Orleans in 1931 and returned to Jefferson City to serve a term for robbery. When last heard from in the late 1930s, he was still there, with no hope of getting out for a long while.

The Licavoli family, Colbeck's liaisons to the Italian underworld, had moved to Detroit and were smuggling whiskey and beer from Canada across the upper Detroit River. After taking a prominent role in the bloody crosstown war between Detroit's Eastside and Westside mobs in 1930-31, the Licavolis racked up several murder indictments and relocated to Toledo, establishing themselves as the city's crime overlords. The Licavolis would be the top gangsters in Ohio and Michigan for decades and would later extend their influence into Nevada and Arizona.

Two other Egan associates were in the news in the 1930s. Willie Harrison would eventually join the Barker-Karpis Gang as an armed robber and valet to Fred Barker, but he incurred the displeasure of his partners and was killed in early January 1935. Elmer Macklin moved to Detroit, where he became a key figure in the crosstown gang war between two factions of the Italian underworld. He made his mark by assassinating Westside mob boss Chester LaMare in February 1931.

Another ex-Rat who shot his way to infamy was Leo Vincent Brothers. After the crew had been sent to prison, Brothers, whose nickname was "Buster," found work in the city's labor rackets as an enforcer for union organizer Edward "Toots" Clark. In August 1929, at the age of thirty, he was accused of the contract killing of John DeBlasi. Buster's main claim to fame would come when he was charged with the dramatic assassination of *Chicago Tribune* reporter Jake Lingle in an underground pedestrian tunnel in downtown Chicago on June 9, 1930. Lingle's ties to the Chicago mob were exposed and publicly aired in a series of embarrassing news articles.

It was generally believed Al Capone had offered up Leo Brothers to the public as Lingle's killer. Despite doubts about his guilt, Brothers was convicted and sentenced to fourteen years, but he served just eight.

Milford Jones, the boyish-faced killer who had started out with the Egan's Rats and later joined the Cuckoo Gang and Fred Burke's crew, continued to be a one-man crime wave, working for anyone who would pay him. Always an independent-minded crook, he traveled throughout the Midwest, driven by his pathological hatred of Italian criminals. His luck ran out in Detroit's Stork Club on the morning of June 15, 1932, when he bumped into members of the Licavoli mob, who remembered him all too well from St. Louis. Jones did not leave the club alive.

Egan nemesis Max Greenberg was named as one of the principals of the 1924 Rondout train robbery near Chicago, which involved the notorious Newton brothers of Texas. Max had an eventful career, becoming infamous as the right-hand man of "Waxey" Gordon and assisting him in importing booze and drugs through New York. Greenberg and Gordon went to work full time for New York gangster Arnold Rothstein just after Max had fled the Midwest, overseeing the distribution of whiskey smuggled from Europe. After Rothstein's murder in 1928, the two men simply carried on his operation.

Max never set foot in St. Louis again. He and Waxey Gordon eventually were targeted by rival mobsters, and hit men invaded their Elizabeth, New Jersey, hotel on April 12, 1933, killing the fifty-year-old Greenberg and another man. Gordon was said to have barely escaped death that night.

John "Pudgy" Dunn was released from Michigan's Marquette Prison on November 21, 1934, and returned to St. Louis. Trying to rebuild his life, Dunn married and became a stepfather, living with his new family in the Ormond Apartments at 758 Goodfellow Boulevard. He was soon drawn back into the only life he'd ever known. Still enormous and tough as nails, Dunn worked as a bouncer as various East Side clubs, notably Vic Doyle's popular gambling house in East St. Louis.

Pudgy also became involved in union racketeering, serving as a "delegate" in the Central Trades and Labor Union as well as the Miscellaneous Hotel Workers union. On July 14, 1937, Pudgy arrived home at 3:50 a.m. after a night's work. As he entered his building, an unknown gunman stepped from the shadows and blew off his right shoulder with a shotgun blast. The forty-two-year-old Dunn bled to death within half an hour.

Isadore "Izzy" Londe won a parole from Michigan's Jackson Prison on March 26, 1936, and returned home to St. Louis. He immediately became involved with what was left of the Cuckoo Gang and also became a fixture in the St. Louis labor rackets. Londe was suspected of participating in several labor bombings and a couple of murders and was nailed by police for bombing a clothing store at Jefferson and Franklin on June 2, 1938.

The chief witness against him, Lee Baker, was abducted that November, driven out into the county, shot full of holes, and buried alive. Baker amazingly survived, despite being blinded in his right eye. His testimony helped secure a twenty-five-year sentence for Londe. While out on bond the next year, Izzy went to

Los Angeles and was captured after a jewelry heist/shootout in Santa Monica. By the beginning of 1940, he was finally shipped to Jeff City.

Senator Mike Kinney continued to represent the Fifteenth District in the Missouri General Assembly until 1968, when he retired after serving fifty-six years, the longest tenure of any state senator in Missouri history. Edward "Jelly Roll" Hogan served five terms in the state house and four in the state senate before retiring in 1960 after losing a reelection bid. He was part of an unsuccessful attempt to recall Governor-elect Forrest C. Donnell in 1941.

Hogan's brother Jimmy spent the early 1920s in court on charges stemming from the robbery and subsequent murder of bank messenger Erris Pillow. After a total of four trials that ended in either deadlocked or hung juries, the case against Jimmy Hogan was dismissed in March 1926. Despite vows from then-Governor Arthur Hyde to press the case until Hogan was convicted, no justice was dispensed on behalf of Erris Pillow, just as it had been denied to so many others.

Dint Colbeck and the boys came up for parole routinely in the 1930s, but all were just as routinely turned down. The world had changed around them: motion pictures now had sound; Charles Lindbergh had flown across the Atlantic solo; the St. Louis Cardinals had won the World Series three times and claimed two more National League pennants; the stock market had crashed, plunging the country into the Great Depression; Prohibition had been repealed; and the rise of the Nazis in Germany was threatening world peace.

But the imprisoned Egans Rats hardly noticed all this. Their routine was one of lockdowns, tedious jobs, and seeing the same faces day in and day out. Any news of the outside world that was allowed inside depended on the warden's whims and policies. But except for the 1926 fight, the Rats maintained spotless prison records, and they began to see daylight at the end of the tunnel. Far from being the angry young men they were when they were first incarcerated, the now middle-aged members of the Egan gang began receiving paroles.

Denouement

On November 27, 1940, just after his fiftieth birthday, William "Dint" Colbeck was paroled from the Atlanta penitentiary and returned to St. Louis. Just after his arrival, looking dapper and fit, Dint appeared downtown at police headquarters and declared he was going straight, saying how he was looking forward to "doing some good for the people of St. Louis," as a master plumber. By the spring of 1941, his fellow gangsters had been released from Atlanta and Leavenworth.

At first, it seemed that Colbeck would keep his promise, but soon he, Chippy Robinson, Steve Ryan, and Oliver Dougherty became interested in the Grand Novelty Company, which supplied pinball machines and slot machines to clubs and underground gambling parlors throughout the St. Louis area. While this was not necessarily illegal in itself, the former Egans jumped back into the news on June 26, 1941, after the murder of racetrack tout Charles "Cutie" Bailey, who was shot to death off Highway 66 in the county.

Colbeck and the rest were rounded up for questioning, but they were kicked loose after Patrick Hogan, a triggerman for fledgling crime boss Frank "Buster" Wortman, was fingered as the primary suspect. Wortman, an ambitious and capable mobster, was seeking to extend his foothold on the East Side, where he was born and raised.

At this time, the St. Louis area's most lucrative crime enterprises were the gambling clubs and casinos in surrounding towns such as East St. Louis, Venice, Madison, Collinsville, and Granite City. With the Shelton mob gradually being squeezed out by reform-minded lawmen and politicians, the East Side was in a state of flux—and into the void stepped Buster Wortman.

If Colbeck and his pals were indeed trying to re-establish their old criminal empire, the new situation must have confounded them. The action was now across the river on the East Side, where Dint and his associates were unfamiliar with the communities, crooks, and politicians. If he *was* trying to reclaim his old position as lord of all he surveyed, Colbeck was playing a dangerous game, one that that may have led directly to his death.

Whatever his criminal intentions might have been, Dint Colbeck took leave of his wife on the evening of February 17, 1943, and headed over the river for a brief visit to Illinois. Who and where he visited remain unknown to this day, but ninety minutes later, after crossing the McKinley Bridge on his way back into St. Louis, Colbeck was ambushed and shot to death. Police found him slumped in his Ford sedan at the corner of Ninth and Destrehan streets, his body riddled by a half-dozen submachine-gun slugs.

In trying to figure out who had delivered the fatal dose of lead to Dint Colbeck, the most astute police detectives went on record as saying the Shelton brothers were probably behind the murder. But by this time, the Sheltons had largely relocated to Peoria, Illinois, and had little interest in what happened on the East Side of St. Louis.

In fact, Colbeck's murder was almost certainly engineered by Buster Wortman. The up-and-coming East Side gangster, recently returned from a federal prison term, had already forged a solid relationship with the Chicago Outfit and didn't need an aging has-been like Dint Colbeck trying to muscle in on his territory. Plus, he would bolster his already considerable reputation if he took out the legendary Egan boss.

Dint's former partners Chippy Robinson, Steve Ryan, and Red Smith seemed to realize this, as they joined Wortman's organization without so much as a hint of protest upon Colbeck's murder. Perhaps they resented their former chieftain, or just recognized that Buster Wortman, not Dint Colbeck, represented the future.

Of course, it's also possible that Colbeck was indeed serious about going straight and was murdered because he refused to step back into a life of crime.

As for who wielded the Tommygun on Ninth Street that February night, it's impossible know. It may have been Monroe "Blackie" Armes, ace Shelton triggerman and submachine-gun expert who had recently defected to Wortman. Perhaps it was Chippy Robinson, who would soon prove he was just as homicidal as when he first went to prison. Or Steve Ryan, taking out the man who ushered him into a life of crime. Maybe Buster Wortman himself, setting an example for his men. Or perhaps it was someone else. But whoever pulled the trigger, the end result was the same.

William "Dint" Colbeck was buried in St. Louis's Calvary Cemetery after a modest ceremony. Perhaps tellingly, none of his old pals attended. To this day, Dint rests peacefully among two large bushes, overlooking West Florissant Avenue.

It could be said that whatever was left of the Egan's Rats died with Dint Colbeck on February 17, 1943. The gang had no substantive organized presence after its principals were imprisoned in November 1924. And when Dint and boys were paroled in the early 1940s, they encountered a vastly different world, one in which there was no place for the old Egan gang. The survivors of Colbeck's inner circle took their positions at Buster Wortman's heel—born followers who simply changed leaders.

In 1944, Wortman violently consolidated his stranglehold on the East Side, and he used the former Rats to do it. In March, he tried to kill Ted Cronin, the main obstacle to a union takeover, while Cronin was driving on Chippewa Street in South St. Louis. On the other side of the river, both Wortman and Chippy Robinson were suspected of killing triggerman Pat Hogan at the Club Royal casino in Belleville on September 29. Hogan's body was never found, and both Robinson and Steve Ryan were charged with his abduction but beat the rap. Blackie Armes had a falling-out with Wortman and was goaded into a fatal bar fight in Herrin, Illinois, on December 13, 1944.

By the following spring, the supremacy of the Wortman Gang was firmly established, although the media still referred to the crew as the "old Egan gang."

Robinson and Ryan were charged with extortion in 1946, but the charges were dismissed. They also assisted Buster Wortman in disposing of the Shelton Gang once and for all.

Driven out of Peoria by a reform mayor, Carl Shelton had retreated to his home turf in and around Wayne County, Illinois. Wortman and Frank "Cotton" Epplesheimer met with the bosses of the Chicago Outfit, Paul Ricca and Tony Accardo, and put a substantial bounty on Carl and his brother Bernie. Carl was shot to death as he drove his Jeep along a country road not far from his home on October 23, 1947. Bernie would be assassinated by a sniper on July 26, 1948, outside his Peoria tavern.

As the 1940s wound down, the surviving ex-Rats mostly disappeared from the limelight. Frank "Cotton" Epplesheimer was the first to go, dying of natural causes in 1948.

Leo Vincent Brothers, convicted killer of *Chicago Tribune* reporter Jake Lingle, returned to St. Louis in 1940, was acquitted of John DeBlasi's murder, and became an active partner in the Ace Service Company, which supplied gasoline to the mob-controlled Ace Cab Company. Brothers eventually ran afoul of someone, and a gunman crept around his Baden Station home after midnight on September 18, 1950, and shot him three times through the rear screen door as he was drinking a beer. Brothers survived his wounds, and upon his release from the hospital he declared he was "quitting the county" and moved into a suite at the Roosevelt Hotel, where he died of heart disease on December 23 of that year.

Former Rat Willie Heeney became a high-ranking member of the Chicago Outfit. Although not an active member of Fred Burke's crew, he was questioned about the St. Valentine's Day Massacre, probably because of his St. Louis background. Heeney, who acted as an emissary to other gangs in other cities, died of cancer on July 13, 1961.

Claude Maddox, a longtime Egan associate and the only one of Capone's American boys to survive Frank Nitti's purge in the 1930s, remained with the Chicago Outfit for many years. He was suspected, along with Tony Accardo, of gunning down Capone hit man Jack McGurn in a bowling alley in February 1936. Maddox died of a heart attack on June 21, 1958.

After serving nearly sixteen years for the 1938 clothing store bombing, Isadore "Izzy" Londe returned to St. Louis in late 1955. Still associating with gangsters, he found his way back into the news on November 13, 1956, when he was picked up for routine questioning. At the Page Boulevard police station, Londe tried to play it tough with two detectives, one of whom was a brawny ex-Marine. Izzy was beaten senseless and tossed down a flight of stairs. After an unsuccessful lawsuit against the police department for brutality, Londe finally managed to stay out of the public eye and retire peacefully. He succumbed to cancer on August 26, 1951.

Louis "Red" Smith was tried for tax evasion in 1955 and was hit with a year in jail and a $1,000 fine. He died of natural causes in September 1959 at the age of sixty-seven.

Bottoms Gang boss Tony Foley fell on hard times during the Depression but remained a dapper, mob-connected gambler for the rest of his days. He died in Nevada in November 1962.

Edward "Jelly Roll" Hogan continued to serve as a state senator until he was defeated in 1960 by Theodore McNeil, the first black man ever elected to the Missouri senate. The seventy-seven year-old Hogan died on August 11, 1963, after a lengthy illness.

Steve Ryan retained his shares in pinball and vending machine companies and retired to a peaceful life in Calverton Park. He died after suffering a heart attack on May 3, 1965, at the age of sixty-eight. Ryan left behind a wife, son, and grandson, and was interred in Laurel Hill Gardens Cemetery, which stands on the same plot of land off of St. Charles Rock Road that once housed the original Maxwelton Club.

Frank "Buster" Wortman continued to rule as the East Side gambling boss and survived the Kefauver Committee's hearings on organized crime in 1950–51. But high living took a toll on his health, and Wortman passed away at the age of sixty-three in August 1968.

Ray Renard, the gangster-turned-informant whose testimony put Dint Colbeck and most of the other Egan's Rats behind bars, settled into a peaceful life in suburban Los Angeles after his release from prison. He shunned the media, yet allegedly found work as a technical advisor for Hollywood gangster movies.

David "Chippy" Robinson and Oliver Dougherty disappeared from sight and their fates are unknown.

Mike Kinney was convicted along with the rest of the principals in the Jack Daniel's "milking" scheme in November 1925, and was sentenced to a year in jail. He remained a state senator for fifty-six years, the longest tenure of anyone to serve in the Missouri senate. Kinney remained soft-spoken, unassuming, and spry in his later years. He died after a heart attack on February 19, 1971, one month after his ninety-sixth birthday. Laid to rest in Calvary Cemetery, Kinney was the last link to the old days, to the Ashley Street Gang, to the birth of the Egan's Rats.

It's extremely unlikely that any members of the Egan's Rats are still alive today. Organized crime in St. Louis has changed dramatically since the gang's heyday. The North Side neighborhoods formerly ruled by the Egans are now challenged by violent drug gangs armed with machine pistols and body armor, whose members—men, women, and often children—are much more brutal and ruthless than their predecessors. The fact that poverty breeds crime is demonstrated as vividly today as it was in the 1890s.

The city itself has changed greatly in the years since the Egans held sway. Election Days are much more peaceful; roving gangs of "Indians" that terrorized the polling places are long gone. Most buildings associated with the Rats also are gone; a notable example is the Hogan house at 3035 Cass Avenue, which now houses Vashon High School. St. Patrick's Catholic Church at Sixth and Biddle, where many of the Egan gang worshiped as children and adults, was torn down in 1973 after falling into disrepair.

Most people today have no idea, as they walk into the Broadway North entrance of the Edward Jones Dome to watch the Rams play football, that the corner was once occupied by Tom Egan's saloon, the peaceful yet dubious home of St. Louis's most legendary gang.

The Bad Lands, home to the Bottoms Gang, now consists mostly of vast vacant lots and large warehouses. Morgan Street is now Delmar Boulevard; Wash Street is now Cole Street; Dickson Street is now James Cool Papa Bell Avenue; the stretch of Franklin Avenue where Willie Egan's place sat is now Martin Luther King Drive. The changes are endless.

The former site of the Maxwelton Club on Olive Road is right across the street from the Olivette Police Department. The site of Snake Kinney's first saloon, at Second and Carr, is now a mammoth vacant lot used for parking at Rams home games. The alley north of Chestnut between Thirteenth and Fourteenth streets, where Elmer Runge was brutally murdered, is long gone; the St. Louis World War I Memorial now stand there. At Vandeventer and Natural Bridge, the saloon outside of which Eddie Linehan killed Patrolman William Anderson has been replaced by a Chinese restaurant (now abandoned) that sits right across the street from Beaumont High School.

Despite the passage of years and the dimming of memories, the Egan's Rats name—much like that of their Detroit counterparts, the Purple Gang—was too colorful to die completely. Due to Fred Burke's grisly *magnum opus* in Chicago, the gang's moniker was etched into the minds of police and newsmen throughout the country. For years afterward, any tough guy who came out of St. Louis was automatically identified as a member of the Egan's Rats, whether he actually was or not.

Although today the gang is largely unknown in the city they once ruled, there *are* those who remember. Many of the men depicted in these pages have living relatives in the city who may or may not be aware of their ancestors' notoriety. While researching this book, the author was surprised and pleased to cross paths at the St. Louis Public Library with a descendant of Thomas "Red" Kane, Fred Mohrle's assassin—who just happened to be there searching for information about her infamous relative.

APPENDIX

Egan's Rats Roster

The following men were members or associates of the Egan's Rats over the years, roughly from the gang's inception in the early 1890s to its dismantling after the mail robbery convictions of 1924. They range from high-ranking gangsters to low-level hangers-on, and all were arrested by the St. Louis police at some point. The listing includes their full name and the decades in which their association was prominent. Not all members of the Egan's Rats are listed here, only as many as the author has been able to discover.

Frank Anthonis (1910s-1920s)

James Barry (1900s)

Lester Barth (1920s)

Frederick Becker (1900s)

Frederick Beumer
(1890s-1910s)

Samuel Boguslaw (1910s)

Byron Bolton (1920s)

Leo Vincent Brothers (1920s)

Charles Burns (1900s)

John "Pudgy" Burns (1910s)

Joseph Byrnes (1900s)

James Callahan (1910s-1920s)

Frank Cammarata (1920s)

Thomas Camp (aka Fred
"Killer" Burke) (1910s-1920s)

Barney Caples (1890s-1900s)

Jerry Caples (1890s)

William Caples (1890s)

Robert Carey (1910s-1920s)

John Carmody (1910s)

Barney Castle (aka Kassel)
(1910s-1920s)

Joseph "Green Onions"
Cipolla (1910s-1920s)

Patrick Clancy (1900s-1910s)

William "Dint" Colbeck (1900s-1920s)

James "The Rat" Collins (1890s-1900s)

John "Kink" Connell (1920s)

Michael "Heavy" Connors (1910s-1920s)

Walter Costello (1900s-1910s)

Patrick Crowe (1910s-1920s)

William "Lucky Bill" Crowe (1910s-1920s)

Bernard "Oklahoma Red" Deaver (1920s)

August Dietmeyer (1910s-1920s)

William "Whitey" Doering (1910s-1920s)

John Dougherty (1910s-1920s)

Lawrence Dougherty (1920s)

Oliver Dougherty (1910s-1920s)

Harry "Cherries" Dunn (1910s)

John "Pudgy" Dunn (1910s)

James Durant (1900s-1910s)

Thomas Egan (1890s-1910s)

William Egan (1890s-1920s)

William Engler (1920s)

Frank "Cotton" Epplesheimer (1910s-1920s)

Harry Exnicious (1900s-1910s)

James "Fats" Feeney (1910s)

Arthur Fineburg (1910s)

Walter Fischer (1910s-1920s)

Harrison "Doc" Fitzgerald (1900s-1910s)

William Fritsch (1890s)

William Gagel (1890s-1900s)

Tony Garrity (1900s)

William "Red" Giebe (1900s-1910s)

Edward Georgan (1910s)

Dewey Goebel (aka Goebbels) (1920s)

Vincent Goedde (1920s)

Abraham Goldfeder (1910s)

Max Greenberg (1910s-1920s)

John Harris (1910s)

William Harrison (1920s)

William Heeney (1910s)

James "Sticky" Hennessey (1920s)

Edward "Dutch" Hess (1900s-1910s)

David Hickey (1890s-1900s)

Don Hoffman (1920s)

Harry Horrocks (1890s-1900s)

William "Red" Houlihan (1890s-1900s)

Charles "Tennessee Slim" Hurley (1920s)

Ezra Milford Jonas (aka Jones) (1910s-1920s)

Andrew "Big Boy" Kane
(1910s-1920s)

Michael Kane (1900s)

Thomas "Red" Kane (1900s)

Edward Kelleher (1890s-1900s)

Timothy Kelleher
(1890s-1900s)

James "Short Sport" Kennedy
(1910s)

Max Ketcher (1900s)

Michael Kinney (1890s-1920s)

Thomas "Snake" Kinney
(1890s-1910s)

William Kinney (1890s-1920s)

John Laker (1900s-1910s)

Thomas Lamb (1890s)

Charles "Red" Lanham
(1910s-1920s)

Joseph Laughlin (1890s)

Edward "Cocky" Leonard
(1920s)

Anthony Licavoli (1920s)

James Licavoli (1920s)

Peter Licavoli (1920s)

Peter "Horseface" Licavoli
(1920s)

Thomas "Yonnie" Licavoli
(1920s)

Edward Linehan (1910s-1920s)

Carl Lohrman (1890s)

Isadore "Izzy" Londe (1920s)

Harry Londo (1920s)

Elmer Macklin (1920s)

Bartley Martin (1920s)

John "Guinea Mack" McAuliffe
(1890s-1900s)

John McHale (1890s)

Michael "Mickey Mack"
McNamara (1890s-1900s)

Michael "Shamrock"
McNamara (1920s)

James McNulty (1910s)

Ben Milner (1910s-1920s)

Sam Mintz (1910s)

Fred "The Yellow Kid" Mohrle
(1900s)

John E. Moore (aka Claude
Maddox) (1910s-1920s)

Pascal Morina (1910s-1920s)

Paul Morina (1910s-1920s)

Louis "Always Broke"
Mulconry (1910s-1920s)

John Munson (1900s)

John Murphy (1910s)

Spud Murphy (1910s)

James Nolan (1900s)

Charles Nelson (1910s)

Frank "Gutter" Newman
(1900s-1910s)

Elmer Norman (1910s)

Raymond "Crane-Neck"
Nugent (1920s)

Thomas O'Brien (1900s)

Bart O'Donnell (1910s)

John O'Hara (1910s)

Daniel O'Leary (1890s)

Anthony Ortell
(1900s-1920s)

Thomas Owens
(1890s-1900s)

Antonio Pittaluga (1920s)

Clarence "Little Red"
Powers (1910s-1920s)

Edward "Big Red" Powers
(1910s-1920s)

John Reid (1910s-1920s)

Arthur Reidy (1910s)

William "Shorty" Regan
(1890s-1920s)

Raymond Renard (1920s)

David "Chippy" Robinson
(1910s-1920s)

William "Skippy" Rohan
(1890s-1910s)

Harry Romani (1910s)

Joseph Rosewell (1900s)

George Ruloff (1910s-1920s)

Elmer Runge (1920s)

Stephen Ryan (1910s-1920s)

Maurice Shea (1900s)

Raymond Shocker
(aka Schulte) (1920s)

Thomas Skinner (1920s)

Louis "Red" Smith
(1910s-1920s)

Timothy Sullivan
(1910s-1920s)

Everett Summers
(1920s)

Daniel Sweeney (1910s)

John Tracy (1890s-1900s)

Lee Turner (1910s-1920s)

Richard Walsh (1890s)

Theodore Werner
(1910s-1920s)

William J. Werth
(aka Beatty Babbitt) (1910s)

John Whelan (1900s)

Peter White (1900s-1910s)

Arthur Wilson (1910s-1920s)

James "Kid" Wilson (1900s)

Martin Wilson (1920s)

August Winkeler (aka Winkler)
(1920s)

George Woelfel (1890s-1900s)

Frederick Woelfel
(1890s-1910s)

Samuel Young (1890s-1900s)

NOTES

Most information in this book was gleaned from newspaper articles, and the following abbreviations are used when citing publications:

Chicago Tribune . . . . .CTR   *St. Louis Post-Dispatch* . . . . .P-D

Detroit Free Press . . . . .DFP   *St. Louis Globe-Democrat* . .G-D

Detroit News . . . . .DN   *St. Louis Star* . . . . .STR

Detroit Times . . . . .DT   *Toledo Blade* . . . . .TBL

New York Times . . . . .NYT

Prologue: Dint Goes Across The River

13-16   Main events   The recreation of Colbeck's murder is drawn from the following articles: P-D, 2/17-20/43, G-D, 2/18-20/43, STR 2/18-20/43.

Chapter 1: Sneak Thieves

17-18   Kerry Patch   A good description of the neighborhood can be found at home.earthlink.net/%7Elilirish/Kerry-Patch.html; ethnic descriptions from 1880 and 1900 census.

18   Egan family   Egan family birth dates are from the Calvary Cemetery office.

18-20   Snake Kinney   A good thumbnail sketch of Kinney's life and career (written by Kinney himself) can be found at P-D 4/03/01.

20   "Bloody Third ..."   These men were frequently arrested in each other's company during the early 1890s. Just about every week in the decade, newspapers detailed how one or a group of these youths were

arrested or chased by police; two examples: P-D
10/14/91, 11/9/96.

21	Frank James	Yeatman, Ted, *Frank and Jesse James*, p. 297. Nashville, TN: Cumberland House, 2000.
21-22	Egan description	P-D 1/21/12, taken from his interview.
22-23	Skippy Rohan	Descriptions of his life and career and be found at P-D 7/24/97, 8/10/97.
23	Egan … workhouse	A list of Egan's early arrests can be found at P-D 6/3/95.
24-25	Kinney's saloon	P-D 9/6/96, 4/3/01. Recreation of the inside is drawn from what's known of similar saloons in the same neighborhood; Kinney's place was undoubtedly no different. "Robbers Roost": G-D 9/20/96.
25-26	Egan shooting	P-D 10/17/94; subsequent aftermath with Dave Hickey, P-D 6/3/95. The escape of Mickey Mack and Eddie Kelleher from the Four Courts is covered at P-D 9/22-23/94.
27-28	Caples murder	The best description is at G-D 11/28/95. Supplemental details at P-D 11/28/95; Gagel's own account can be found at 11/6/96.
28	1896 tornado	http://en.wikipedia.org/wiki/1896_Tornado.
28-29	Lincoln Steffens	The muckraker's unflattering comments about St. Louis can be found at http://www.spartacus.schoolnet.co.uk/USAstlouis.htm
29	Baldy Higgins	G-D 9/20/96. Stapleton killing at P-D 11/7/94, 12/8/94.
29-31	Kinney's write-up	P-D 9/6/96. Article describes the rough-and-tumble world of St. Louis saloons and street crime with sarcastic prose and detailed illustrations.
32-33	Kinney/Higgins	Their fight is reconstructed from G-D 9/20/96. Supplemental details at G-D, P-D 9/22/96. While the article of 9/20 says nothing about who accompanied Kinney that night, it was most probably **Tom** Egan, brother Mike Kinney, and others in the Ashley Street hierarchy, who were seldom far from his side. Snake would not have gone into mortal combat with Baldy Higgins with anything less than Tom Egan and his tough guys watching his back.

Chapter 2: The Butler Machine

| 35-48 | Ed Butler | Colonel Ed Butler's rise, career, and downfall are covered in Kirchten, p. 306-329. |
| 36 | Emboldened … | P-D 11/9/96 includes the laundry list of crimes the Ashley Street Gang committed that weekend; with two of them attacking police officers, their |

		daring and recklessness seems to be peaking by the fall of 1896.
36-37	Beimfohr murder	P-D 6/17/97. Skippy Rohan's capture: P-D 6/18/97.
37-38	Carl Lohrman	P-D 8/9-10/97. Lohrman's snitching is the author's speculation; it is quite odd that Lohrman was the only one of the bandits to make bail in the Beimfohr murder, and that the police knew just where to find Rohan in the maze-like streets of the Kerry Patch. Bresnehan, Lohrman's killer, was the leader of a rival gang, but his murder of the Ashley Streeter sparked no retaliation, implying tacit approval by Tom Egan and company; they most probably arranged to have Mike Bresnehan waiting for Lohrman.
38	Rohan's escape	P-D 8/31-9/1-2/97, G-D 8/31-9/1-2/97. More details in P-D 9/4/97; bribery, P-D 12/23/97. Rohan's subsequent acquittal, P-D 5/18, 21/98. His "reformation," P-D 5/23/98.
39	Bullet Dwyer	P-D 10/5/96, 5/4/00. Description is taken from a sketch in P-D 5/4/00. G-D 5/4/00. Tough Bill Condon's bio can be found at STR 1/6/02.
39-41	Jack Williams	Personal descriptions and accounts of the Nineteenth Ward riot, P-D and G-D 3/16-19/99.
41-42	New Year's ...	P-D 1/2/00. Democratic split found at P-D 1/11/00.
42	Dwyer murder	P-D and G-D 5/4-5/00.
43	Curley Keyes	G-D 10/1/00. Condon successfully pleaded self-defense.
43	Hussey shooting	P-D 11/6/00. While Frank Hussey initially survived his wound, it would occasionally reopen and bleed, and might have hastened his death a decade later.
43	Foxy Regan	No newspaper account appeared immediately; the shooting is referred to in P-D 8/20/03.
43	Red Houlihan	P-D, G-D 3/15/01 for details.
44-45	Gam Lee's body	P-D, G-D 3/29-30/01. In his statement, Condon seemed genuinely surprised that everyone was so upset—a telling look at his sense of right and wrong.
46	Irish Nationalists	P-D 8/11-12/01. The Williams Gang's try on Joseph Graham's life is detailed at P-D 8/21-23/01.
46	"preach and pray"	P-D 8/30-31/01, also P-D 10/26/01.
46-47	Ryan shooting	P-D 12/23/01 provides the best account. Ryan wanted to press charges against Mike Kinney, but nothing came of his efforts.
47	George Williams	Physical description at P-D 2/28/07. McBriarty killing: P-D 4/24/98. Most witnesses agreed the derelict was killed needlessly, but Williams was exonerated.

| 47-48 | Condon shooting | The best account, complete with Tough Bill's dying statements, is at STR 1/6/02. Also see P-D 1/6/02. |
| 48 | Bad Jack's death | His trip to Arizona is announced in P-D 7/2/02. His life, career, and death are covered in P-D 10/7/02. |

Chapter 3: On The Rise

51	Shea shooting	P-D 3/5/02; Egan ... Caples; P-D 6/10/09.
51-52	Cuddy ... badge	P-D 12/24/02
52	Lahmer killing	P-D 1/20-21/03. Cuddy Mack's fight with John Ryan is at P-D 5/3-4/03.
52-53	Kinney interview	This article can be read in its entirety at P-D 5/3/03, complete with a sketch of the ward politician.
53	Churchill killing	P-D 5/30/03. Perhaps the first well-known gangster in St. Louis history, Mike Churchill was notorious in the 1880s and '90s, but virtually forgotten by the time of his murder.
54	Saloon description	From Tom Egan's interview in P-D 1/21/12.
54-55	McAuliffe killing	Heavily covered by the city's newspapers, details can be found at P-D, G-D, STR 8/20-24/03. No charges were filed against the officers involved in the shooting. Why they did it is open to question, ranging from plain callousness, determination to avenge the wounded brother officer, or even an internal Egan gang plot; perhaps Tom Egan decided to do away with his friend for whatever reason, but the account is purposely ambiguous to allow readers to draw their own conclusions.
56	Sloan shooting	P-D 2/19/04. This would be the last time that Kinney would be involved in drunken saloon disputes. Around this time, the papers stopped referring to his men as the "Kinney gang," suggesting Snake took some kind of lesson away from this episode.
56	Egan ... stood in	P-D 2/27/04 includes a complete list of the convention's delegates.
57	Wreaked havoc	Election Day terror tactics by the "Indians" are highlighted in P-D 2/29-3/1/04. Hawes' victory in P-D 3/13/04.
57-58	1904 World's Fair	An excellent overview of the event can be found at: www.mohistory.org/content/fair/wf/html/Overview.
58-60	Scheel shooting	Details found in P-D, G-D 9/19-24/04. Accounts were quite confused, and it would take many months to iron out who did what that day.

60	Election details	P-D 11/8-11/04. Tom Egan's father Martin passed away about this time and was interred in Calvary Cemetery.
60-61	St. Louis Tommy	One of the most mysterious of St. Louis's gangland murders, Sullivan's demise was barely noticed by the media. The only real coverage is at G-D 1/30/05. A slightly more detailed account is at P-D 3/9/07. Eddie Kelleher's reaction to his indictment at P-D 2/4/05.
61	Frank Hussey	Background on Hussey at G-D 8/4/11, P-D 5/19/06.
61-62	Bottoms Gang	These men would often be identified as members of this gang in the coming years. A good cross-section of the gang is identified in both P-D 9/2/06 and 1/18/09. Assassination attempts are covered at P-D 12/21/05, 2/2/06. Hussey mug shot, P-D 1/18/09. Additional picture at G-D 8/4/11.
63	Scheel ... Giebe	P-D 10/22/05. Giebe's surrender is detailed in P-D 5/30/06.
63	Kinney's bills	A list of his accomplishments are presented in both P-D 8/1/07, 5/15/12.
63-65	Atlantic City	Kinney's Atlantic City jaunt is covered at P-D 8/24/06.
65-66	Egan ... inner	These men would be key witnesses for Egan in the following year, see P-D 6/19/07. The others had been frequently arrested in his company and would play a key part in Egan-related gang activities in the future.
65-66	Sam Young	A brief sketch of his life can be found at P-D 4/4/09. Frequently arrested in the company of Tom Egan and Snake Kinney, Young's place in the Egan food chain was undoubtedly high. Upon his murder in 1909, the gang went to extraordinary lengths to avenge him.
66	confrontation ...	P-D 10/6/06 details the election-day clash between the two factions, without specifically naming either gang, but the names of the perpetrators are known members of both groups.
67	Election Day	Results can be found at P-D 11/6-8/06.

Chapter 4: Changing Times

69	Jolly Five	Due to the catchy name of this political roost, it stuck in the heads of local newsmen, who often incorrectly labeled it a Egan hangout in subsequent articles. Policy game busts are detailed at P-D 12/8/06.
69-71	Gagel shooting	No newspaper account appeared until P-D 1/26/07. Additional details at P-D 1/27/07, 6/19/07. Gagel's killing of Jerry Caples would

later be garbled by St. Louis newsmen whenever they did a gangland retrospective. Caples would be called "Yatz Kelley." No such hoodlum existed. There was a George "Yatz" Quigley, but he wasn't killed by Willie Gagel and had nothing to do with the Egan's Rats. This mix-up probably occurred due to the fact that record keeping a century ago wasn't as Johnny-on-the-spot as it is today. Gagel's thoughts as he enters the Jolly Five are artistic liberties on my part.

70-71	Don't be a louse ...	The story of how the Egan's Rats earned their nickname can be found at P-D 1/21/12.
71-73	Tony Foley	His assault on Patrolman Stapleton is found in P-D 2/11-13/07. Brother Tim's death is at P-D 12/22/06.
73	Fingerlin killing	P-D 2/14, 15, 22-24/07. Abusing Italians: P-D 9/22/05. Cuddy Mack's retirement announced at P-D 6/1/07.
73-75	detective fight	This event was the top St. Louis news event of early 1907, and was heavily covered by all major newspapers just about every day until mid-summer. P-D, G-D, STR, 2/28-3/5/07 were used for main events. Killian's dismissal is at P-D 12/19/05. The Sullivan murder case is recounted at P-D 3/09/07. Williams trial is covered from P-D 7/10-15/07.
75	McDonald murder	P-D 3/4/07. Real name Regiole Loiseau, Rex McDonald appears to have defected to the Bottoms Gang from the Egan's Rats in the last months of 1906. Not a typical gangster, McDonald was handsome, well-educated semi-pro baseball player, but he carried a notorious reputation from when he snitched off his common-law wife three years earlier in Illinois during a counterfeiting case.
75-76	Bottoms crimes	An overview of the Bottoms Gang's rampage can be found at P-D 3/11/07. The shootout with police is at P-D 8/2/07.
76	Egan trial	Overview of the case, as well as some rare photos of gang members and a from-life sketch of Tom Egan at P-D 6/19/07.
76-77	Kid Wilson	Account of killing at P-D 10/23/07. Egan's subsequent trial at P-D 1/22/08.
78	City Hall raid	The Bottoms Gang's reign of terror that day is covered in P-D 4/14/08.
78	Red McAuliffe	One of the founding members of the Bottoms Gang, he was known as something of a "clay pigeon" in the underworld. His shooting at P-D 9/1/08, his final passing at P-D 9/9/08.

Notes

79-80	Hutton shooting	This evening garnered the Bottoms Gang a ton of ink, as the shooting was covered daily until early February. Main coverage at P-D 1/18-25/09. "Kid" Gleason's spree is covered in P-D 1/29/09. When Gleason was finally freed a decade later, he would be killed while fleeing from a detective in January 1919: P-D 1/7/19
80-81	St. Louis ... 1909	A good site with multiple links to local history is at www.usgennet.org/usa/mo/county/stlouis/index.html. Mickey Mack's status is at P-D 4/7/06. Skippy Rohan updates at P-D 1/8/16
81	Young killing	The best accounts are at P-D 4/4-6/09. Additional info at P-D 6/4/09.
82-86	Mohrle shooting	One of the most shocking St. Louis events of the decade, it was covered daily at least half of the summer. Main events are covered in P-D, G-D, STR 6/4-10/09. Egan's Rats first used on P-D 6/4/09. *Weatherbird* ... P-D 7/10/09. Wright's shooting of his friend is at P-D 7/1/09.
86-88	Marie Mohrle	Her suicide attempt is covered in P-D 7/10/09.

Chapter 5: "We Don't Shoot Unless We Know Who Is Present"

89-91	Kane's trial	Covered in P-D 10/11-19/09. The second trial and dummy plot are detailed in 11/23-25/09. Kane's death: P-D 12/23/10, 1/6/11.
91	Election Day	P-D 11/8-11/10. Kinney's fight detailed P-D 5/15/12, also P-D 4/21/19.
92	Egan smuggling	Evidence concerning Egan's liquor smuggling network can be found at http://www.american-mafia.com/Feature_Articles_159.html Hussey's death P-D 8/4/11
92-93	Edward Devine	P-D, G-D 11/1/11. Von der Ahe murder at P-D 11/15-16/11.
93	Regan murder	P-D 12/26-28/11.
93-97	Egan interview	Taken exclusively from the Sunday magazine of P-D 1/21/12. Contains excellent sketch from life of the gang boss.
97-98	Kinney death	Removal to Kirkwood in P-D 4/17/12. Death and career recounted at P-D 5/15/12. Funeral at P-D 5/19/12. Political revenge at P-D 10/20/12, 11/5-7/12, 4/21/19.
98-99	height ... power	Many of the men named here were most probably attached to the gang before this time, but they all rose to prominence in the early 1910s. One of them, Willie Heeney, would eventually move to Chicago and become an important fixer in Al Capone's Outfit: home.earthlink.net/~lilirish/KerryPatch.htm.

99	Dunn brothers	Harry's description from photo in STR 9/19/16. Escape from workhouse in G-D 3/4/14. John's description, from P-D 7/14/37.
99-100	Foley saloon	"Crime incubator" P-D 4/6/13. Cotty killing: P-D 9/29/12.
100	Carroll murder	P-D 4/2-4/13. G-D 4/2-4/13. MacDonald shooting: P-D 4/5/13.
101	Albert Kapp	P-D 8/16-18/13.
101	baseball betting	The issues of P-D 7/10-11/13 provide a glimpse into the world of St. Louis bookmaking. While Tom Egan is not mentioned in the articles, given the tight fist he had on the city's rackets, it's inconceivable he didn't have some kind of a squeeze on them.
101-102	Friendly Ten	This double homicide is detailed in P-D, G-D 2/10-13/14, including an illustration of the room where the bodies were found.
102-103	Simons trial	Unlike it's predecessors, this killing didn't make quite as big a news splash. Full coverage in P-D, G-D, STR 3/2-5/14.
103-104	liquor ... drugs	For information on Tom Egan's smuggling network and other Egan cells around the country, check: http://www.americanmafia.com/Feature_Articles_159.html An interesting article on drug use in early 20th century St. Louis can be found at P-D 6/12/14. "King Coke-Head": P-D 6/28/12. Articles in P-D 7/23-24/10 gives insight into St. Louis opium usage.
104	Mintz ... Sweeney	Mintz's murder is found in P-D 12/6-7/14, 9/16/15, Sweeney in P-D 3/13-14/15.
104-105	Skippy Rohan	Details of his intervening years found at P-D 1/8/16.
105-106	Fred Burke	Information on Burke's early years graciously provided by Ann Tinsley in a series of e-mails. A good sketch of Fred Burke and his mannerisms can be found at P-D 12/18/29.

Chapter 6: Rotten Cherries

107	Koch killing	CT 11/8/14.
107-108	Details ... hazy	This theory is first alluded to in STR 11/1/21. No confirmation is given, but given the circumstances, I find it plausible and have included it .
108	private quarrel ...	P-D 12/16, 18/15. A John Murphy was present at the Chicago murder of Robert Koch. Whether that same Murphy died on December 16 is unknown.
108-109	Groenwald killing	The best account is in P-D 12/21/15. Supplemental details in P-D 1/10/16. Dunn finally publicly named as suspect in P-D 9/19/16.

109	Reutilinger murder	P-D 12/30/15.
109-110	Rohan murder	P-D, G-D 1/8-9/16. Once again, the positive ID on Harry Dunn was not made public until after his own murder.
110	Schoenborn	His homicide charge at P-D 8/10/12.
111	Romani murder	P-D 8/21/16.
112	Dunn killing	P-D, G-D, STR 9/19-22/16. Supplemental material in STR 11/1/21. Dunn's killers ID'd in G-D 11/1/21. According to his death certificate, Dunn was born on October 28, 1892, making him just shy of his 24th birthday upon his killing.
113	Schoenborn hit	P-D, G-D, 10/5/16
113-115	Gang murders	The weekend killings are covered in P-D, G-D, STR 10/21- 24/16. Fennell/Carroll homicides are at P-D 3/11/1917. Dutch Hess killing at P-D 4/14/17, Bryan Walsh killing at P-D 5/31/17, 11/22/18. Pudgy Dunn's oath at STR 11/1/21.
115-116	Gutter Newman	Both witnesses of the killing and St. Louis newspapers gave wildly differing accounts of this shooting. I've reconstructed the most plausible version of Newman's murder from the following articles: G-D, STR 6/9/17. P-D 6/9, 10, 12/17.
116-117	Costello shooting	P-D, G-D 7/25/17.
117-118	Tom and Willie	The differences between the two are commented on at STR 11/1/21.
118	Reid, Carey	Johnny Reid's birthdate provided by head office of Evergreen Cemetery, Detroit, Michigan. Carey's birthdate from his WWI Service card at www.sos.mo.gov/archives/soldiers. Additional info from 1900 and 1910 census. Carey's burglary bust covered at DN 3/16/24. Ortell's longtime-association with the Rats and his later presence in Detroit indicates that he knew the men for a long time and may well have facilitated their joining the Egan gang.
118-119	Giambrone	The first Italian mob boss of St. Louis remains to this day shrouded in mystery. The murder of the beheaded witness (Salvatore Leone) found here: P-D, G-D, 1/19-22/12. A couple of other murders he was involved in at P-D 12/1/22, 3/18/23.
119	Cuckoo Gang	No seems to know the origin of their nickname. They first appeared in the Soulard district at pickpockets and burglars circa 1910, headed by John "Jack" Lyons. After the end of the Bottoms-Egan war, their crimes became much more violent and daring, especially when the small handful of Bottoms Gang survivors joined their ranks. While their story is too complex and far-reaching

for this book, the Cuckoos would cross paths quite a few times with the Egans in the future.

119   Hogan brothers   Background on Edward Hogan at http://www. crimelibrary.com/gangsters_outlaws/family_epic s/louis/4.html. Additional info on both at P-D 3/30/23. James' murder of Michael Lynam at P-D 8/29, 9/2/15.

119-120   Joseph Cipolla   His killing of rope bandit Heywood Wilson at P-D 10/4/17.

120   McNulty shooting   P-D 10/15/17. Reidy killing and funeral mass brouhaha at P-D 10/18, 20/17.

120-121   W.W. I service   The service cards of all the Egans mentioned here can be found at www.sos.mo.gov/archives/ soldiers. Ortell robbery: P-D 8/19,20/18.

121   Beatty Babbitt   After the killing of Walter Costello, Babbitt was perhaps the most dangerous man in the Egan gang, but his habits of mixing business with pleasure would hasten his downfall. Details of his killing found at P-D 11/21-23/18.

122   Powers brothers   P-D 2/25/23. Leavenworth; their sentences covered at P-D 11/22/20.

122   new members   Physical descriptions of all gang members can be seen at P-D 1/15/25. Doering's pardon at P-D 4/20/23.

122-123   Big Boy Kane   P-D 8/6/23, STR 3/27/25.

123   Dunn collared   Mixed up in a mysterious murder in a Lindell Boulevard mansion, his arrest at P-D 1/3-6/19.

123   Hot Springs   This robbery and its aftermath are mentioned in article about Ruloff's murder at P-D 12/2/21.

123-124   Baden robbery   P-D 4/10,11/19, STR 3/6/25. The eight robbers were never publicly named, but two men suspected of taking part were Max Greenberg and Abe Goldfeder, both of whom would soon defect to the Hogan Gang.

124   Egan death   P-D 4/21/19.

Chapter 7: Dawn of a New Era

125   Colbeck   STR 3/7/25. Burke ... detoured; his bust detailed at P-D 3/26/31, DN 3/16/24.

126   Mulconry ... safe   P-D 5/20/19.

126-127   Water Tower   P-D 1/21-23/20. Account of Lowell Bank job at P-D 4/9/20. While the Water Tower job isn't on Ray Renard's master list of Egan robberies in STR 3/6/25, I'm convinced the Egans did indeed pull this job, mainly due to the fact the MO matches that of the Baden robbery so closely, right down to the same costumes. The dead robber, Walter Fischer, was the recipient of a gubernatorial pardon, something most criminals couldn't dream of, indicating he had a powerful friend helping him; Tom Egan makes a handsome suspect.

127	Egan ... inattentive	http://www.americanmafia.com/Feature_Articles _159.html. Johnny Reid's shooting found at NYT 5/16/21.
128	sergeant-of-arms	P-D 9/9/22. Ireland robbery detailed in article covering Colbeck and Robinson's trial: P-D 4/18/23.
128	Giannola brothers	These two men would dominate Italian organized crime in St. Louis in the early to mid 1920s. Information on their rise to power can be found at STR 11/22/27. Additional history at http://www. crimelibrary.com/gangsters_outlaws/family_epics /louis/2.html
128	Cuckoos	Becker murder at P-D 4/16-20/19. The Cuckoos went on an extended crime spree in the wake of Becker's murder. Lyons killing at P-D, STR 6/14-16/20.
128-129	Hogan ... fight	P-D 10/3/20. Job duties and list of Hogan gang members found at P-D 3/30/23. Overview of Jacob Mackler's career at P-D 2/22/23. Ambs murder: P-D 12/16-17/18.
129	Cody murder	P-D 9/3/20.
129-130	Egan members	Hennessey description: STR 12/13/23. Londe description: P-D 3/30/23. Londe and Runge: STR 3/13/25. More info on "Astor" Runge at P-D 12/6/23.
130	Okie Red	His first meeting with Colbeck is detailed by Ray Renard at STR 3/23/25.
130-131	Georgan killing	This murder was reported in P-D 4/20/19. The tit-for-tat sniping over it is detailed in the following issues: P-D 8/3/20, 8/22/20, 9/1/20.
131-132	Greenberg beef	Details of the double cross in P-D 3/30/23. Bar fight at Egan's in P-D 10/16/20. Detroit smuggling: http://www.crimelibrary.com/gangsters_outlaws/ family_epics/louis/3.html. The story of Greenberg smuggling whiskey from Canada in late 1920 has been told frequently over the years. I haven't been able to find any conformation for it. Greenberg did indeed seem to disappear from St. Louis in the fall and winter of 1920/21, and I find the story plausible under the circumstances.
132-133	Milner shooting	P-D, STR 11/22-24/20.
133-134	Sweeney murder	Details found at P-D, G-D 3/12-14/21. Max Greenberg may have returned to St. Louis to recruit the Hogan Gang as customers for his new Detroit booze pipeline. Egan could have easily learned of

his presence in town and coerced him into the meeting. What Egan may have done to the gunman who accidentally wounded him and failed to kill Greenberg is unknown. Suffice to say, the triggerman (whoever he was) probably didn't go off to live a carefree life in the Bahamas.

134   payroll heists   Info on Egan forays into southern Illinois found at http://www.americanmafia.com/Feature_Articles_159.html

134-135   North St. Louis   Details of the robbery can be found at P-D 4/4-5/21.

135-136   Informants   McNamara murder: P-D 4/11, 12, 17/21. Pillow shooting at P-D 5/10-12/21. Morris murder at P-D 5/13-15/21.

136   Regan murder   P-D, G-D 4/26/21. The shootout at Joe Mount's saloon was a big story in wartime St. Louis; details in P-D 1/23-25/18.

136   robberies   The stories of these heists are found at P-D 9/23-24/21: P-D 10/24/21. Egan involvement is confirmed at STR 3/6/25.

Chapter 8: Combat

137-139   Egan murder   Main accounts taken from P-D 10/31-11/1-5/21. Also G-D, STR 11/1-3/21. Nine-year-old Abe Stein, witness of the killing, allegedly saw the shooters just before they did the work; he added the tantalizing claim that one of the hit men dressed as a woman. Young Stein eventually changed his story and his credibility diminished. As usual with such events, different eyewitnesses had different stories, so I recreated the most plausible scenario out of the varying statements.

138   gasped out ...   P-D 12/2/21.

138   John Dougherty   While not a major member of the Egan gang, he would become a city sheriff in later years and give assistance to the remaining members of the crew when they re-entered the St. Louis rackets in the 1940s: P-D 3/14/45.

139   Egan paternity   P-D 11/7/21, 1/9/22.

139   Renard ...   At this point in the history of the Egan's Rats, turncoat Ray Renard gives his unprecedented testimonial in the St. Louis *Star* between February-April 1925. As with most mob informants, Renard's statements reflect his own point of view. He often comes across as self-righteous and a bit arrogant, and sometimes his accounts differ from those of contemporary newspaper articles. However, Renard was a high-ranking

member of Egan gang during Prohibition, the only of the Rats to leave a first-person account of his crimes. Often his remorse and fear seem to jump off the pages, especially when he describes murders he claims to have witnessed first-hand. Therefore, I have decided to use Renard's statements as primary source material. All dialogue is taken from his accounts. In some places of the narrative, some words are blanked out, obviously denoting curse words. In the interest of keeping the natural flow of said dialogue, I have inserted probable curse words in the place of the blank, expletive deleted spaces. Every thing else is untouched. Gangsters, then and now, are profane men, and I believe this adds a touch of realism to the dialogue. If the reader is offended, I apologize.

139-140	McAuliffe trial	P-D 11/15-20/21.
140	refining company	Curiously, Renard doesn't mention this episode in his testimonial. P-D 11/26-28/21, 12/1/23.
140	Ruloff murder	The best account is in P-D 12/2/21. Another article and description/photo of Allies Restaurant at P-D 12/29/21. No one ever fit the pieces of this killing together; the only motive ever given was he was killed because he "talked too much."
141	Maxwelton move	P-D 3/7/25.
141	Greenberg	This conversation and bounty disclosure at STR 3/4/25. Jelly Roll Hogan would later publicly claim that John Doyle had been in an Ohio jail at the time of Egan's murder: P-D 3/29/23. His claim has yet to be verified. The question of who actually shot Willie Egan that night was never definitely settled.
141-143	Cipolla killing	Main accounts of the double murder and Dupo bank job from come from P-D, G-D 12/23, 27-29/21, STR 3/11/25. Cipolla's brother Charles would eventually take up arms with the Hogan Gang in an attempt to avenge Joseph: P-D 6/11/22.
143-144	Market Street	This gunfight is covered in P-D 12/30-31/21. Powers' remark at G-D 2/25/23.
144-145	Londe ... Doyle	Accounts of both shootings in P-D 1/6/22. Supplemental material of Doyle's shooting at P-D 1/7-8/22, 4/19/22.
145	Maplewood	Account of robbery at P-D 1/17/22, STR 3/6/25.
145-146	Ray Nugent	One of the most mysterious of all Egan's Rats. A determined search by the author has uncovered virtually no leads on his past. He may have been

Notes

a native of New Orleans, but I have not confirmed this. Nugent appears to have come to St. Louis from Ohio, specifically the Cincinnati area. He always seemed to return to this state when the excrement hit the fan. His veteran service confirmed by his wife in the 1950s. Nugent's description from photo in the Helmer book on the St. Valentine's Day Massacre.

146	Burke hideouts	A brief overview of his St. Louis activities can be found at P-D 12/18/29, 3/26,27/31.
146	Gus Winkler	Real name and birthdate at Helmer/Mattix p.28. Most records list him as being born in 1898, while his tombstone further muddles the matter by giving a 1901 birthdate. I concur with 1900 as the correct year. Cuckoo Gang connection at P-D 10/10/33. Military service card at www.sos.mo.gov/archives/soldiers.
147-148	Colbeck attack	STR 2/14/24, 3/4/25.
148	robberies	Chouteau Trust: P-D 3/3/22. Gravois Bank: P-D 3/6/22. Both are on Renard's master robbery list at STR 3/6/25.
148-149	Vance shooting	P-D 3/21-22/22. Water Tower holdup: P-D 4/4/22.
149-150	Kennedy murder	The best accounts are drawn from G-D 4/18/22, STR 3/17/25. Additional coverage used from P-D 4/18-19/22.
150	Hogan ... holes	P-D 9/9/23. He virtually dropped off the face of the Earth after Kennedy's death, and his whereabouts were a great source of speculation during the gang war.
150-151	May shootings	Descriptions of these episodes found at P-D 5/18-19/22. Dialogue from Ray Renard's article in STR 3/4/25.
151	Robinson shooting	P-D 6/5/22.
151-152	Truce	Details of Father Dempsey's mediation found at P-D 6/7/22.
152-153	Jelly Roll caught ...	P-D 6/11/22. Greenberg's departure: P-D 9/8/22.
153	Tower Grove	This robbery covered in P-D 7/5/22. Ray Renard gives his account at STR 3/6/25. Diamond heist at P-D 7/24/22.
153-154	Maxwelton	A good description and diagram of the gang's headquarters and their antics there can be found at STR 3/6/25.
154-155	Robinson	Renard's description of Chippy Robinson is at STR 3/18/25. Although the article doesn't specifically name Robinson (his name is blanked out) it's obvious he's talking about him. Over the years, Robinson is repeatedly referred to as the "sharpshooter" or "bad man" of the gang: STR

4/1/25. An outline of the mystery killer's face is seen at STR 3/14/25. A comparison of gang members' facial features from mug shots shows it's Chippy's face in the silhouette.

155-156 Double shooting   P-D 9/2-3/22. New York gunmen theory pushed in P-D 9/8/22. Ray Renard's account at STR 3/4/25. A mug shot of Max Gordon is at P-D 6/15/30.

156-157 Dint's personality   Ray Renard draws an excellent portrait of the gang boss in STR 3/7/25. Renard's misadventures in STR 3/6/25.

157 Beer concessions   More on Colbeck's business dealings in STR 3/7/25.

158 Lange murder   P-D 11/16,17/22.

158 Berg killing   P-D 12/4/22, STR 3/24/25.

159-160 Jack Daniel's   The story of the warehouse robbery can be found at P-D 12/9/22. Renard's account at STR 3/10/25.

Chapter 9: Maelstrom

161 Anderson ...   P-D 1/12/23, STR 3/6/25.

161-162 Deaver murder   P-D 2/11/23, STR 3/23/25. Gus Dietmeyer was identified by witnesses as the shooter but was turned loose due to a lack of evidence: P-D 4/10/24. His murder of Joseph Toomey at the behest of Cherries Dunn is at P-D 9/19/16.

162-163 Mackler hit   Details of Mackler's murder from P-D 2/22-23/23. Renard's description at STR 3/16/25.

163-164 Little Red   The murder of Powers is covered in P-D, G-D 2/26/23, as well as at STR 3/20/25. Wilson's death: P-D 4/19/23.

164-165 St. Louis Trust   P-D 3/11/23. Ray Renard's account at STR 3/6/25.

165 Wellston bank   P-D 3/16-19/23. Renard was ID'd by a handkerchief embroidered with an "R" found at the scene. He claimed it wasn't his. Renard gives his story of the robbery in STR 3/5/23.

165-166 Hogan house   The best account of this shooting and Hogan's precautions is at P-D 3/22/23. Additional details in STR 3/4/25.

166-167 running fight   Details of shooting and Hogan's remark at P-D 3/25-26/23. Medical care: P-D 2/18/43. In STR 3/4/25, Renard describes how the boys passed the hat around the Maxwelton and got up a purse of $500 for Bickel's care.

167 Lindell gunplay   P-D 3/27, 28/23. Renard's claims on STR 3/4/25.

167-169 Hogan interview   This article can be found in it's entirety at P-D 3/29/23, as can Father Dempsey's comments.

169-170 pictures ...   A large portion of the Friday issue: P-D 3/30/23, was devoted to the gangs. The comments of both the police official and reporter are found within.

170-171 Colbeck ... Details of his peace proposal and the letters in STR 3/5/25.

171-173 mail robbery The downtown mail robbery is one of the biggest events in the history of the Egan's Rats. Immediate news accounts are at P-D 4/2-3/23. Also in STR 11/1/24, P-D 11/1-2/24.

173-175 Constable Neu Basic events in P-D 4/4/23, 11/1/24. Renard's version of the shooting (curiously absent from the *Star* series of 1925) is at P-D 7/30/31. Clarence "Dizzy" Daniels drew a life sentence for the murders of off-duty St. Louis policeman William Griffin and produce merchant John Surgant during a South St. Louis County robbery spree on June 10, 1923: P-D 6/10-14, 9/18/23. Daniels' rebuttal and Renard's reaction at P-D 11/21-22/33.

175 aftermath ... The morning after the constable's shooting is described in STR 11/1/24.

176 Renard's legals ... P-D 4/9-10/23, STR 3/7/25. Renard's acquittal for a February 1923 bank robbery in East Alton, Illinois at P-D 4/17/23.

176 Big Bill Rush P-D 4/6/23, STR 3/27/25.

176-177 Lucky Bill P-D 4/12-13/23, 12/6/23.

177 Colbeck's trial P-D 4/18-20/23.

177 Doering ... His bust is covered at P-D 4/19-23/23.

177-178 Burke distillery While this crime has never been officially linked to Fred Burke, I believe he and his pals did indeed pull off this distillery heist. Especially given Burke's presence in St. Louis at the time and his later penchant for using police uniforms to fool victims; this job has his name written all over it. According to later reports, the idea of using police uniforms to fool victims may have originated with Bob Carey. P-D 4/25/23, CTR, DN 8/1/32.

178-180 Powderly murder P-D 6/4/23, STR 3/12/25.

Chapter 10: Depraved Indifference

181-183 Staunton heist P-D 5/27-28/23, 11/10-14/24.

183 easy come ... STR 3/6/25.

183-184 Pocahontas ... The inside story of this job from Ray Renard is found at STR 3/28/25. Lee Turner's flying skills: P-D 8/8/23.

184-186 Young murder P-D 6/13/23. Ray Renard's first-hand account at STR 3/18/25. Linehan description at STR 3/21/25.

186-188 Pocahontas ... STR 3/28/25. Turner's crash landing at P-D 8/8/23.

188-189 UR heist P-D 7/3/25, 11/10/25, 3/26/31. Renard's account at STR 3/5/25. The only confirmed participants were Burke, Dougherty, and Turner. The other bandits who took part were never named by Ray Renard and their identities are uncertain to this day. They probably were not members of Burke's sub-group, as Renard stated that when Fred told Dint about the job he said he needed some "good men" to help pull it off, which suggests that Gus Winkler, Bob Carey, et al., were unavailable for whatever reason.

189	Turner flight	His airshow for the boys is detailed at P-D 8/8/23.
189-191	Maxwelton	The Rats' attempted destruction of the old Maxwelton is at P-D 8/6/23, STR 3/7/25.
191	Big Boy	Brothers' involvement is speculation on my part. Ray Renard indicated that Kane's killer was a "hanger-on" who didn't go to prison with the rest in 1924. Brothers was arguably the most dangerous former Rat in St. Louis when Renard's testimony came out. His reputation would have gotten a boost by killing Kane. By the time Brothers was charged with murder in 1929, he was already locally notorious. Details at P-D 8/6/23, STR 3/27/25.
191-192	fatal flight	P-D 8/8-9/23.
192-193	whiskey theft	Renard's account of the milking operation is at STR 3/10/25. Participants named in P-D 11/2/25.
193-195	Jimmy Hogan	An update on his situation and the story behind his attempted murder at P-D 9/10,11,13,17/23, STR 3/25/25. Colbeck's comments in P-D 9/13/23.
195	whiskey theft	The milking scam's press coverage at P-D 9/21-22/23.
195-198	Billy Grant	His career and subsequent demise: P-D 10/23-24/23, While Renard's account in STR 3/14/25 differs from the above articles, the gangster claimed to have witnessed the triple homicide himself, so his report deserves respect.
199	Park Savings Trust	P-D 11/6/23, STR 3/6/25.
199	Catanzaro	P-D 11/16/23, STR 3/26/25.
199	Consolidated ...	STR 3/6/25.
199-200	Doering shooting	P-D 11/19/23, STR 3/27/25.
200-202	Londo, Runge	Their murders are detailed at P-D 12/1, 5, 6/23. STR 3/13/25.
202-203	Hennessey	His death and Londe's statement are at P-D 12/13/23.

Chapter 11: Downfall

206	West St. Louis	P-D 1/15/24, STR 3/6/25.
206	tobacco ...	Renard's account of the failed heist at STR 3/6/25
206-208	Linehan, Renard	Their argument with Colbeck is at STR 3/9/25, as is the account of Patrolman Anderson's murder. Supplemental material at P-D 2/11/24.

Notes

208-211 Linehan murder — A graphic eyewitness account from Ray Renard, complete with illustrations, is at STR 3/21/25. More coverage of the killing and Colbeck's comments at P-D 2/13-14/24, STR 2/13-14/24 While the names of the perpetrators are blanked out, it's fairly obvious that Colbeck himself and his four top henchman were responsible.

212 Maplewood ... — P-D 2/26/24, STR 3/6/25. Info on Barth and Goebel at P-D 11/22/30. Goebel's real name was Goebbels, two of his brothers, William and Harry, assisted him. Their service records at www.sos.mo.gov/archives/soldiers.

212-214 Renard ... — Colbeck's reaction to his acquittal at STR 3/29/25. His decision to run at STR 3/30/25.

214 indictments — P-D 4/10/24.

214 Granite City job — P-D 4/25/24, STR 3/6/25. Italians ... STR 11/22/27.

215-216 Renard's return — STR 3/30-31/25.

216-218 Kinney shooting — This event earned multiple headlines in the city's newspapers. Accounts used from P-D 6/3-7/24, G-D 6/4-6/24.

218 Renard's letter — P-D 11/1/24, STR 3/31/25. Colbeck's arrest: P-D 8/13/24. "Blind Walter" Kelly was quite an enigmatic figure. Active in St. Louis city politics for nearly thirty years, he always seemed to be on the fringes of crime and graft, and had emerged unscathed from the Folk trials of the early 1900s. Wellston bank job: P-D 9/19/24, STR 3/6/25.

219-220 downtown trial — Main accounts from P-D 10/30-31, 11/1-4/24.

220-224 Staunton trial — The Egans final trial and convictions were thoroughly covered by the St. Louis media. Primary sources include: P-D 11/10- 16/24. Their Leavenworth were covered at P-D 11/16, 17, 19/24. Grand and Olive: P-D 1/19/25.

224 Re-trial — The Egans re-trial on the downtown mail robbery at P-D 1/16-20/25.

224 Eagle Park — P-D 11/17/24, 10/5/25.

224-225 Mazda Lamp — P-D 12/6/24. Barney Castle's last job at P-D 4/7/25.

225 Wellston crew — Their crimes accelerated after the imprisonment of the Egan leadership, but the days of high-risk robberies were closing fast. The Wellston boys frequently got shot during their capers. When killed in the Creve Coeur shootout, both Vincent Goedde and James Tully had partially healed bullet wounds from previous gunplay. Account of the gun battle at P-D, G-D 10/5/25. "Hell's Half-Acre": P-D 3/9/12.

226 Colbeck ... — His comments on the Renard series at STR 4/1/25.

Chapter 12: The One That Got Away

227	Burke crew	Lists of those involved with Fred Burke in Detroit can be found at DN 3/16/24, 8/1/32, 11/27/33. DFP 1/5/25.
227-228	Kay robbery	DN 3/11, 13, 16/24. Carey's threats at DN 8/1/32. Waugh manuscript p.134. A list of Burke's crimes can be found at DN 3/27/31 and P-D 3/26/31.
228-229	"snatch racket"	DN 9/8/27, 6/15/32. Helmer/Bilek p.80, Waugh p.151.
229	Pudgy Dunn	DN 1/18/24. Hurley shooting at DFP 1/8/25.
229	Bishop shooting	DN 1/10/25. While Isadore Bernstein is listed as having been present, this is unlikely as he was barely 17 years old at the time. Joe is much more likely to have been there, probably using his younger brother's name at his booking.
230	Louisville ...	Info on this bank robbery was drawn from P-D 3/26/31. His chase through St. Louis: P-D 6/5/25, Helmer/Bilek p.136.
230-231	Londe's escape	NYT 7/5/25, P-D 11/19/38.
231	Burke's acquittal	P-D 11/12/25.
231	North St. Louis	This bank robbery detailed at P-D 5/18/26, 3/26/31. STR 12/20/30. Five of the six men involved in the robbery would eventually die violent deaths, a grim reminder that the gangster lifestyle often ends with a bullet.
231-234	Reid, Dipisa	The gang war between was heavily covered by Detroit newspapers; Broadway gun battle at DN 8/11/26, café shooting at DN 8/12/26, DT 8/12, 14/26. Brush Street gun battle at DT 8/14/26. Double murder: DN 8/26, 27/26. Reid's terms at DN 6/28/28.
234	St. Louis shooting	This mass murder, in the midst of a ferocious gang war between the Cuckoo Gang and the Green Ones, persuaded Vito Giannola sue for peace with Cuckoo boss Herman Tipton. P-D 9/24-26/26.
234-235	Loveley	This robbery and the subsequent misadventures of its perpetrators is at DN 8/1/32.
235	Hurley shooting	DN 9/20/26. Rhodes' suicide attempt at DN 10/30/26.
235-236	Reid murder	DN 12/27-29/26, 11/28/33. Dipisa's brother Leo was killed in the attempted robbery of their Macomb County roadhouse in November 1926. The shooters were found to be Canadian hijackers. Whether or not they had anything to do with Johnny Reid is unknown. DN 11/24, 25/26. Mike Dipisa would eventually get his, killed by a constable after he murdered a Polish bootlegger

named Gus Nykiel who resisted his extortion demands. DN, DT 6/28/28.

236   Weinberg murder   DN 2/4/27. Joseph Bloom and George Cohen were from New York City originally. Their real names were William Harrison and Isaac Riesfield, respectively. Harrison/Bloom had beaten a 1925 murder indictment there: DT 3/29/27.

236-237   Ellis, Snyder   DN 3/17/27, 8/1/32.

237-238   Milaflores ...   The best account is in DN 3/29/27. Supplemental details in DN 3/30/27, DT 3/29-30/27. Many accounts say 110 bullet holes were found in the walls of the hallway; this seems to have been an exaggeration, since ballistic expert William Cavers determined the submachine gun was fitted with a 50-round drum, and a .45 revolver and .45 automatic were used as well. One of the Siamese Twins apparently whipped out a second pistol when his gun came up empty, as Cavers stated that a .38-caliber revolver had been used as well. This was why the number of shooters at first was believed to have been four; it was later amended to three. All told, there were probably around seventy shots fired in the fusillade.

238-239   Werner   His murder detailed at P-D 4/18/27.

239-240   Capone meeting   Helmer/Bilek p.81, 83-85.

240   Burke ...   Details about his imitators at Helmer/Bilek p.84.

240-241   Oakland Avenue   Fred Burke's retaliation against the Purples found at DT, DFP 7/22/27. Fein snatch at DN 9/12/33; Abe Axler and Eddie Fletcher would continue on as the Purple Gang's top killers until November 1933, when they were taken for a "one-way ride" by their own friends: DN 11/27-29/33.

241-242   Shocker ...   A lower-level of both the Egan's Rats and the Burke crew, his attempted murder is at DN 9/7-8/27, 11/27/33.

Chapter 13: "Nobody Shot Me"

243   Capone's gang   A partial list of Burke's Chicago associates is at Helmer/Mattix p. 118-123.

243-244   Fred Goetz   Good sketches of his life and career found at p. 36 of *Public Enemies* by Bryan Burrough, Penguin Press, New York, NY, 2004; also at Mario Gomes' excellent website: http://www.myalcaponemuseum.com/id107.htm

245   horsing around   Info on Burke at www.myalcaponemuseum.com/id91.htm The golf caddy story related in *Sports Illustrated* 11/6/72.

245	"American boys"	Helmer/Bilek, p. 84-85.
246	Toledo heist	Info on the armored truck robbery at TBL 4/17-18/28. Also at Helmer/Bilek, p. 136-137, Helmer/Mattix p. 113.
246-248	Yale murder	NYT 7/2/28. Helmer/Bilek, p. 91-94, Schoenberg, p. 201-203.
249	North Siders	The on-and-off strife between the groups is discussed at Helmer/Bilek, p 19, 47-54, 87-88, 93-94.
249	Couderay ...	The plotting of the massacre and it's main participants are found the FBI's file at p. 38-39; http://foia.fbi.gov/stvalen/stvalen1.pdf. Also at Helmer/Bilek, p. 231-233.
250-252	Gusenberg ...	Pete Gusenberg's final thoughts are artistic license on my part. For years it was assumed that the North Siders had congregated in the garage to await a shipment of stolen booze, but this is convincingly refuted in Helmer/Bilek, p. 131-132.
252-255	massacre ...	My account of the St. Valentine's Day Massacre draws from Schoenberg, p. 207-229; Helmer/Bilek, p. 3-8.
255-256	Chicago police	The investigation in St. Louis and disassembly of one of the murder cars at Helmer/Bilek, p. 127-45. Helmer/Mattix, p. 122. Capezio allegedly received his nickname of "Tough Tony" from this incident. According to the FBI report, one of the men who helped him dismantle the Cadillac was Raymond Shocker. http://foia.fbi.gov/stvalen/stvalen1.pdf
256	"James Ray"	CTR 3/5-6/29 Helmer/Bilek, p. 139-144.
256-257	killers ...	Helmer/Bilek, p. 232-234; Helmer/Mattix, p 118-123. I have based my conclusions based on the above two sources, both linking Burke and Goetz to the police uniforms. The Peerless was found near Maddox's home, which indicates that he may have driven it. Winkler, while capable of killing, was at his best behind the wheel of a car, and probably drove the Cadillac. Bob Carey and Ray Nugent were best utilized as triggermen, and were most probably the two "detectives." Byron Bolton later said in his FBI confession that he watched for Bugs Moran from a room across the street. Both a letter addressed to him and possibly a vial of prescription medicine were later found in this room by police.
257-258	scattered ...	The immediate aftermath for the killers is found at Helmer/Bilek, p. 154-155.
258	autumn ...	Helmer/Bilek, p. 177-178. Peru bank robbery: Helmer/Mattix, p. 126

Notes

258-259	December ...	The bond story, murder of Patrolman Skelly, and attendant fallout at Helmer/Bilek, p. 178-184.
259-260	Burke in hiding	Burke's marriage, hiding out, and subsequent fate are covered in Helmer/Bilek, p. 188-190. Bonner murder in P-D 7/14/30. Merchants Trust robbery from Helmer/Mattix, p. 164. Additional info at P-D 3/26-27/31.
260	Winkler ...	The beginnings of his problems with the Chicago outfit are covered at Helmer/Bilek, p. 199-200.
260-261	Nugent ...	His time in Miami and disappearance covered at Schoenberg, p. 265, Helmer/Bilek, p. 201; sand dune rumor at DN 8/1/32.
261-262	Bob Carey	His downfall and death are covered at DN, P-D, NYT, 8/1/32; It's possible that Carey and Rose Sanborn were murdered. NYPD never specified how the suicide verdict was reached. True crime author Rose Keefe spoke with a former truck driver for George "Bugs" Moran who said he talked with Moran circa 1932 and that Moran mentioned that he had just returned from "the coast" and "had taken care of Bob Carey." How Moran would have known Carey was one of the St. Valentine's Day Massacre gunmen is unknown. The author leans toward the original murder-suicide verdict but agrees it's feasible that Bugs Moran may well have gotten some little-noticed revenge for the St. Valentine's Day Massacre. This theory is at Helmer/Bilek, p. 249-250.
262-263	Gus Winkler	His troubled final months and murder detailed at Helmer/Bilek, p. 202-211, 290. CTR, P-D 10/10/33. In a tragic footnote, Winkler's grief-stricken wife, Georgette, attempted to kill herself after his funeral but was stopped by Fred Burke's wife, Bonnie. She would survive to write her memoirs, which provide an interesting glimpse into the Burke crew in the late 1920s. Helmer/Bilek, p. 248
263	George Goetz	Goetz's murder detailed at CTR 3/21/34, Helmer/Bilek, p. 221- 222.
263-264	Byron Bolton	Bolton's claims are detailed in Helmer/Bilek, p. 227-241. Also available is the FBI file on Bolton's claims: http://foia.fbi.gov/stvalen/stvalen1.pdf

Chapter 14: Denouement

265	Spirits ...	Martin's suicide at P-D 7/4/26. Info on brawl at P-D 6/17/30, 2/18/43, http://www.americanmafia. com/Feature_Articles_159.html

266	theology ...	Colbeck's time as a chaplain's assistant and radio operator at P-D 12/5/30, 11/22/33. Capone as cellmate at this first-rate website by Jim Brasher, whose great-uncle William "Bow-Wow" McQuillen, was a noted member of the Cuckoo Gang: genealogyinstlouis.accessgenealogy.com/Brasher.htm
266	Cuckoos ...	Cuckoos-Green Ones war covered at STR 11/29-12/3/27. Cuckoo internal war reviewed at STR 4/15/32. Information on how the Sheltons instigated the Cuckoo civil war and their gradual departure from East St. Louis is at Pensoneau, p. 145-149, 181- 194.
266-267	Hurley	G-D 10/28, 11/2/27.
267	Barth, Goebel	Mogler murder: P-D 12/2-6/29, 11/22/30. Valmeyer shootings: P-D, G-D, STR 10/2-4/30. Double murder at P-D 11/22-23/30. The three killers of Barth and Goebel were said by a witness to have fired nearly 300 rounds from their Tommyguns.
267	Mulconry	P-D, STR 12/19-20/30. Mulconry's killers (one of whom was suspected to be Tommy Hayes) were driven away in a too-late rescue attempt by a deadeyed machine-gunner riding in the same maroon Hudson used in the Hill shootings. The Cuckoo Gang's internal war ended with the murder of Hayes: P-D, STR 4/15-17/32.
267	Ortell	DN 8/1/32.
267-268	Licavolis ...	Their involvement in Detroit's bloody Crosstown War is at Waugh, p. 221-251. Their takeover of the Toledo underworld and subsequent fates at Waugh p. 277, 307.
268	Harrison	Helmer/Mattix, p. 226.
268	Macklin	DN 2/6-9, 10/28/31. Waugh p. 247-248.
268	Brothers	DeBlasi murder at P-D 8/3-4/29. Lingle killing and Brothers's part in it at Schoenberg p. 277-285.
268	Jones	DN, DFP, 6/15-16/32, 2/9/33.
268-269	Greenberg	P-D 4/13/33.
269	Dunn	His prison release at DFP 11/22/34. Dunn's murder was covered heavily by St. Louis newspapers (gang murders had become rare by then): P-D, STR 7/14-16/37.
269-270	Londe	Londe's parole and re-imprisonment at P-D 11/19/38, 3/2/40.
270	Hogan dismissal	P-D 3/13/26.
271	Dint's parole	P-D 2/18/43.
271	Bailey murder	P-D 6/25-26/41.
271-272	Buster Wortman	Newspapers failed to mention Wortman at all, as he still flew under the radar in 1943. As noted in

		Taylor Pensoneau's book, by this time the Sheltons had little to no power on the East Side of St. Louis. The man who benefited most from Colbeck's murder was Buster Wortman.
273	1944 ...	Cronin shooting at P-D 3/3/44. Hogan disappearance at P-D 9/29-30, 10/2-6/44. Robinson and Ryan charged at P-D 10/12/44. Armes' death at P-D 12/13/44. 1946 extortion at http://www.crimelibrary.com/gangsters_outlaws/family_epics/louis/4.html
273-274	Shelton deaths	The murders of the two brothers and the role of Wortman in setting a bounty at Pensoneau, p. 219-242.
274	Epplesheimer	P-D 2/18/51
274	Brothers	P-D 9/18, 12/23/50, Schoenberg, p. 285.
274	Willie Heeney	http://www.myalcaponemuseum.com/id120.htm
274	Maddox	His fate at Schoenberg, p. 357. McGurn murder at Helmer/Bilek, p. 244-245.
274-275	Londe	P-D 11/13-14/56
275	Red Smith	http://www.crimelibrary.com/gangsters_outlaws/family_epics/louis/4.html
275	Tony Foley	His misfortune during the Depression is covered at P-D 11/24/34. Foley's age cross-checked with Social Security death index to determine death date and location.
275	Jelly Roll Hogan	Obit at P-D 8/13/63; also at http://www.crimelibrary.com/gangsters_outlaws/family_epics/louis/4.html
275	Steve Ryan	P-D 5/4/65.
275	Buster Wortman	A good retrospective on his career at P-D 8/11/68.
275	Renard	P-D 11/22/33.
275	Robinson ...	Author could find no leads on the later years of Chippy Robinson and Oliver Dougherty.
275-276	Kinney	Senator Kinney's obituary at P-D 2/20/71.

SELECTED BIBLIOGRAPHY

Fontaine, Walter. *The Rise and Fall Of Dinty Colbeck*. American Mafia.com, 2001.

http://www.americanmafia.com/Feature_Articles_159.html

Helmer, William, and Rick Mattix. *Public Enemies: America's Criminal Past, 1919-1940*. New York: Checkmark Books, 1998.

Helmer, William, and Arthur J. Bilek. *The St. Valentine's Day Massacre: The Untold Story of the Gangland Bloodbath That Brought Down Al Capone*. Nashville, TN: Cumberland House Publishing, 2004.

Kirchten, Ernest. *Catfish and Crystal: The Story of St. Louis, U.S.A.* Garden City, N.Y.: Doubleday, 1960.

Pensoneau, Taylor. *Brothers Notorious: The Sheltons: Southern Illinois' Legendary Gangsters*. New Berlin, IL: Downstate Publications, 2002.

Schoenberg, Robert. *Mr. Capone*. New York, N.Y.: William Morrow & Company, 1992.

Waugh, Daniel. *Misplaced Wiseguys: The Forgotten Gangsters of Early 20th Century Detroit*. Unpublished manuscript, 2001.

INDEX

Index

Index

Index

Index

Index

Index

Index